The Christian Call
to Justice and Peace

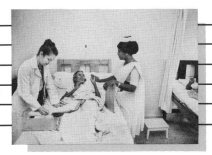

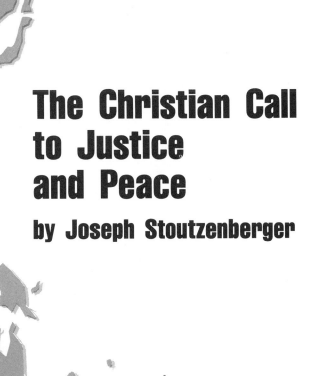

The Christian Call to Justice and Peace

by Joseph Stoutzenberger

Saint Mary's Press   Christian Brothers Publications

To Timothy and to your generation:
May the dream of a just and peace-filled world
become a reality through God's grace
and through your creative endeavors.

Nihil Obstat: Rev. Msgr. William T. Magee
            Censor Deputatus
            3 December 1986
Imprimatur: †Loras J. Watters, DD
            Bishop of Winona
            3 December 1986

Consultants for this course book included John Groch,
Frank J. Kieliger, Noreen Kromm, Jack Palmer, and
Gery Short. The publishing team included Stephan
Nagel, development editor; Donnarae Lukitsch, man-
uscript editor; Carolyn St. George, designer and il-
lustrator; and Mary Kraemer, production editor and
indexer.

The acknowledgments continue on page 288.

Printed in the United States of America

Printing: 6 5 4 3 2 1
Year: 1994 93 92 91 90 89 88 87

ISBN 0-88489-180-1

Contents

Introduction

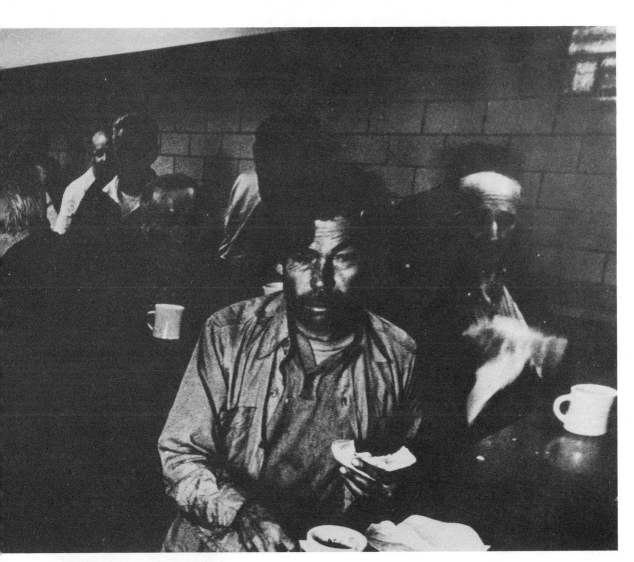

Which Was Neighbor?

> Jesus replied, "There was a man going down from Jerusalem to Jericho who fell prey to robbers. They stripped him, beat him, and then went off leaving him half-dead. A priest happened to be going down the same road; he saw him but continued on. Likewise there was a Levite who came the same way; he saw him and went on. But a Samaritan who was journeying along came on him and was moved to pity at the sight. He approached him and dressed his wounds, pouring in oil and wine. He then hoisted him on his own beast and brought him to an inn, where he cared for him. The next day he took out two silver pieces and gave them to the innkeeper with the request: 'Look after him, and if there is any further expense I will repay you on my way back.'
>
> "Which of these three, in your opinion, was neighbor to the man who fell in with the robbers?" (Luke 10:30–36)

In the story of the good Samaritan, Jesus portrays a world of stark reality, striking contrasts, and unexpected twists. His parable begins innocently enough: a man sets out on a journey. Immediately, however, Jesus tells us that the man is victimized by a band of thieves. Jesus follows this brutal incident with a description of the reactions of three passersby. The first two, who are leaders in the Jewish community, completely ignore the victim. But giving the story a sudden twist, Jesus tells how a foreigner, one of the hated Samaritans, stops to help the beaten man and to graciously care for him.

We are familiar with the kind of tough world that Jesus depicts. We know about victims and thieves. We hear constantly about people who are victims of hunger and poverty, oppression and war, and other such injustices. We know that these victims exist in faraway places sometimes called the *Third World* or *developing countries,* as well as in overcrowded ghettos and forgotten sectors in our own country. We also know that victims of injustice are living in our own neighborhoods—in nursing homes, hospitals, factories, and private homes.

Frequently we feel that we ourselves are victims:

- We may be afraid to walk down city streets late at night.
- We may wish to travel to exotic lands. But even if we had the resources to do so, we might hesitate because of the threats of terrorists.
- We may look forward to a life of creative and meaningful work, but monetary needs and economic instability lead us to place financial security above creativity and service.

- We may like to believe that we have friends whom we can depend on, yet we fear that in difficult times we will find ourselves alone.
- We may enjoy life, but reminders of people suffering throughout the world make us uneasy.
- We may look forward to a long and healthy life, but news reports of the increasing weapons buildup and nuclear accidents around the world threaten that hope.

In too many ways we feel that we are victims in a world that is out of control.

So the beginning of Jesus' parable rings painfully true—the world is filled with far too many victims and thieves. The second part of the story, however, baffles us. Why didn't the priest and the Levite, or lawyer, stop to help the victim? It seems to be the natural thing to do, as well as the expected moral response. In our terms, these two passersby represent the **haves**—the rich, the talented, the educated, the beautiful people—the people we look up to and most wish to be like. In Jesus' story, however, they pass by, refusing to help a human being in need—one of the **have-nots**. We can only guess why Jesus gives us two such puzzling examples of uninvolvement and inhumanity.

Oddly, the fourth character of the story is himself a victim. He is a Samaritan; that is, to the Jews he is a despised foreigner. In our vocabulary, the label *samaritan* has often been reduced to meaning a do-gooder. But when Jesus told this story, his Jewish audience knew who the Samaritans were. For several centuries, hostility and guerrilla warfare characterized the relations between the Jews and their northern neighbors, the Samaritans. Furthermore, if the roles in the parable had been reversed, if a Jewish traveler had come upon a wounded Samaritan, the Jew would certainly have known that Samaritans are to be scrupulously avoided as unclean. Herein lies the unexpected turn in Jesus' story, for it is the Samaritan who has enough moral, human feeling to recognize a "neighbor" in need and to want to do what he can to help. As the theologian John McKenzie has noted, "There was no deeper breach of human relations in the contemporary world than the feud of Jews and Samaritans, and the breadth and depth of Jesus' doctrine of love could demand no greater act of a Jew than to accept a Samaritan as a brother."

In this parable Jesus is asking us in clear and vivid terms: Which side are we on? Do we help those in need or do we pass them by? Do we stand with the victims, working with them to alleviate their pains and to care for their needs? Do we allow our brothers and sisters to die, or do we take the side of life? Are we uninvolved, throwing up our hands in despair, or do we have hope that creative solutions can be found to lessen the pain of all people victimized on their journeys through life?

Three Steps to Becoming a Good Neighbor

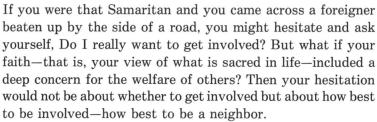

Part A: Justice and Christian Faith

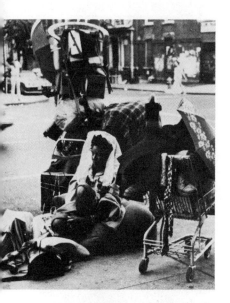

If you were that Samaritan and you came across a foreigner beaten up by the side of a road, you might hesitate and ask yourself, Do I really want to get involved? But what if your faith—that is, your view of what is sacred in life—included a deep concern for the welfare of others? Then your hesitation would not be about whether to get involved but about how best to be involved—how best to be a neighbor.

For this reason our course begins by exploring the link between our faith and our concern for others. Chapter 1 examines our concern for others in light of the term *justice.* If the word is to have meaning for us, we must look at it in relation to today's world with its unique problems and concerns. We must realize that justice deals with the pains and triumphs of real people and with how we should relate to them as neighbors.

Next, chapter 2 examines the scriptural basis of concern for others. Put simply, the Scriptures reveal to us that our God is clearly on the side of the victims of the world. Not only the parable of the good Samaritan but the entire Bible, the whole Judeo-Christian story, challenges us with this message.

Chapter 3 then discusses how justice has been manifest throughout the Church's history. Judeo-Christian teachers, from biblical prophets to our present popes and bishops, assert that our faith cannot be separated from acting on behalf of those in need. Throughout its history the Church has attempted to transform the world into the one Jesus spoke of, where victims hold a special place and all people are neighbors. As in the story of the good Samaritan, church movements to help those in need sometimes have arisen not from official leaders but from the victims themselves.

Finally, chapter 4 deals with some practical implications of working for justice in today's world. We will consider the underlying causes of injustice; the long-term solutions, as well as the immediate ones; and the possible contributions of individuals, through works of mercy and through works of social action.

Part B: Justice and Human Needs

The second step to our becoming good neighbors is to get to know our neighborhoods. Recently many schools and parishes have begun local programs to visit elderly and sick persons. Frequently volunteers for such programs exclaim with surprise, "I never knew that so many people were without families or in need of food or lonely in my own neighborhood!" So this course will examine the various groups of people that are in need of our concern and help.

Chapters 5 and 6 speak of poor people and, closely related, of hungry people. Studies of the world situation indicate that the number of poor and hungry people is staggering—especially given our technologically advanced and affluent societies. Many experts suggest that enough food exists to provide basic nourishment for everyone. Moreover, recent official church statements affirm that adequate food is a basic right of all people. In this light, chapters 5 and 6 present poor and hungry persons as victims whose needs we can and must meet.

When we look at victims in our world, we discover the stinging truth that more often than not they are women. Accordingly, chapter 7 discusses how sexual groups are oppressed today, emphasizing the modern women's movement and its call for the liberation of both men and women.

Chapter 8 deals with the many people in our world who are victimized because of their race. Whenever we speak about poor and hungry people, we cannot help but be struck by the inordinate number of them who are black, Native American, or Hispanic. Just as the Samaritan saw the foreigner as his neighbor, so we are called upon to recognize members of other races as our sisters and brothers.

Modern medical advances have made longer lives a reality. For that reason, older people are frequently called "our fastest-growing minority." To deal with a continually increasing life span, we need to examine our personal and social attitudes and practices toward older people. Therefore, chapter 9 looks at old age from the perspective of justice.

To be good Samaritans, should we act neighborly toward nature? Chapter 10 suggests that our call to justice does involve caring for the earth. As the chapter makes clear, failure to justly treat nature damages not only nature but also each of us.

Part C: Peace and Christian Faith

We often think of peace as a goal but not as a means to that goal. For instance, it is often said that justice is the means to achieve a peaceful world. Chapter 11 views peace more dynamically, as an activity or process called *peacemaking*. It examines the implications of peaceful responses to conflict and investigates the modern Church's challenge to look at war with an entirely new attitude.

Chapter 12 looks at peacemaking in the nuclear age. The existence of nuclear weapons has brought our world to a crisis point. Chapter 12 suggests that the Christian message speaks to the nuclear age and can provide hope and direction in this critical era.

Tapping Your Energy for Justice and Peace

Once a speaker was invited to deliver the opening talk at a high school retreat. She recommended that her topic be justice and peace because these are such significant concerns today. The teacher who had invited her warned her that students are not interested in justice and peace. "Talk about justice and peace frustrates most students and makes them feel guilty, turns off the students who don't see these issues affecting them anyway, creates a sense of powerlessness, and generally makes people feel bad."

Contrary to that discouraging viewpoint, this course presents justice and peace as important concerns of yours. It seeks to tap within you the desire to take control of your life and to shape your future. It is hoped that the course will be energizing and not frustrating.

The call to justice and peace is a call to love, compassion, imagination, and creativity. May you find these qualities burning within you, and may this course provide you with an opportunity to share them with others.

Part A:
Justice and Christian Faith

1
The Call to Justice

To answer the call to justice, we need to know where that call is leading. Thus, this first chapter discusses the concept *justice* in light of the Christian vision of a just world. In order to ground the concept in present reality, we will also look at certain values in our society that can distract us from answering the call to justice. Therefore, this chapter contains descriptions of two worlds, one of justice and one that hinders justice. By learning to discriminate between these worlds, we can see more clearly what the Christian call to justice means for us.

The Story of Two Brothers

Two brothers shared a farm. The younger brother was married and had seven children. The older brother was single. They worked hard on land that was good. So for many years the harvests were abundant, and each year the brothers split the wealth of the land evenly. Thanking God for their prosperity, they gathered the grain into their separate barns.

After one harvesttime, the older, single brother thought to himself: "It is not right that we should divide the grain evenly. My brother has many mouths to feed and he needs more. I have only myself to look after. I can certainly get by with less." So each night the single brother would take grain from his barn and secretly transfer it to the married brother's barn.

That same night the married brother thought to himself: "It is not right that we should divide the grain evenly. I have many children who will look after me in my old age. My brother has only himself. Surely he will need to save more for the future." So each night the married brother would take grain from his barn and secretly transfer it to his older brother's barn.

So, as it happened, each night the brothers gave away their grain; yet each morning they found their supply mysteriously replenished. Neither brother told the other about this miracle.

Then one night after a month or so, the brothers met each other halfway between the barns. They realized at once what had been happening. They embraced one another with laughter and tears. And on that spot they built a temple in which to worship God. (Adapted from John Shea, *An Experience Named Spirit*, pp. 7–8)

A Vision of a Just World

The world fashioned by these two brothers is a beautiful one. In this world the words *love* and *sharing* ring loudly and clearly. Each brother is genuinely concerned about the other's welfare; each gladly shares the earth's resources with the other. Both brothers work to tip the scales in favor of the one in need. Indeed, this world of the two brothers is a sacred place, a proper location for a holy temple in which to worship God.

We Christians are called to do our part in fashioning such a world. However, our task looms large and seems overwhelming. In today's world our brothers and sisters are not simply on the other side of a farm; they are also on the other side of the earth. Often they do not speak our language. Typically, they do not possess an adequate share of the earth's goods—while we enjoy more than an abundance of resources. Too often we think of them not as sisters and brothers but as strangers who want to take from us or dominate us. Given the makeup of today's human family, we would have great difficulty finding a sacred place upon which we might build our temple.

Nevertheless, we want such a world. Its beauty is too alluring to dismiss. It is the world of God's reign proclaimed by Jesus—the "kingdom come" (Matthew 6:10). With God's help it is not an impossible ideal but a developing reality, a gradual building up of a holy place. This sacred world cannot be created alone or without hard work or pain; nevertheless it can be created. How we can move the human world along toward becoming such a sacred place is the subject of this course.

The Four Elements of a Just World

The world described above—where family, friends, and strangers share their resources freely and care for each other's needs—is what we will call a just world. As we will see, such a world mirrors God's design, embodies the message of Jesus, and reveals the concerns expressed in many of the Church's recent teachings. Taking the time to discuss the following characteristics of a just world will give us a better idea of what that world is like and of the steps that we can take to create it.

1. Concern for Basic Needs

> God destined the earth and all it contains for . . . all people so that all created things would be shared fairly by all [humankind]. . . . (Vatican Council II, *The Church in the Modern World*, no. 69)

Recent official church statements declare that people have a right to basic life goods—
- food
- clothing
- shelter
- health care

along with a right to the means to attain these basic life goods—
- equal opportunity
- education
- employment

So as Christians we need to be concerned about whether or not such basic needs of people are being met.

The disturbing truth is that even though our present resources could provide for the basic needs of all people, the majority of the earth's population cannot meet its basic needs. Therefore, the vision of a just world challenges us to move toward a fairer distribution of basic goods. Saint Ambrose, an early leader of the Church, addressed this point to the rich church members: "You are not making a gift to the poor man from your possessions, but you are returning what is his. For what is common has been given for the use of all, [but] you make exclusive use of it. The earth belongs to all, not to the rich."

Similar testimony comes from our biblical roots: Ancient Jewish law called for regular periods of redistribution of property and wealth. Every fifty years, during what was called a *Jubilee year,* the law required that land be returned to its original owners. Likewise, all debts were to be canceled. This special year was an attempt to ensure a fair distribution of wealth and thereby prevent a widening gap between rich people and poor people.

2. Concern for Personal Dignity

> Then God said: "Let us make [people] in our image, after our likeness. . . ." (Genesis 1:26)

The second component of a just world—a concern for personal dignity—considers the psychological dimension of people's basic needs as being on a par with their physical needs. All people not only share basic needs, but also possess God-given worth and dignity. Thus people have a right to a sense of self-esteem and personal power. Therefore, working for a just world involves concern for personal dignity. The following incident illustrates this dimension of justice:

> A service club in a suburban Catholic high school decided to collect toys and clothing for children living in an inner-city parish. They planned on dressing up in Santa Claus outfits and personally distributing the gifts on Christmas Eve.
>
> The pastor of the inner-city parish visited their club to speak to the students. "I appreciate your work on behalf of our children," he told them, "but I can't have you delivering toys to the children yourselves. Parents should be Santa Claus for their children, not wealthy young people from the suburbs. It would diminish the self-esteem of our parents if you brought the gifts to their children. Instead, I suggest that you bring the toys and presents to the church hall the week before Christmas. Then our parents can come and choose the things that they feel would be best for their children. In that way the children will receive gifts at Christmas, and the parents will also participate in the giving."

This second element of a just world requires that we work toward the empowerment of people. People who are presently far removed from the centers of power must be included as members in our decision-making. They must share the power to shape our world and not simply remain pawns in the hands of a domineering elite.

We all know how much greater our sense of personal satisfaction is when we help to design or create something for ourselves. Conversely, we probably can recall science-fiction stories about beings from another galaxy who impose their idea of a "perfect" civilization upon earthlings. Because people have no say in its design, the perfect world ends up being an inhuman nightmare.

A United Nations committee

3. Concern for Solidarity

> Furthermore since work which [people] share together causes them to have common hopes, sorrows, desires, and joys it unites their wills, their minds, and hearts. For when [people] work they recognize one another as [brothers and sisters]. (Pope Paul VI, *On Promoting the Development of Peoples*, no. 27)

Working for justice means working *with*, not working *for*. Where an inequality of power exists, a redistribution of power is called for. In the opening story each brother has the ability to give to the other; it is not the haves giving to the have-nots. Each brother considers himself to be someone capable of giving, not simply an object of someone else's giving. In a similar way, people concerned about helping poor people do not simply cry, "We need to feed the poor." They also say: "We need to empower the poor. We need to teach people to read. We need to give the voiceless a voice. We need to share important decision-making among rich and poor people alike."

Solidarity is that quality of justice that breaks down barriers between people: the powerful and the powerless, rich and poor, black and white, young and old, those in prison and those free. As Christians we naturally lean toward solidarity since Jesus so radically identified himself with the sufferings and joys of all people, especially of the penniless and voiceless. Solidarity implies a spirit of mutuality—the recognition that we need each other and that the good of one person coincides with the good of all people.

4. Concern for Social Structures

Society should be so structured that it is easy for people to be good. (Attributed to Peter Maurin, co-founder of the Catholic Worker Movement)

Almost all of us want to do what we can to create a just world. We are haunted by images of starving children, by stories of older people wasting away in poor housing, and by the sight of homeless people crowding the busy sections of our cities.

Yet, when we view the enormity of our problems alongside the limits of our abilities, we easily become discouraged. In any action for justice we eventually find ourselves butting our heads against social structures that promote injustice. For that reason, our work for justice calls for a concern for the social system as a whole.

Because the way that our society and our world is structured plays such an important role in creating a just world, we

will look at this dimension of justice throughout the book, especially in chapter 4. For now, here is an example to illustrate the importance of social structures:

> Being disabled creates special problems for many people. We would like to help the disabled in any way that we can. If we know persons confined to wheelchairs, for instance, we might go shopping for them or transport them to their doctor when needed. However, we can become frustrated by the limitations of our efforts. What happens when we cannot help these persons? What about the many disabled persons who do not have someone to help them?
>
> At this point we might ask, what changes in society can occur that would help all disabled persons? For instance, many communities require that sidewalks be built with ramps at intersections so that people in wheelchairs can travel by themselves. Special parking places and ramps at public buildings also help to make disabled persons more self-reliant. While such changes cannot replace our personal efforts, they can do as much for the disabled as many hours of volunteer help from caring individuals.

In a similar fashion, we can examine a society's educational systems, transportation systems, patterns of governmental spending, use of natural resources, and other areas of social life. For example, the amount of our tax money spent on education is one indication of our society's commitment to education. Likewise, the amount a society spends on public transportation or on low-cost housing suggests its degree of commitment to poor people and to the environment.

Concern for social structures is an important consideration in working toward a just world. The goal is *the transformation of society's structures* in order to create a society that provides for its people's basic needs and self-esteem.

Reading the Signs of the Times

> "... If you can interpret the portents of earth and sky, why can you not interpret the present time? Tell me, why do you not judge for yourselves what is just?" (Luke 12:56–57)

If we are to work for justice realistically, then we need to develop our awareness of the "signs of the times"—that is, the current direction and present values in human society. Here is one symbolic description that portrays a harsh but realistic picture of our own society:

The earth is like an ocean liner that contains first-class, second-class, and third-class passengers. The first-class passengers, making up about one-fourth of the ship's list, have insisted on bringing along their automobiles, their freezers, their hair dryers, their television sets, their kitchen disposal units, and their pets. They have indiscriminately filled a number of the ship's holds with empty cans, bottles, discarded plastic, old newspapers, and broken appliances—the residue of their excessive consumption. In other holds they keep cattle, which are periodically slaughtered to sustain their customary, first-class eating habits. And in still other compartments they keep grain reserved for feeding the cattle.

These privileged passengers have some dangerous personal habits as well. They flush garbage down the toilets, blow smoke and gasoline fumes into the ship's ventilation system, and insist on unlimited use of the ship's limited electricity and water. Every once in a while they have a major brawl among themselves and threaten to sink the ship, and "just in case," they constantly improve their assorted bombs with which to do so.

The ship has no captain because the first-class passengers are afraid to give anyone authority to steer a new course or to change the ship's arrangements. Instead, there is a committee, which has no power and is not allowed access to the bridge. The committee is permitted only to discuss possible future directions and to make highly tentative suggestions. (Adapted from Adam Daniel Finnerty, *No More Plastic Jesus,* pp. 2–3)

Admittedly Adam Finnerty paints a grim picture of our world and especially of its first-class passengers. Before we reject Finnerty's scenario as unreal, however, we would do well to see what characteristics of his ocean liner match those of our world. Below are five characteristics that were presented in the ocean-liner image that also apply to our world. An antidote to each negative characteristic is also described.

1. The Crisis of Limits

North Americans have had a long love affair with the frontier. Throughout most of our history, more land was available "out West." If one locality could no longer support a population, then it was always possible to move on. North America seemed to offer limitless land, limitless resources, and limitless opportunities. Even when all the land was parceled out and some of our resources showed signs of running out, we put our faith in space as "the last frontier."

The ocean-liner image awakens us to a different reality—the crisis of limits. Recently, many experts on the future of the earth's resources have been waving a yellow flag of caution. They warn us that if we continue to use up our resources at the present rate, we will be facing drastic shortages of essential elements in the future. Because replacing key resources with substitutes from space remains an unlikely solution, the experts point out that if we are to survive, we had better change our ways.

Living simply. An antidote to our present crisis of limits is a commitment to what comes under the general label *simple living*. **Simple living** refers to reducing the amount of energy and resources that we use in our daily living. Riding a bicycle instead of a car to school is an obvious example of simple living. Recycling paper, metal, and glass is another example. Getting an appliance fixed instead of replacing it is another. On a social level, expanding the uses of nonpolluting wind and solar energy conserves other limited energy resources—and the environment. Many individuals and groups are now attempting to live more simply. From their experiences they are finding that not only is simple living good for the earth, in many ways it is also good for the human spirit.

2. Consumerism: Possessed by Possessions

Think of the TV commercials or magazine ads that you have seen recently. Chances are that many of them have tried to convince you how much better your life would be if you possessed whatever it was that they were selling. As the ocean-liner story points out, we do tend to bring an excessive number of possessions with us on our life journeys.

In God's bounteous goodness, the earth offers us a great variety of exciting things that we would like to have around us and at our disposal—tropical fish, exotic trees and plants, animals suitable as pets, and a great many delicious fruits and vegetables. In addition, our technologically advanced society constantly presents us with new inventions that promise to make our lives more comfortable, more interesting, more fun, or more rewarding. Looking to the Scriptures for guidance, we find that material things are seen as good: "God looked at everything he had made, and he found it very good . . ." (Genesis 1:31). However, looking elsewhere in the Scriptures we see that we need to keep our wishes for material things in perspective. Take for instance, the episode of the rich young man, who wanted to know what he had to do in order to get to heaven. He said that he had followed the Commandments all of his life.

> When Jesus heard this he said to him: "There is one thing further you must do. Sell all you have and give to the poor. You will have treasure in heaven. Then come and follow me." On hearing this he grew melancholy, for he was a very rich man. When Jesus observed this he said: "How hard it will be for the rich to go into the kingdom of God! Indeed, it is easier for a camel to go through a needle's eye than for a rich man to enter the kingdom of heaven." (Luke 18:22–25)

Consumerism is a term that refers to the harmful attitude toward possessions suggested in Jesus' statement above. Specifically, **consumerism** is the distorted desire to possess things, all out of proportion to our needs or normal wants. Rather than our using things for practical or even noble purposes, consumerism allows our passion for possessions to control our actions until possessions become ends in themselves. One writer recently described this distorted desire in this way: "We buy things we do not want to impress people we do not like."

The ocean-liner story hints at the dangers of consumerism. We need much more guidance about what to buy or not to buy than what thirty-second TV commercials provide us with. Given the fact that a multitude of third-class passengers desperately need the minimal essentials of life, we must be much more cautious about how we spend our money and use our resources.

Consumerism is such a pervasive disease in modern society that we can easily overlook its impact. Consumerism preaches the message "You *can* buy happiness." However, when we do buy the new car, the VCR, or the computer, we eventually find that we have more possessions but not necessarily more happiness. Consumerism hides the simple truth that happiness is a state of *being*, not of *having*. Of themselves, material goods do not bring happiness: Affluent persons sometimes commit suicide, and impoverished persons sometimes struggle heroically to hang on to life in any way they can. Depression can strike rich people, as well as poor people.

Finally, consumerism can change people into commodities. Just as we may feel that we need to own a particular make of car, we may also feel compelled to wear a certain hairstyle or certain clothes, or to be seen with certain types of people. In this way consumerism makes commodities of us and of the people around us. We shape ourselves into packages to be bid and bargained for like any other consumer goods.

Going from riches to rags? The antidote to consumerism is to put possessions into their proper perspective. Looking to our history, we find Christianity peopled with heroes who joyfully gave up a life of riches to live simply and to be with poor people. Such models include Saint Francis of Assisi in the Middle Ages and in our own day Jean Donovan, whose short, dramatic life led her from the upper-middle class in the United States to martyrdom in El Salvador.

Our society offers us a very different type of hero, namely, the poor person who becomes rich. Jesus spoke about the dangers of wealth and the lure of possessions more than about any other social issue. If he felt the need to stress these dangers in his comparatively simple society, how much more in our highly affluent society do we need to remain vigilant to the dangers of consumerism?

3. The Throwaway Society

Our discussion on consumerism might seem to imply that in our society we value material things. In fact, this is not the case. We have so many things, and we are so struck with the possibility of possessing many other things, that we seldom take time to value what we do have. As a result, ours is a "throwaway society" in which the things we craved yesterday become the junk of today. Consequently, our world—like the ocean liner—is overburdened with our junk.

Regarding human relationships, we need to ask: Do the characteristics of our throwaway society apply in any way to our treatment of people? We may personally agree with the saying "God doesn't make junk," but how well do the policies of our society reflect its truth? Our jails, our mental institutions, our homeless population, our pockets of poverty reveal a lack of care for many members of our society. Human junkyards exist where another motto, "Out of sight, out of mind," prevails.

Seeing people as sacraments. To counteract the devaluing of people and things that can accompany the throwaway mentality, we need to look to the past and to the future so as not to be overwhelmed by the changes of the present. We need to be rooted in our past and maintain a basic fidelity to our religious tradition, which sees both people and all of nature as sacraments. Also, we must concern ourselves with the future and ask ourselves, Are we going in the direction of valuing humanity and the earth's resources? We can chart a course toward justice only when we ocean-liner passengers remember where we have come from and when we care about where we are going.

Above: Rhode Island Medical Center's patients displaced by fire
Left: Inmates at a prison in Mansfield, Ohio

4. Individualism and Competition

Western society glories in its history of rugged individualism. "I've got to be me" and "I did it my way" are basic social themes. Consequently, on both the personal and political levels, competition is valued much more highly than cooperation. When circumstances suggest that we might need other people or other countries, we immediately react by calling for greater independence. At the political level, a reliance on military power has accompanied our excessively competitive spirit.

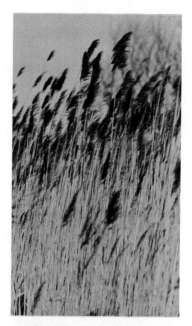

The ocean-liner story merely hints at the dangers of competition. Given the precarious nature of our world at this time, we will perish together unless we learn to work and live together. Our world is a "global village" in which all segments are dependent upon one another. We live in a rich nation, blessed with many and varied resources. Nevertheless we rely heavily upon others. We are not independent or dependent. Rather, we are interdependent. For example:

- Changes in prices by oil-producing countries affect the cost of consumer goods throughout the world.
- Accidents at nuclear energy plants in the USSR continue to affect levels of radioactivity in North America.
- The U.S. heartland serves as the breadbasket of the world in that it provides a large portion of the earth's grain. In similar fashion, Brazil's enormous jungles act as the earth's oxygen tank, producing much of the oxygen that we breathe. A drought in the United States' farmland would spell disaster in Africa. Likewise, destruction of Brazil's rain forests would damage the earth's air supply.

Fostering interdependence and cooperation. The perspective of rugged individualism is a false and destructive myth. Unless we acknowledge our interdependence and work for solidarity, we will steer our ocean liner to disaster. Because we need to direct all of our energies toward the survival of our planet and all the people on it, we can no longer afford to use so much of our energy and so many of our resources to maintain, not merely military equality, but military superiority.

5. Fatalism: "There's Nothing I Can Do"

The ocean-liner story describes a world out of control. We can easily allow the many problems facing us to create a spirit of defeat. We may sense that the world and its problems are too big for us, that we can do little against the overwhelming power of darkness pervading our world. We seem to hear about a new crisis or trouble spot every week. What can we do? Where do we start? How do we counteract **fatalism**—that is, the belief that the world is out of our control and in the hands of blind fate?

Having high-energy hope. The Christian call to justice always involves hope. Hope is a virtue, that is, a quality that we acquire through practice. Too often we use the word *hope* only when things are out of our hands. For example, we might say, "That police officer just saw me driving way over the speed limit. I sure hope she doesn't give me a ticket." Genuine hope is not throwing up our hands in despair but lending a helping hand where it is needed. In short, hope is a high-energy attitude: when we are hopeful, we are in a state of intense readiness to size up and seize opportunities.

Hope counteracts the spirit of fatalism that characterizes our world today. Hope reminds us that all things are possible and challenges us to work to make them happen. In the words of Robert Kennedy: "Some men see things as they are and say, Why? I dream things that never were and say, Why not?" The following story suggests how individual effort might make all the difference in changing the world:

"Tell me the weight of a snowflake," a squirrel asked a wild dove.

"Nothing more than nothing," was the answer.

"In that case I must tell you a marvelous story," the squirrel said. "I sat on the branch of a fir, close to its trunk, when it began to snow, not heavily, not in a raging blizzard, no, just like in a dream, without any violence. Since I didn't have anything better to do, I counted the snowflakes settling on the twigs and needles of my branch. Their number was exactly 3,741,952. When the next snowflake dropped onto the branch—nothing more than nothing, as you say—the branch broke off."

Having said that, the squirrel scampered away.

The dove, since Noah's time an authority on the matter of peace, thought about the story for a while and finally said to herself: "Perhaps there is only one person's voice lacking for justice and peace to come about in the world." (Adapted from "The Weight of Nothing," quoted in Mary Lou Kownacki, editor, *A Race to Nowhere*, p. 85)

Conclusion: A Just World Is Possible

In this chapter we have considered where we would like to be and where we presently are. Obviously we have powerful obstacles to overcome in creating a just world. Yet our Christian call to justice commits us to bring about such a world. In working toward that goal we experience the deep joy that Jesus promised his followers,

> Blest are they who hunger and thirst for holiness; they shall have their fill.
>
> (Matthew 5:6)

For Review

1. List the four elements of a just world.
2. Along with their antidotes, outline the five signs of the times discussed in this chapter.
3. Explain the terms *solidarity, consumerism,* and *fatalism.*

For Reflection

1. The story of the two brothers presents an image of a just world. Using a poem, story, or visual art, create your own image of a just world. Be attentive to the elements of a just world mentioned in this chapter.

2. People have a right to have their basic needs met. List what you consider to be the basic needs of people. Which of the needs that you have listed are protected by the Bill of Rights?

3. Concern for personal dignity is an element of justice that requires a sensitivity to the language that we use. Rewrite the following statements to reflect a concern for dignity:
   - Let us pray for those who are less fortunate than we are.
   - You look good for your age.
   - Women libbers just want to be like men.
   - We need to help the crippled—they can't take care of themselves.
   - People on welfare are lazy.

4. Justice means working *with,* not working *for.* Describe in writing how you might address the following problems, first using a working-for approach, then using a working-with approach.

- A classmate is receiving failing grades.
- A friend of yours develops a drinking problem.
- Your local neighborhood is in serious disrepair.
- You live near a prison and would like to help those leaving prison who have no place to go.
- Your grandmother is alone and housebound.

5. Concern for social structures means that we take time to examine the effects of various institutions on people. Research and write a brief analysis of one of the following topics:
   - Who does our school system educate most effectively?
   - What groups are found most often in our prison system?
   - Who does our welfare system help?
   - Does our health-care system help all those who are in need of care?

6. Complete one of the following activities:
   a. Write a sample newspaper article related to one of the signs of the times mentioned in this chapter. The article could be a news story, an editorial, a movie or TV review, a comic strip, or an advice column. Remember to consider both the problem and the antidote.
   b. Collect newspaper or magazine articles and advertisements that reflect the five signs of the times. Put them into a collage or a folder. Write about what you learn from your collection.
   c. Make your own list of signs of the times that hold implications for justice or peace in today's world. Write a brief essay on each.

7. Advertising reflects consumerism. Watch the ads on a typical evening of commercial television and list the possessions that the ads suggest lead to happiness. Also, describe the techniques that are used to sell these products.

8. Read the book *Salvador Witness,* by Ana Carrigan, and write a brief report on the life of Jean Donovan as described in that book. In your report, include two key influences on her values and describe how she worked *with* people.

9. The signs of the times discussed in this chapter paint a negative picture of our world. Of course, this is only part of the picture. List and describe what you see as signs of hope in our world. Bring to class several magazine articles that include signs of hope.

2
The Scriptures' Call to Justice

Throughout the Scriptures we hear the call to justice. From the opening story of Creation to the concluding vision of a new heaven and a new earth, the Bible beckons us to work with God to make justice reign over the world. In this chapter we will examine the key themes present in the Scriptures' call to justice.

God Loves Stories

Once upon a time a great rabbi saw misfortune threatening his people. He went into a certain part of the forest, lit a fire, and said a special prayer. Miraculously the misfortune was averted.

Many years later a disciple of the rabbi had occasion to call upon heaven. He went to the same place in the forest and said: "Master of the Universe, listen! I do not know how to light the fire, but I am still able to say the prayer." Again a miracle occurred, and misfortune was averted.

Still later a third rabbi, in order to save his people, went into the forest. There he said: "I do not know how to light the fire, I do not know the prayer, but I know the place and this must be sufficient." It was sufficient, and another miracle occurred.

Finally, it fell to a fourth rabbi to overcome misfortune. Sitting in his armchair, his head in his hands, he spoke to God: "I am unable to light the fire, and I do not know the prayer. I cannot even find the place in the forest. All I can do is to tell the story of the rabbis who knew these things. This must be sufficient." And it was sufficient because God loves stories. (Adapted from Elie Wiesel, *The Gates of the Forest*)

Our God is the God of all people, not only perfect people. Our God loves both sinners and saints. The Bible, our sacred storybook, is filled with stories about God and about the flesh-and-blood people through whom God chose to be revealed. Although these biblical stories can be interpreted in different ways, clearly justice is a central theme. It seems that our God is a lover of stories, especially stories about justice.

The Scriptures and Justice: An Opening Comment

As we shall see, the biblical understanding of justice centers on relationships. The Bible's stories describe people who struggle with important questions about their relationships with God, about their relationships with the rest of Creation, about what it means to be human, and about how people should treat one another. We can thus use the Scriptures to help us in our own struggles with the central questions of life. Retelling these stories may rekindle God's message of justice in our own lives.

Genesis and Creation

According to the early chapters of Genesis, God created a harmonious world where all things have their places. God's Creation is the sacred world of earth and animals and humans. In this paradise, human beings play a special role as stewards commissioned by God to take care of the world. In this role as caretakers, human beings are to uphold the original beauty and order of God's Creation.

> . . . "Let us make [people] in our image, after our likeness. Let them have dominion over the fish of the sea, the birds of the air, and the cattle, and over all the wild animals and all the creatures that crawl on the ground." (Genesis 1:26)

Yet things soon fall apart. Human beings seek to lord it over the rest of Creation, each other, and even God. Rather than seek to cultivate and care for the world, people attempt to refashion it to serve their selfish wants.

1. Adam and Eve: In our first encounter with human beings in the Scriptures, we find Adam and Eve at home in paradise, on direct speaking terms with God and nature. The world is presented as a unified whole: all things are interrelated. The vision of Eden affirms the goodness and harmony of all Creation.

Nevertheless, Adam and Eve desire to set themselves above the created order, to "be like gods" (Genesis 3:5). As a result, their eyes are opened to their isolation and separateness. The first human beings no longer trust each other, and nature is no longer their friend. For protection and from embarrassment, they cover themselves. In shame the first human couple hides from God, only to be thrust from paradise into the world of struggle, pain, and death.

2. Cain and Abel: The next event in the human drama deepens the rift within the natural order. Driven by jealousy, one family member kills his brother. When confronted by God, Cain replies, "Am I my brother's keeper?" (Genesis 4:9). Looking at the story from the outside, we know the correct answer: Yes, Cain, you are your brother's keeper, as we all are responsible one for another.

3. Noah: In the next story in Genesis, God despairs of the entire human race and so destroys the world, except one righteous person. With Noah, with his descendants, and with all

the creatures who share the ark with him, God makes a covenant, or agreement. God will never again destroy the world, but God requires that human beings return to their original role as responsible caretakers: ". . . I will demand an accounting for human life. . . . Be fertile, then, and multiply; abound on earth and subdue it" (Genesis 9:5,7).

4. **The tower of Babel:** The last of these early stories returns to the theme of human beings attempting to be godlike. In the story about the tower of Babel, the people seek to build a great city and tower in order to "make a name for [themselves]" (Genesis 11:4). God thwarts their efforts by confusing their language "so that one will not understand what another says" (Genesis 11:7). Even more so than the stories that precede it, the story of the tower of Babel becomes a universal symbol of disharmony, producing the various human races.

The Stories of Genesis Speak About Justice

The early scriptural stories in Genesis speak about God, Creation, and humanity—and about the relationships that exist among the three. In the stories the natural order is always referred to as *creation* and is always seen in relation to the Creator. Therefore, Creation—including humanity—is viewed as an expression of God, just as a painting is an expression of the mind and will of an artist. The stories thus affirm the goodness of Creation and the unity of all Creation.

As mentioned earlier, human beings play the special role as caretakers of Creation. Significantly, the same Hebrew word is used when God charges Adam to *care* for the earth as when God queries Cain about being his brother's *keeper*. Whenever human beings allow narrow or selfish interests to lead them astray from their original role as caretakers, they suffer consequences that are natural outgrowths of their actions. Adam and Eve, for instance, are banished from paradise. Cain, who decisively cuts himself off from humanity by killing his brother, is condemned to be a friendless and homeless wanderer. The builders of the tower of Babel, who desire to be better than their neighbors, find that they can no longer communicate with their neighbors.

In all of these stories, God's Creation mirrors the specific concerns of justice:
- the sharing of goods
- the care for the earth and for one another
- the interdependence of all Creation

When human beings work against God's created order, the results are shame, violence, destruction, and chaos.

Fortunately, the stories in Genesis do not end here. Every one of the early stories ends with a note of hope. Even the story about the tower of Babel, which describes the division of nations and the resulting misunderstanding, is followed immediately by the story of Abraham. Here we learn that Abraham's descendants, the Jewish people, are to be a blessing to all the nations, living reminders of God's just Creation. So these early stories remind us that Creation is good and that justice is part of the natural order of things.

The Exodus: A Universal Story

In Genesis, we do not find many heroes with whom we can identify. The Book of Exodus, however, tells a story paralleling every hero's story—the story of injustice overcome, of a fearful journey through the wilderness, and of a prize won. Thus, the Exodus story features characters and settings that we can identify in our own stories of struggle: Egypt, the pharaoh, Moses, the Hebrew slaves, the desert, and the Promised Land.

In the early stories of Genesis, God is the Creator; in the Book of Exodus, God emerges as the compassionate Liberator:

> . . . "I have witnessed the affliction of my people in Egypt and have heard their cry of complaint against their slave drivers, so I know well what they are suffering. Therefore I have come down to rescue them from the hands of the Egyptians and lead them out of that land into a good and spacious land, a land flowing with milk and honey. . . ." (Exodus 3:7–8)

Too many people today find themselves in "Egypt," that is, in the land of slavery. Too many children are enslaved by illiteracy: even in North America the illiteracy rate is surprisingly high. Too many old people find themselves slaves to hunger, poverty, and loneliness. Too many women in our society are enslaved by stereotypes that result in inferior jobs and unjust wages. A disproportionate number of blacks, Hispanics, and Native Americans find themselves in low-paying jobs with little hope of advancement. In other words, for too many people the slavery and oppression of "Egypt" are painful realities, not distant history.

The Exodus and Liberation

The cry of liberation often arises from people seeking justice. Women seeking justice call themselves members of the "women's liberation movement." Poor or unemployed people seldom ask for handouts. Usually they call for liberation, which to them means the freedom to provide for their own needs. Dr. Martin Luther King, Jr. (one of the most famous U.S. advocates of justice) saw the struggle for civil rights as a freedom movement. In his moving speeches he frequently linked civil rights for blacks and poor people with the story of the Exodus from Egypt to the Promised Land. On the night before he died, Dr. King said: "I have been to the mountaintop. And I've looked over, and I've seen the promised land. I may not get there with you. But I want you to know tonight that we as a people will get to the promised land."

Center, front: Civil-rights activist Dr. Martin Luther King, Jr.

In your life, reflect on some of the ways in which you experience lack of freedom:

- Perhaps at home you submit to rules not of your choosing and far from your liking.
- If you had a choice, you would probably avoid a large part of your school experience.
- You think about things that you would like to own and realize that due to your financial limitations, you cannot purchase them. Of course, a job might solve that problem, but then working limits your free time.
- Maybe you want a full scholarship to college, but you are held back by SAT scores that place you below the top 10 percent in ranking.
- At a party you meet "Mr. or Ms. Right," but you do not feel free to ask him or her for a date.
- You want to be a basketball star, but the coach tells you that people who are only five feet tall cannot make the team.

We could continue this list for a long time. Each of us experiences lack of freedom in our lives, each of us feels the weight of oppression, and each of us groans for liberation. The Book of Exodus provides us with a powerful story of liberation. In the Exodus story, justice is grounded in the compassion of God for people. Because God's love has been demonstrated to the people in freeing them from slavery, those who are faithful to God will also show compassion to others in need.

Often we do not see God in the light of the Exodus story. We tend to think of the God of the Jewish Scriptures as the fierce and jealous Yahweh. The justice of Yahweh is depicted as a strict brand of law and order: if the Jews don't follow the rules, God will smite them and that's that! Yet as we have seen in the creation stories, the God of the Bible genuinely loves Creation. The Exodus story underlines this very compassionate view: God comes to the rescue of the Jews in Egypt in response to their sufferings. Thus the justice of Yahweh is more closely related to *love* than to law.

The Prophets' Role in Transforming Society

Leaving Egypt, the Hebrew slaves do become free and enter the Promised Land. However, their moment in the sun is short-lived. Soon they acquire a system of government, military power, alliances with other countries, an established social system, and a king to rule over them. Unfortunately, they also acquire the dissension, corruption, and injustices that accompany culture. During this historical period of the Jewish people, a unique group of people arises who speaks loudly a message of justice that still has an impact today.

The Hebrew word for prophet—*nabi*—means "mouthpiece." A prophet, therefore, is a person who speaks for God. Moses is the greatest of the Jewish prophets in that he speaks most clearly the message of God. For Christians, Jesus is the foremost prophet. Indeed, John's Gospel calls Jesus not simply one who speaks the words of God but one who is himself the very Word of God. Although Moses and Jesus possess many characteristics in common with other Jewish prophets, for our purposes we will be focusing on those prophets mentioned in the Scriptures who lived during the eighth and seventh centuries before Christ.

You can read about these prophets—most notably Amos, Hosea, Isaiah, and Jeremiah—in the books of the Bible that are named after them. In their preaching, the prophets address the specific religious, political, and social problems of their time. For us to understand the prophets' unique contributions to the Scriptures' call to justice, we need to examine at least briefly what kind of people they were.

The Prophets' Personal Traits

The scriptural prophets are among the least likely people that we would expect to speak for God:

■ The prophet Amos is a shepherd from the southern kingdom

of Judah who speaks to the people of the northern kingdom of Israel. He is both a member of the lower class and a foreigner!

- When Jeremiah is called by God to prophesy, he responds, "I know not how to speak; I am too young" (Jeremiah 1:6).
- Hosea's being chosen as a prophet rests upon his dubious distinction of having a wife, Gomer, who is constantly unfaithful to him.
- Moses has difficulty speaking and has to bring along his brother, Aaron, to speak for him before the pharaoh.
- In the Gospel the three Magi seeking the Messiah naturally go to King Herod's palace in Jerusalem. Instead, Jesus is born in the unlikely little town of Bethlehem—in a stable! Jesus later says of himself,

> The stone which the builders rejected
> has become the keystone of the structure.
>
> (Matthew 21:42)

A true prophet, then, does not hold an official or exalted position and is often uneducated, reluctant, emotionally wounded, and ridiculed for telling people what they do not want to hear. The prophets' strength lies in their powerful messages, not in their personal affluence or influence.

United Farm Workers' organizer Cesar Chavez

The Message of the Prophets

The biblical prophets call for conversion—that is, personal and social transformation. They call for a return to the past when the Jewish people "knew God," and they look forward to the day when God's word will once again rule Israel. The prophets identify "knowing God" with "doing justice":

. . . .
Did not your father eat and drink?
    He did what was right and just,
    and it went well with him.
Because he dispensed justice to the weak and the poor,
    it went well with him.
Is this not true knowledge of me?
    says the LORD.

(Jeremiah 22:15–16)

Thus the prophets speak not only on behalf of God but also on behalf of those who have no voice.

The biblical prophets despise any practice of religion that is not linked to working for justice. Consequently, they condemn the religious hypocrisy of their day. Amos, one of the earliest prophets, puts the case clearly:

I hate, I spurn your feasts,
    I take no pleasure in your solemnities;
Your cereal offerings I will not accept,
    nor consider your stall-fed peace offerings.
Away with your noisy songs!
    I will not listen to the melodies of your harps.
But if you would offer me holocausts,
    then let justice surge like water,
    and goodness like an unfailing stream.

(Amos 5:21–24)

Civil-rights activist Jesse Jackson

The prophets do not separate religion from politics or from the social conditions of their day. They recognize that many political decisions contradict God's call for justice:

> . . . .
> Because you have trusted in your chariots,
>   and in your many warriors,
> Turmoil shall break out among your tribes
>   and all your fortresses shall be ravaged. . . .
> (Hosea 10:13–14)

Evangelist Billy Graham, right, speaking in Wittenberg, East Germany

For the prophets, religion, politics, and social conditions are all matters of justice. Through the prophets, God calls for social, as well as personal, conversion:

> Thus says the LORD of hosts, the God of Israel: Reform your ways and your deeds, so that I may remain with you in this place. . . . Only if you thoroughly reform your ways and your deeds; if each of you deals justly with his neighbor; if you no longer oppress the resident alien, the orphan, and the widow; if you no longer shed innocent blood in this place, or follow strange gods to your own harm, will I remain with you in this place, in the land which I gave your fathers long ago and forever. (Jeremiah 7:3–7)

The view of justice propounded by the prophets is a highly realistic one. Injustice is seen not simply as a bad attitude or ignorance. Rather it is grounded in behavior—specifically the mistreatment of weak or needy persons. Likewise, the effects of justice are portrayed concretely as freedom from slavery and oppression, harmony in the community, and hope in the face of continuing sinfulness:

> This, rather, is the fasting that I wish:
>   releasing those bound unjustly,
>   untying the thongs of the yoke;
> Setting free the oppressed,
>   breaking every yoke;
> Sharing your bread with the hungry,
>   sheltering the oppressed and the homeless;
> Clothing the naked when you see them,
>   and not turning your back on your own.
>
> . . . .
>
> Then light shall rise for you in the darkness,
>   and the gloom shall become for you like midday;
> Then the LORD will guide you always
>   and give you plenty even on the parched land.
> He will renew your strength,
>   and you shall be like a watered garden,
>   like a spring whose water never fails.
>
>   (Isaiah 58:6–11)

The biblical prophets were not well heeded in their own time. Yet their words were preserved by their admirers, and their powerful message of justice has profoundly influenced the Christian moral vision that centered on the mission and ministry of Jesus.

Jesus and Justice

The Messiah Is Among Us

For years the old monk had lived alone in the woods near the monastery. Often the other monks wanted to hear from this wise, old man who in his youth had a reputation as a great teacher. However, they respected his desire to live alone and to keep his thoughts to himself.

Then one evening after a bitterly cold spell, one of the monks was sent to him to inquire about his provisions. When he arrived at the small hermitage, the monk found his colleague cheerful and welcoming. He was invited to join the older monk in a cup of tea. After sitting mostly in silence for some time, the younger monk risked asking the hermit, "In the monastery all of us wonder what truth, what knowledge you have gained from your years in solitude with God. If there was one message that you would share with the other monks, what would it be?"

The old monk replied quickly and starkly, "The Messiah is among you."

The younger monk thanked him and returned to the monastery. He gathered the other monks in the chapel and told them of the message: "The Messiah is among us."

All of the monks looked upon their wise, old brother with great reverence, so they treated his message very seriously. Yet what could he mean? Did he mean that one of them was the Messiah? Could it be old Brother Jerome who took such loving care of the books in their sparse library? Could it be Brother Gregory who cooked their meals and kept the kitchen running smoothly? Could it be Brother Timothy, the one who smelled like the animals because he spent so much time caring for them?

Each monk pondered the old man's message and realized that any one of them could be the Messiah—indeed, even oneself! From that day on, every monk treated each of his brother monks as if he were the Messiah. People who visited the monastery marveled at the aura of holiness that emanated from these monks.

Jesus: God with Us

In the opening chapter of Matthew's Gospel we find this famous message:

> "The virgin shall be with child
> and give birth to a son,
> and they shall call him Emmanuel,"
> a name which means "God is with us."
>
> (Matthew 1:23)

The very last line of Matthew's Gospel repeats this theme:

> And know that I am with you always,
> until the end of the world!
>
> (Matthew 28:20)

The message "God is with us" deserves the prominence it is given in Matthew's Gospel because it expresses a central tenet of Christian belief—that in Jesus, God is in our very midst. Just as the old monk's message, "The Messiah is among us," leads the other monks to view themselves and one another in a new light, so Jesus' message that God is close at hand leads to a new insight about the relationship between God and ourselves.

Jesus does not depart from the core message of the earlier scriptural writings—the stories of Genesis and Exodus or the teachings of the prophets. Yet, as God among us, Jesus embodies the reconciliation of Creation and Creator. He personalizes within himself the rule of God that is proclaimed in the creation stories, demonstrated through the Exodus, and yearned for by the prophets. Also, Jesus broadens the interpretation of God's rule, thus pointing out implications often overlooked.

Jesus' Radical Vision of God's Kingdom

> When the book of the prophet Isaiah was handed [to Jesus], he unrolled the scroll and found the passage where it was written:
> "The spirit of the Lord is upon me;
> therefore he has anointed me.
> He has sent me to bring glad tidings to the poor,
> to proclaim liberty to captives,
> Recovery of sight to the blind
> and release to prisoners. . . ."
>
> (Luke 4:17–18)

Through his vision of God's reign, Jesus reminds us of both

our dignity and our responsibility. Regarding dignity, Jesus proclaims that God's Kingdom is inclusive and not exclusive. That is, he welcomes into God's reign not only poor and outcast people but also those people considered "bad." Other Jewish teachers of his day speak of God's reign as Jesus did, but their vision divides Jews from Gentiles, law keepers from lawbreakers, and the good from the bad. In Jesus' vision of God's reign, every person has innate worth and dignity.

Jesus teaches the dignity of all people through both his actions and his words:

- Constantly he seeks out the undignified of his day—lepers, tax collectors, prostitutes—with whom to share a meal or to spend some time.
- He also uses parables to express the universal worth of all people. In the parable of the day laborers (Matthew 20:1–16), Jesus speaks approvingly about a vineyard owner who pays the same wages whether a person works a full day or a half day.
- Elsewhere, Jesus describes the reign of God as a wedding banquet to which the invited guests do not come. Instead, unlikely guests are invited from the streets to enjoy the banquet: "The servants then went out into the byroads and rounded up everyone they met, bad as well as good. This filled the wedding hall with banqueters" (Matthew 22:10).

Maryknoll sister Rosemary McCormack in Peru

The flip side of Jesus' message, the call for responsibility, can be summed up in one quotation: ". . . You shall love your neighbor as yourself" (Matthew 22:39). As already mentioned, in his interpretation of the reign of God, Jesus understands the word *neighbor* in an all-inclusive sense. Therefore, the command "love your neighbor as yourself" has radical implications for those seeking to be part of God's Kingdom. Hard sayings such as "love your enemies, pray for your persecutors" (Matthew 5:44) and "as often as you did it for one of my least brothers, you did it for me" (Matthew 25:40) make sense only in light of Jesus' radical vision of God's Kingdom.

Perhaps because of the radical nature of Jesus' vision, it is often thought that the Kingdom of God is heaven. In fact, because of the Jewish reluctance to use the name of God, Matthew in his Gospel generally speaks of the "kingdom of heaven." Yet, when we use this phrase, we may begin to think mistakenly that Jesus' vision is *spiritual* in the otherworldly sense of the term.

In truth, Jesus's vision is of a kingdom that "has overtaken you" (Matthew 12:28). Our allegiance or conversion to God's Kingdom demands specific actions at all the levels at which we act within the human reality—namely, personal, interpersonal, and political.

1. Changes are demanded at the personal level. Persons who choose to live in the Kingdom of God become the "poor in spirit" that Jesus describes in the Beatitudes. As such, their self-images are based firmly on their identities as God's children—and not on power, possessions, or prestige:

- They are willing to sell their possessions, to do without luxuries, and to give the money to poor people because their values are those of God's Kingdom, not of consumerism.
- They thirst for justice rather than power, as Jesus himself did.

2. Kingdom people are also changed interpersonally, that is, in their relationships with others:

- They do not seek to get ahead of others but work with God to give all people their due.
- Believing the comment of Jesus that the person who wishes to be first must be the servant of others, they willingly care for those in need.
- The people of God do not use religion to gain power or to "look good" in their communities. Rather, they find in their religion the comfort and challenge that lead to action on behalf of others.

3. To be a kingdom person means being changed politically. This may seem surprising, but in fact the values of God's kingdom have obvious implications in the political sphere:

- The parable of the day laborers mentioned earlier suggests that people are paid according to their needs, not because of their talents or productivity. How does this compare with the indignation we often feel when we hear that an unemployed person receives as much as someone lucky enough to have a job?
- Throughout history, religious authority has often been used to support those in power against those in need. Jesus' teaching of the Kingdom of God stands clearly against this: "You know how those who exercise authority among the Gentiles lord it over them; their great ones make their importance felt. It cannot be like that with you. . . ." (Matthew 20:25–26). In the Kingdom, authority is understood as service to people in need, not as the power to dominate them or silence their pleas.
- When Jesus tells us that there is no difference between Jews and Gentiles, slaves and free people, men and women, he is speaking directly against racism and sexism in a way that still challenges our thinking today.

Civil-rights activists Coretta King
and Dorothy Day

Conclusion

By definition, religion seeks to lead us to God. However, no other religion's scriptures link God and justice together as tightly as our Bible does. Throughout the Scriptures, the message is clear: to know God means to do justice. For those of us who believe that God speaks to us through the Bible's stories, that message is the promise and the challenge of the Scriptures' call to justice.

For Review

1. What relationships does the biblical understanding of justice center on?
2. According to Genesis, we are commissioned to be "stewards of Creation." Explain what this phrase means.
3. Describe the growing disharmony in the world as portrayed in the early stories in Genesis.
4. The beginning of Genesis refers to nature as *creation*. What does this term imply about the relationship between God and nature?
5. What does it mean to say that the Exodus is a universal story?
6. What image of God is presented in the Exodus story?
7. Is the God of the Bible a God of law or of love? Explain your answer.
8. Briefly describe the message of the biblical prophets.
9. What is the reconciliation that Jesus embodies?
10. In what sense is Jesus' teaching about God's reign inclusive?

For Reflection

1. Often the meaning of a word comes to life when we think about its opposites. List all the possible antonyms for the word *creation* that you can think of. Then write a brief essay entitled "Creation and Its Opposites in My Life."

2. Reflect on your own life in light of the elements of the Exodus story. Have you ever experienced a journey from slavery to liberation? Write your own liberation story. Is justice one of the themes in your story? Explain.

3. During the last two centuries in the southern United States, slaves desiring their freedom found solace in the Exodus story. Describe in writing two current situations to which the message of the Exodus could be applied.

4. Reflect on the personal characteristics and the message of the biblical prophets as described in this chapter. Choose someone whom you believe to be a prophet in our era. Write a brief essay describing how that person is performing or has performed a prophetic role in creating a more just world.

5. Jesus serves as a reminder that "God is with us." What are some implications that this central message of Jesus holds for justice and peace? In writing, complete the following sentence in four different ways: "If God is with us, then . . ."

6. The text makes this comment about Jesus: "Constantly he seeks out the undignified of his day—lepers, tax collectors, prostitutes—with whom to share a meal or to spend some time." With this statement in mind, complete the following exercise:
   a. Describe in writing one activity that you imagine Jesus would do if he were to visit our world today.
   b. Write an account of Jesus' activity from the perspective of a newspaper reporter.
   c. Write an account of Jesus' activity from the perspective of someone who has been touched by him.

3
The Church's Call to Justice

While the Scriptures issue a clear call to justice, how has the Church echoed that call in its teachings and practices? A look at its history reveals that the Church has challenged its members to respond to the call and has itself been challenged by the call to justice. This chapter examines four historical periods and the way that the Church's response to justice has manifested itself in different cultural situations.

The Road to Emmaus

> Two of them that same day were making their way to a village named Emmaus seven miles distant from Jerusalem, discussing as they went all that had happened. In the course of their lively exchange, Jesus approached and began to walk along with them. However, they were restrained from recognizing him. He said to them, "What are you discussing as you go your way?" They halted, in distress, and one of them, Cleopas by name, asked him, "Are you the only resident of Jerusalem who does not know the things that went on there these past few days?" He said to them, "What things?" They said: "All those that had to do with Jesus of Nazareth, a prophet powerful in word and deed in the eyes of God and all the people; how our chief priests and leaders delivered him up to be condemned to death, and crucified him. We were hoping that he was the one who would set Israel free. Besides all this, today, the third day since these things happened, some women of our group have just brought us some astonishing news. They were at the tomb before dawn and failed to find his body, but returned with the tale that they had seen a vision of angels who declared he was alive. Some of our number went to the tomb and found it to be just as the women said, but him they did not see."
>
> Then he said to them, "What little sense you have! How slow you are to believe all that the prophets have announced! Did not the Messiah have to undergo all this so as to enter into his glory?" Beginning, then, with Moses and all the prophets, he interpreted for them every passage of Scripture which referred to him. By now they were near the village to which they were going, and he acted as if he were going farther. But they pressed him: "Stay with us. It is nearly evening—the day is practically over." So he went in to stay with them.
>
> When he had seated himself with them to eat, he took bread, pronounced the blessing, then broke the bread and began to distribute it to them. With that their eyes were opened and they recognized him. . . . (Luke 24:13–31)

In the passage above, the disciples recognize Jesus only when he breaks bread and shares it with them. Echoing the events of the Last Supper, the Emmaus story underlines certain values that made the early Church a phenomenon in history.

The Early Church: Caring Communities

Ask yourself, Given the fact that its founder died ignominiously, that it had its origins in lowly Israel, and that its early history was one of persecution, how did Christianity end up dominating the Roman Empire? Historians today emphasize that early Christianity's appeal lay in the way it valued and taught about justice. Marked by this concern for its members and a special concern for poor and needy people, the Christian communities offered a fresh alternative to the Roman worldview.

The Roman world in which Christianity bloomed valued justice highly. Yet it equated justice with law and the protection of rights. In fact, the word *justice* is derived from the Latin word *ius,* meaning "law." Doing no one harm, preserving the common good, and protecting personal property were the underlying principles in the Roman tradition.

In contrast to this strictly legal view of justice, the early Christian Church saw justice as linked more closely to love than to law. As we saw in the last chapter, this view of justice was grounded in the biblical vision of God as love, embodied in the loving deeds of Jesus.

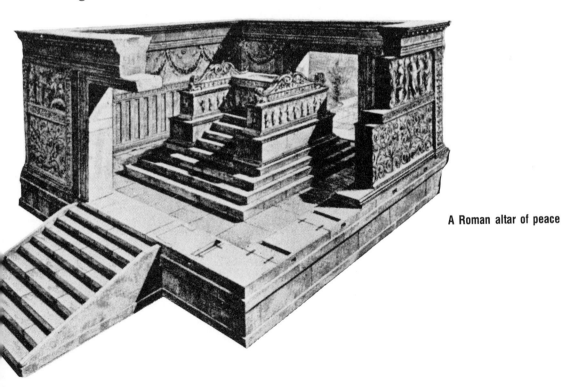

A Roman altar of peace

The Church's Revolutionary Values

So within one of the most highly developed legal systems the world had yet known, the early Church proclaimed a revolutionary set of values. For example:

- To the principle "Do no one harm," Christianity added Jesus' very challenging teaching: "Do not return harm with harm." Christian writers before the fourth century A.D. condemned killing and participation in warfare.

- With its stress on community, the early Church de-emphasized the distinction between public and private property. Instead of protecting private property, early Christians viewed all possessions as intended to be placed at the service of all community members, especially of poor and needy people.

What could be more challenging as basic values than these denials of self-defense and of private property? As the Acts of the Apostles describes it:

> Those who believed shared all things in common; they would sell their property and goods, dividing everything on the basis of each one's need. They went to the temple area together every day, while in their homes they broke bread. With exultant and sincere hearts they took their meals in common, praising God and winning the approval of all the people. Day by day the Lord added to their number those who were being saved. (Acts 2:44–47)

Although they did not always measure up to these challenging values, the early Christians brought a spirit of freedom and faith to a culture that had grown legalistic and selfish. Saint Augustine of Hippo, a church leader in the late fourth century, rephrased a popular Roman slogan to reflect the new, more compassionate Christian standpoint:

> Let no one say, "Let us eat and drink for tomorrow we die," but rather . . . "Let us fast and pray, for tomorrow we die." I add . . . a third step . . . that as a result of your fast the poor man's hunger be satisfied; and, should you be unable to fast, that you give him more to eat. . . . Let Christians therefore say, "Let us fast and pray and give, for tomorrow we die."

Saint Augustine of Hippo

Communities of Compassion

The term that best describes the early Christian Church is *compassionate*, a word that literally means "to suffer with another." Early Christians viewed themselves as members of the Body of Christ, sharing in the joys and sorrows of all the other members. The Archbishop of Constantinople John Chrysostom (A.D. c. 347–407) put this viewpoint into these words: ''Don't you realize that, as the poor man withdraws silently, sighing and in tears, you actually thrust a sword into yourself, that it is you who received the more serious wound.''

This spirit of compassion naturally held an appeal for the poor and outcast members of society. However, it also attracted a surprising number of rich and powerful adherents. These people saw that Christianity offered a vital faith in place of selfish fatalism, that it provided deep joy instead of their shallow pleasures, and that it was a wellspring of religious experience from which to quench their spiritual thirst. In short, the early Christians discovered the essential Christian mystery and truth: by sharing in Christ's continuing suffering they also shared in the joy of the Resurrection.

The Medieval Church: Christendom as God's Kingdom

When the Roman Emperor Constantine pronounced his Edict of Milan in A.D. 313, he set the stage for uniting Christianity with the Roman Empire. After years of persecution, the edict finally granted Christians the freedom to practice and preach their religion. Although earlier forced to live on the fringes of society, Christians now took their places at the center of Western civilization. As a result, Christian communities now had to accommodate large numbers of converts.

The Christian Church inherited much of the wealth and power of the Roman Empire, which began breaking up soon after Constantine's reign. For over one thousand years, the tensions that occurred between the Church and the imperial institutions shaped Western European history. During this period, which is called *the Middle Ages*, the loose federation of principalities that appeared in Europe found unity in their common religion. Christianity became referred to as *Christendom*, in which society and the ruling powers were seen as mirroring Christian principles.

The Well-Ordered Universe

People of the Middle Ages had a passion for order. This is evident in the formal quality of their art, in their logical systems of thought, and in their clearly defined social structures. For medieval Christians all of nature fit into an order that was called *the Great Chain of Being.* The first link in this chain was God, followed by angels, people, animals, plants, and finally inanimate objects. Society also was seen as hierarchical, with distinct levels or links. Both the Church and the secular society adopted this hierarchical structure.

The medieval understanding of justice also assumed a well-ordered universe. From lords to knights to serfs, every social group had its specified rights and responsibilities. The nobility ruled by their inherited "divine right," just as the serfs and their descendants were bound to the land because of their inherited positions. Although such a system obviously lent itself to abuses, it took a later age to question the structure itself. During the Middle Ages, church leaders felt that God's justice was best served by maintaining the correct order of society and by assuring that rights were protected and responsibilities were carried out: the lord who did not provide protection for his serfs was judged irresponsible, and a serf who did not work in his lord's fields was regarded as disobedient.

In short, many medieval Christians assumed a less challenging position regarding justice. The medieval theologian Saint Thomas Aquinas recommended Christian values in terms that harked back not so much to the early Christian writers as to the even earlier Greek and Roman philosophers:

> For the good life of the community three things are required. First, that the community should be established in the unity of peace. Secondly, that the community, united in the bond of peace, should be directed to good action. . . . Thirdly, that through the ruler's diligence there should be a sufficient supply of the necessities for a good life.

Although Aquinas's guidelines are good ones, they do not reflect the radical message found in the Scriptures and the early Christian writings.

Saint Thomas Aquinas

Saint Francis of Assisi: The Flower of the Middle Ages

Into this world of kings, knights, and peasants, an exceptional person was born—a man who challenged the prevailing medieval view of justice. The British historian Kenneth Clark has called **Francis of Assisi** (c. 1181–1226) the greatest spiritual figure that Europe ever produced.

As a young man, Francis recognized that money and power

A woodcut depicting the activities of various classes in medieval society

too often lead to corruption. To free himself, Francis did more than commiserate with the needy or even share his wealth with them. Instead, in his early twenties, Francis renounced his father's wealth and married "Lady Poverty." From that time on he kept no possessions and urged his followers to do likewise.

Yet Francis's embrace of poverty was not life-denying or morose. Indeed, he sang with joy as he extended himself in compassion to all creatures and all people. He thought of himself and his followers as being the clowns of God. Francis's odd riches-to-rags decision was intended to remind people of the two strange decisions at the core of Christian faith—the decision of God to enter the world in poverty and the decision of Jesus to die in humiliation in order to show us the way to a new and glorious life.

Francis was particularly concerned about the connection between possessions and warfare: "If we have possessions, we must have weapons to defend them, from which come quarrels and battles." He also saw that greed had a stranglehold on many people, diminishing their capacity to enjoy the simple things of life and preventing them from seeing the persons suffering around them.

Francis challenged his era by calling it back to the purity and simplicity of Christ's message. In a society in which burgeoning cities offered new opportunities for wealth, Francis preached voluntary poverty. In a Church dominated by the clergy, Francis refused priesthood for himself. In a world in which Christians were fighting Muslims, Francis went to Egypt to speak personally with a Muslim leader.

Although he did not denounce the institutions and authorities of his day, Francis's example powerfully pointed to their inability and unwillingness to care for the needy and to free people from their greeds. Declared a saint only two years after his death, Francis inspired other grassroots reforms that continued to change the face of the Church as it left the Middle Ages behind. Today Francis's example continues to inspire people working for justice, peace, and the ecology.

New Worlds and New Challenges

The Ninety-five Theses that Martin Luther posted on the doors of the church in Wittenberg, Germany, in 1517, initiated the collapse of Christendom and the beginning of a new era marked by the rise of an attitude called *nationalism*. People now identified more with their own nations (England, France, and Spain, for example) than with Christendom. This new era was also marked by Europe's exploitation of the lands of America, Africa, and India. In addition, many other developments—such as the breakdown of the feudal system, a growing middle class, the expansion of cities, and the Protestant break with the Catholic Church—created new challenges for the Church in responding to its call to justice.

Saint Francis of Assisi receiving
from Pope Honorius III the charter
of the Franciscan order, approved
in 1223

— have to involve laity

New Responses to Injustice

While these changes brought new forms of injustice, church people emerged who boldly and effectively addressed these problems. The seventeenth to the nineteenth centuries were peopled with many saintly women and men who felt the suffering around them and took steps to alleviate that suffering:

- In the 1600s in France, Vincent de Paul and Louise de Marillac founded orders of women that addressed the needs of the hungry and sick in the crowded cities.
- John Baptist de La Salle (1651–1719) organized men to teach homeless boys and prisoners in Paris.
- In the early 1800s, Elizabeth Ann Seton and other women began orders of women to teach the increasing Catholic population in the United States.

In addition, missionaries traveled to foreign lands in order to introduce peoples there to Christianity. Sometimes these missionaries were the only voices that demanded that these native Asians, Africans, and Americans be treated with respect and compassion.

The legacy of these efforts is today's Catholic hospitals and schools, convalescent homes, hospitality centers for the hungry and homeless, and various other social-service organizations. Even public school systems and community hospitals are by-products of works by these and other reformers who believed that every person has a right to education, health care, and basic community services. Although Christianity emerged from this period split into Protestant and Catholic factions, individual groups of Christians in both factions kept alive the Church's response to the call to justice.

The Modern Era: Catholic Social Teachings

Karl Marx Challenges Christianity's Stance on Justice

Karl Marx (1818–1883) was one of the shapers of the modern world. Along with his colleague Friedrich Engels, Marx deplored the effects of industrialization on working people in England and in his native Germany. He saw men, women, and even children and older people working long hours in inhuman conditions at less than living wages. Marx observed that working-class people lacked political power; the wealthy few controlled the new industrial society.

Saint Elizabeth Ann Seton

Marx also deplored the Christianity of his day: "Religion
is the sigh of the oppressed creature, the heart of a heartless
world, the soul of soulless conditions. It is the opium of the
people." In other words, Marx saw religion as a drug that kept
people from facing the reality of their suffering and from working to better their lives. In his view, Christian faith was a
private affair between individuals and God that taught people
not to worry about this life and to expect happiness only after
death. Marx therefore denounced religion as an instrument used
by the powerful elite to keep the powerless workers from com-
plaining or trying to better their conditions.

Marx proposed a radical restructuring of society. With his
battle cry "Workers of the world, unite!" he called for an
equalization of work and a sharing of resources. In this way,
all people would be workers and owners. No one would be required to work excessive hours; everyone would be free to pursue cultural enrichments that were previously reserved for the
wealthy few. In other words, the world would become a workers'
paradise.

Karl Marx

The Church Responds:
Pope Leo XIII and *Rerum Novarum*

Pope Leo XIII

The plight of workers was a concern not only of Marx but also of the Church. The landmark church document that first addressed the rights of workers and the conditions that were produced by industrialization was **Pope Leo XIII**'s letter titled *Rerum Novarum* (*On the Condition of Labor*), written in 1891. This **encyclical**, which is an official papal letter, was the first of many modern church documents to deal with matters of social justice.

Rerum Novarum criticized the socialism preached by Karl Marx. The encyclical condemned socialism because it gave to the state the rights belonging to the individual and family. As a result, socialism can jeopardize the dignity of the individual. Pope Leo's fear has been borne out by the loss of personal liberties in the Communist countries that were established after 1900.

Although socialism was condemned by Pope Leo, his encyclical shocked many capitalists of that time because he also strongly criticized aspects of capitalism. Today we take for granted the existence of trade unions and the freedom to strike. However, in the late 1800s these practices were considered subversive of the established social order. Yet *Rerum Novarum* supported the right to form trade unions and to strike—as well as advocated fair wages and decent working conditions.

Later popes felt strongly enough about Pope Leo's call for justice that they wrote their own social encyclicals on the fortieth, seventieth, eightieth, and ninetieth anniversaries of *Rerum Novarum*'s publication. A reading of these encyclicals and other related church documents makes it clear that today's Church is very concerned about human suffering and about the social conditions that cause poverty and oppression.

In Europe many political parties sprang up that embraced the Church's social teachings. Also, workers' unions and other labor organizations based on Christian principles became popular. Begun earlier in this century, these church-led developments are still reflected in the current face of European politics. In the United States specifically, the Catholic Worker Movement founded by Dorothy Day and Peter Maurin has been one of the most influential movements in the modern U.S. Church.

The official Church, along with many individuals and groups within the Church, has continued to discuss concerns about justice with Communists, socialists, and capitalists—that is, with the whole spectrum of the political arena. The U.S. bishops ask the following questions about every economic and political system: "What does the economy do *for* people? What does it do *to* people? And how do people *participate* in it?" (*Economic Justice for All,* no. 1).

Catholic Social Teaching Today

Since the time that Pope Leo issued *Rerum Novarum,* the modern Church has focused more attention on justice-related concerns. During this period, the geographical focus of Christianity in general and of Catholicism in particular has been changing. For example, Latin America contains the largest concentration of Catholics in the world today. By the year 2000, Africa will have more Catholics than the United States. At the present time, one of the fastest-growing Catholic communities is in South Korea.

Catholicism's shift from being predominantly a European religion to one of truly global dimensions has created new questions in regard to justice. Because its presence is now worldwide, extending beyond the interests of one country or one continent, the Church is uniquely suited to speak on global justice-related issues.

Justice in the World, a 1971 statement by the Synod of Bishops meeting in Rome, made this understanding of the Church's global role particularly clear. The document states:

> Action on behalf of justice and participation in the transformation of the world fully appear to us as a constitutive dimension of the preaching of the Gospel, or, in other words, of the Church's mission for the redemption of the human race and its liberation from every oppressive situation.

In other words, the Church has responded strongly to critics like Karl Marx by insisting that it has been called by Jesus to speak about justice. The Church does not offer a brand of religion that numbs people to present injustices with the promise of salvation after death. On the contrary, the salvation after death that was promised by Jesus cannot be separated from peoples' liberation from injustice now:

> In their pilgrimage to the heavenly city Christians are to seek and relish the things that are above: this involves not a lesser, but rather a greater commitment to working with all [people] towards the establishment of a world that is more human. (Vatican Council II, *The Church in the Modern World,* no. 57)

Recent church documents about justice have provided general guidelines and some challenging concrete proposals. The U.S. bishops, for instance, have published numerous statements on justice-related concerns—most recently statements on peace, focusing on nuclear weapons, and on the U.S. economy.

Liberation Theology: Voices from the Third World

In Latin American countries, a small percentage of the population usually controls the wealth and power while the vast majority of the people live in poverty. This situation exists despite the fact that Latin America is overwhelmingly Catholic. This scandal has led many Latin American church leaders and theologians to ask, How can the Good News of Jesus and the Church's social teachings be applied to our world? Out of this question has emerged an innovative and influential school of thought called *liberation theology.*

Liberation theology primarily echoes the Church's teaching that Jesus' message of liberation means liberation from existing oppressive forces, as well as salvation from sin and death. In that sense, liberation theology also harkens back to the spirit of the early Church when Christians represented the voice of the oppressed. Liberation theology has helped to give a voice to the many poor people of the world who are crying out for justice. It also has influenced papal pronouncements on justice. For instance, Pope John Paul II has made a number of visits to Latin America to discuss church teachings on justice and the situation of poor people.

Liberation theology has become an important basis for political change not only in Latin America but also in many of the world's poorest countries. These countries are usually called *developing* countries. Collectively they are known as the *Third World.* For the most part, the Third World comprises the southern half of our planet, including Latin America and most of Africa and Asia.

Although it first developed in response to the conditions in the Third World, liberation theology has become a challenge to the more prosperous countries as well: it has pointed out that the current world order makes it very difficult for poor countries to make needed improvements. The 1971 Synod of Bishops shared this belief:

> Unless combatted and overcome by social and political action, the influence of the new industrial and technological order favors the concentration of wealth, power and decision-making in the hands of a small public or private controlling group. (*Justice in the World*)

Because so much wealth and power reside in the Western democratic countries (sometimes called the *First World*), liberation theology presents a challenge to those countries to recognize their complicity in fostering conditions that lead to misery in the needy countries of the Third World. It also challenges the so-called *Second World,* or Communist countries, to realize that their atheistic socialism lacks a concern for personal dignity and spirituality.

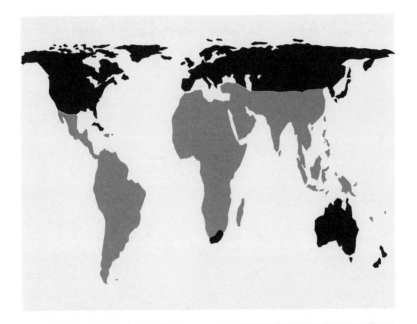

This world map shows the First and Second Worlds (in black) and the Third World (in color). This map is based on a projection that gives a clearer picture of the relative sizes of the continents than does the more familiar Mercator projection.

Three Worlds, One Earth

Catholic Social Teaching and Peace

The arms race is a threat to [people's] highest good, which is life; it makes poor peoples and individuals yet more miserable, while making richer those already powerful; it creates a continuous danger of conflagration, and in the case of nuclear arms, it threatens to destroy all life from the face of the earth. (The Synod of Bishops, *Justice in the World*)

The twentieth century has been a century of wars—two world wars and countless smaller conflicts no less tragic in their toll in human suffering. We live under the threat of annihilation by nuclear war while our country and much of the rest of the world gears itself up for warfare. We glance at newspaper headlines fearful that we will learn about another troubled spot

**Anglican Archbishop Desmond
Tutu of South Africa**

where conflict is occurring. In our country most scientists, many industries, and a large percentage of federal employees direct their energies toward the business of war or preparing for war. The world community spends enormous amounts of money on weapons, monies that could be spent alleviating poverty and solving other problems.

In its social teachings the Church recognizes war and peace as justice-related issues and recognizes the links between peace and other concerns about justice. Later on this course will address war and peace specifically. For now it is important to note that recent Catholic social teachings view with alarm the powder-keg world in which we live. Likewise, individual Catholics and church-related organizations have been active in working for peace. The Church and many of its members have devoted themselves to dealing with this crucial issue.

Conclusion

The gathering that began with a simple breaking of bread two thousand years ago has become a church of global proportions, the largest of the world religions. Throughout its history the Church has expressed in different ways what it means to break bread together and to be a community of faith. Today the liberating message of Jesus remains as challenging and hopeful as ever.

For Review

1. Describe the Romans' concept of justice.
2. What revolutionary values did early Christianity propose?
3. What term best describes the early Christian Church? Explain. *compassion*
4. How did Christianity's role as it emerged during the Middle Ages affect its understanding of justice?
5. Describe Saint Francis of Assisi's attitude toward poverty.
6. List the new problems that faced the Church following the collapse of Christendom. *p 60*
7. Describe Karl Marx's attitude toward religion. What did he propose in contrast to the religion of his day?
8. What rights did Pope Leo XIII's letter *Rerum Novarum* advocate for workers? *unions, strikes, fair wages, decent conditions*
9. According to the U.S. bishops' letter on the economy, what does the Church ask about economic and political systems?
10. Where did liberation theology originate? What is its message?
11. How does today's Church view war and its relationship to justice?

For Reflection

1. The early Church strove to be communities of compassion. Look up the word *compassion* in a dictionary. Spend time thinking about its meaning. Write a brief essay about what a community of compassion would be like for you.

2. Because of its position of power, the medieval Church was deeply involved in political issues of its time.
   a. Record your response to each of the following statements by choosing *agree strongly, agree, disagree,* or *disagree strongly:*
      1) Priests, nuns, and other religious should never hold political offices.
      2) Church leaders should not make political statements about elections or specifically political issues.
      3) Since many issues of justice and peace, such as the arms race and unemployment, are also political issues, these concerns should not be addressed in sermons during the Mass.
      4) The Church should be concerned about all areas of life. Therefore, the Church and its leaders should be involved in political issues.

    b. Write a one- to two-page paper explaining your position on one of the above statements.

3. Research the life of Saint Francis of Assisi. Write an essay on one of the following topics:
   - Saint Francis and Lady Poverty
   - Saint Francis and Peace
   - Saint Francis and Nature

4. Research one of the following persons and write about how she or he attempted to address people's needs:
   - Vincent de Paul
   - Louise de Marillac
   - John Baptist de La Salle
   - Elizabeth Ann Seton

5. Review Karl Marx's criticism of the religion of his day. Based on your experience, do you find Marx's criticism valid for Christianity today? Write a one-page essay to support your position.

6. Numerous church statements on justice have been written in this century. Read one of them, such as the 1971 statement *Justice in the World.* Make a list of the key teachings on justice that are found in the document.

7. Write a report on one of the following topics:
   - The Church in Latin America
   - Liberation Theology
   - Archbishop Oscar Romero of El Salvador

8. This chapter discusses the Church and justice. According to the Second Vatican Council, the Church is "the soul of human society in its renewal by Christ and transformation into the family of God" (*The Church in the Modern World,* no. 40). Write a two-page essay describing what you see as the *unique perspective* that the Church can bring to justice-related concerns today.

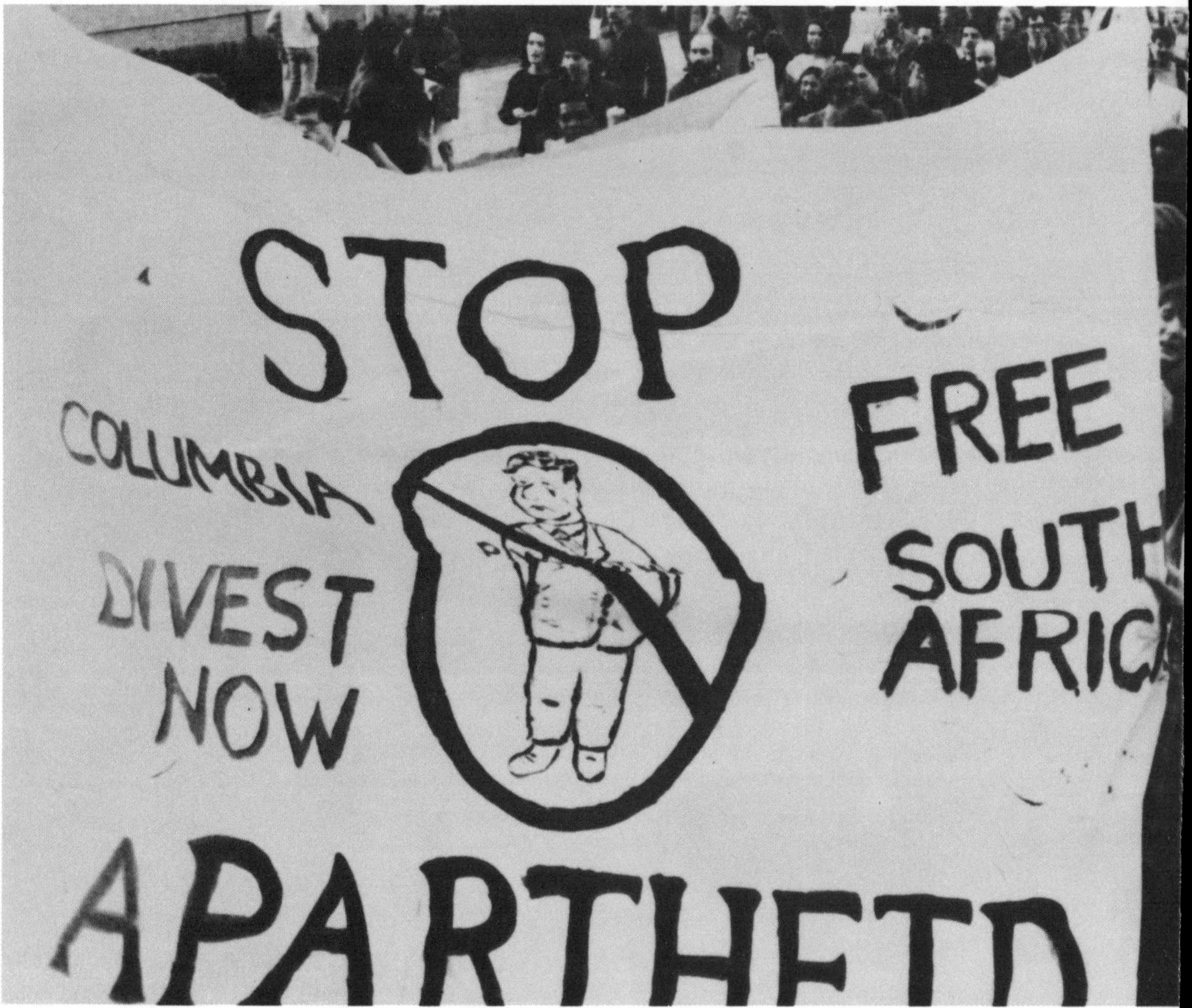
STOP
COLUMBIA
DIVEST
NOW
FREE
SOUTH
AFRIC
APARTHEID

4
Our Response to the Call

The call to justice is a call to action. When deciding where this call will lead, we need to consider how best to be of service. This chapter describes two broad categories of possible involvement: the works of mercy and the works of social action. Also we must reflect on our particular talents and on how we as individuals can best respond to the needs of justice. Finally, we need to be sensitive to the setting in which our involvement occurs.

Dr. Albert Schweitzer, a Nobel Peace Prize winner, at his clinic in Lambaréné, Gabon, in 1953

How Do We Save the Babies?

Once upon a time there was a small village on the edge of a river. The people there were good and the life in the village was good. One day a villager noticed a baby floating down the river. The villager quickly jumped into the river and swam out to save the baby from drowning.

The next day this same villager was walking along the river bank and noticed two babies in the river. He called for help, and both babies were rescued from the swift waters. And the following day four babies were seen caught in the turbulent current. And then eight, then more, and still more.

The villagers organized themselves quickly, setting up watch towers and training teams of swimmers who could resist the swift waters and rescue babies. Rescue squads were soon working 24 hours a day. And each day the number of babies floating down the river increased.

The villagers organized themselves efficiently. The rescue squads were now snatching many children each day. Groups were trained to give mouth-to-mouth resuscitation. Others prepared formula and provided clothing for the chilled babies. Many [people] were involved in making clothing and knitting blankets. Still others provided foster homes and placement.

While not all the babies . . . could be saved, the villagers felt they were doing well to save as many as they could each day. Indeed, their priest blessed them in their good work. And life in the village continued on that basis.

One day, however, someone raised the question, "But where are all these babies coming from? Who is throwing them into the river? Why? Let's organize a team to go upstream and see who's doing it." The seeming logic of the elders countered: "And if we go upstream who will operate the rescue operations? We need every concerned person here."

"But don't you see," cried the one lone voice, "if we find out who is throwing them in, we can stop the problem and no babies will drown. By going upstream we can eliminate the cause of the problem."

"It is too risky," [decided the elders].

And so the numbers of babies in the river increase daily. Those saved increase, but those who drown increase even more. (Inter-Religious Task Force for Social Analysis, *Must We Choose Sides?* pp. 114–115)

Responding with Justice as Christians

In our Christian tradition, two approaches to justice developed: works of mercy and social action. Because both approaches are considered necessary to bring about a just world, let's spend some time describing the contributions they can make.

Works of Mercy: Justice as Giving Direct Help

Feed the hungry.
Give shelter to the homeless.
Visit the sick and imprisoned.
Educate the unschooled.

When we see people in need, our hearts cry out to help. The empty bowl held by a starving child begs to be filled. The sudden illness of a classmate calls for a visit or some other sign of care. When a neighbor's house is destroyed by fire, we want to do what we can to provide for the family.

As the story above suggests, when we directly help people in need, we are performing works of mercy. Such works have been espoused by Christianity since its beginnings and are rooted in the example of Jesus himself. For instance:

- In the Acts of the Apostles, Peter declares that Jesus ". . . went about doing good works and healing all who were in the grip of the devil . . ." (10:38).
- As noted already, care for widows and orphans, sharing bread with the hungry, and other similar acts of mercy set the early Christian communities apart from their neighbors.
- Either through institutions, such as Catholic hospitals and Catholic Charities organizations, or through the acts of individual Christians, the Church today continues to relieve suffering and help people in need.

Clearly Christians are called to perform works of mercy in whatever way possible. Moreover, as the word *mercy* suggests, Christians are called to help others without judging them and without expecting reward. Let's take a moment to discuss this traditionally Christian understanding of justice.

In modern Western societies, it is conventional to talk about the "truly needy" as opposed to merely lazy or conniving people who are said to be not worth helping. Often this distinction has been used as an excuse to avoid helping any needy persons.

Interestingly, this complaint about needy persons is almost as old as the Church itself. But so is the Gospel's answer, essentially given in the passage above from the Acts of the

Apostles: in short, Jesus was more concerned about healing people than about judging them. He also pointed out that we all fit that category—in need of healing. Jesus came to save and transform all of us into the images of God that we are meant to be.

As far back as the second century, Clement of Alexandria stated the Church's position in more formal terms:

> You must not try to distinguish between the deserving and the undeserving. You may easily make a mistake, and, as the matter is in doubt, it is better to benefit the undeserving than, in avoiding this, to miss the good. We are told not to judge.

The 1985 Live Aid concert in London

In the fourth century, John Chrysostom defined the Church's position even more forcefully in his preachings on justice. To those who complained that poor people were merely lazy, Chrysostom replied that if the rich themselves were not giving to the poor, then they were just as lazy because helping poor and needy persons is the work God wants us to do. To this retort to the rich he added, "If you are prompt in showing mercy, the man who is poor will soon be rid of idleness and you of cruelty."

The Christian work of mercy, then, means that we stand *with* other people as brothers and sisters, ministering generously to their needs. We are not to stand *above* them as judges, administering justice in cold, narrow, legal ways. That's because love, not law, lies at the heart of Christian justice.

Mother Teresa: A Model of Mercy

Mother Teresa of Calcutta won the Nobel Peace Prize in 1979. At that time, her careworn face framed by a simple Indian veil became a universal symbol of mercy. In India she is known simply as "Mother." Her speeches are so often punctuated with the word *love* that she would sound naively sentimental if her actions did not proclaim love so strongly. Whether working among the starving and homeless of Calcutta, the garbage pickers of Mexico City, the oppressed aborigines of Australia, or the lepers in Africa, Mother Teresa and her followers embody mercy in its clearest form.

Appropriately, Mother Teresa's order of sisters is called the Missionaries of Charity. Along with the traditional religious vows of poverty, chastity, and obedience, they take a crucial fourth vow of "wholehearted, free service to the poorest of the poor." They take Jesus at his word when he said, "I assure you, as often as you did it for one of my least brothers, you did it for me" (Matthew 25:40). In so doing they bear witness to the dignity and worth of every human person.

For herself, Mother Teresa cares little about political action and changing social structures. She cares about people—helping the poorest of the poor and encouraging others to love in whatever capacity they are capable. She views her calling as working among the numberless people who fall between the cracks of the social structures.

Does she, then, reject social action as inappropriate or worthless? In fact, Mother Teresa has said:

> If there are people who feel God wants them to change the structures of society, that is something between them and their God. We must serve Him in whatever way we are called. I am called to help the individual; to love each poor person, not to deal with institutions.

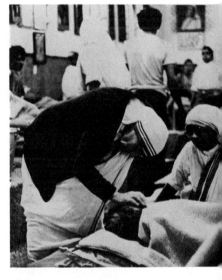

Mother Teresa of Calcutta

Through her untiring work of mercy, Mother Teresa celebrates the value of every human person. She also symbolizes the spirit of compassion that must characterize all Christian service. If questioned about how to help those in need, she would simply say: "What you can do, I can't do, and what I can do, you can't do, but together we can do something beautiful for God."

Social Action:
Justice as Changing Society's Structures

> Give people fish; you feed them for a day. Teach people to fish; you feed them for a lifetime. (A Chinese proverb)

The story about the townspeople helping the drowning victims demonstrates mercy in action, but it also raises important questions: Can more than that be done? Can we address the underlying causes or provide long-term solutions to an immediate problem? The story suggests that alleviating causes is appropriate action on behalf of people who are suffering. At this level of justice, social structures must be examined and creative changes explored.

In the story, for example, the villagers could have decided to investigate the situation upstream to discover the cause of the grave injustice to the babies. What if they found that a village much larger than their own was dealing with a food shortage in this perverse manner? Or, what if the villagers discovered that the central government was coercing the villagers upstream to drown their children in order to deal with overpopulation at the national level? Very quickly, the villagers downstream could find themselves dealing with social structures and legal systems.

Like works of mercy, social action is a work of love. It is concerned with meeting people's needs and protecting their dignity. However, social action is aimed more directly at the other two concerns of justice as defined in chapter 1, namely, the concerns for solidarity and for just social structures. In terms of the story about the drowning victims, social action considers underlying social causes and long-term solutions to injustices.

South Africans sitting on benches designated for blacks only

Archbishop Tutu: A Model of Social Action

Desmond Tutu, Anglican archbishop from South Africa, won the Nobel Peace Prize in 1984. Archbishop Tutu received the award in recognition of his work challenging the South African system of racial segregation known as *apartheid* (ə-'pär-tāt). Because of his country's policy of apartheid, blacks and other nonwhites lack freedom and basic rights, are denied equal treatment under the law, and suffer a standard of living well below that of the ruling white minority. Archbishop Tutu wants this unjust system changed. As Mother Teresa models mercy, so Archbishop Tutu models social action.

Because he wants structural changes in his country, Archbishop Tutu links political action with his religious beliefs. He does not simply want individuals suffering under apartheid to be helped; he wants to eliminate the system of apartheid so that blacks, as well as whites, share power. He believes that the underlying cause of this injustice is that apartheid is written into South Africa's constitution. In Archbishop Tutu's view, systemic change offers the only long-term solution to the problems of South Africa's black population. To bring about change he encourages workers' strikes, rallies and marches, economic boycotts from other countries to exert pressure, and other forms of nonviolent protest.

Archbishop Tutu possesses vision—the vision of a just world. The Nobel Peace Prize affirms that his work for South African human rights is an important step in creating a just world. In his own words he describes the transformation that he envisions:

Archbishop Desmond Tutu

> What we are looking for is a new society where we are saying, "Hey, you are not going to be free, white people, until we are free. We are bound with one another. . . . let's try [going] hand-in-hand together, black and white, into this glorious future that God opened up for us in this wonderful land so that we together—black and white— can walk tall and know that we count not because of the color of our skin, but we count because we are each creatures of infinite value made in the image of God."

The Two Feet of Justice

The works of mercy and of social action are often called "the two feet of Christian justice" because to walk in justice we must walk with both feet. Although we may find one or the other approach more appropriate to our talents or interests, we must understand the interplay and differences between the two:

Works of Mercy	*Works of Social Action*
1. Are concerned with the present symptoms of injustice	1. Are concerned with the underlying causes of injustice
2. Focus on individual needs	2. Focus on changing social structures
3. Look for immediate solutions	3. Look for long-term solutions
4. Provide a direct service with temporary results	4. Provide indirect help that is aimed at permanent change
5. Involve haves sharing with have-nots	5. Involve haves and have-nots working together
6. Require no change in social structures	6. Require working toward changes in the social structures

The following case further illustrates these two methods of working for justice:

> In the United States the current level of unemployment is unacceptable by all standards. To deal with this problem, government agencies provide financial assistance to the unemployed. In addition, private groups—including churches—offer some economic help. These agencies and organizations seek to provide an immediate solution to the present problem and temporary assistance to those in need. In other words, they perform acts of mercy for people who are out of work. Yet these are stopgap measures: that is, they do not pretend to produce anything other than temporary and incomplete results. Of course, temporary help might be all that is necessary.
>
> As the rate of unemployment continues at a high level, people have begun to ponder the reasons that the rate is so high. Some people have concluded that "the unemployed are lazy" and that changes in our employment system would not alter the present situation. Other people have found, however, that high unemployment exists because of many underlying factors. For instance, sufficient numbers of unskilled jobs are not available, and many unemployed people are not trained to fill the skilled positions that are available. In this case, steps can be taken to provide long-term solutions to the problem of unemployment. Agencies and groups might put at least some of their efforts into developing job-training programs and supporting new businesses.
>
> People who are unsuccessful at finding a job over a period of years feel powerless over their own lives and find that their fate is in the hands of others. They become have-nots who are dependent on the charity of the haves. In the face of such an unequal distribution of power, justice aims to change the social structure so that both haves and have-nots can gain skills with which to support themselves and contribute to society. Once employed, people are no longer powerless; they can be givers, as well as receivers.

"Power Over" Versus "Power With"

Of the two feet of justice, social action is the more difficult step to take. The reason has to do with the difference between "power over" others and "power with" others.

People engaged in works of mercy can choose to "give till it hurts," yet they retain their power of choice. That is, they can withdraw their help, and those on the receiving end of this charity have no say in the matter.

Social action, on the other hand, involves sharing decision-making power with others. The people who need help are consulted and participate in making decisions that affect them. Consequently, social action demands consensus and even compromise. At bottom, social action means transforming power *over* others into power *with* others.

Here is a case that illustrates changing the distribution of power by altering political and corporate structures:

> A *multinational* corporation is a business that operates in more than one country. Having international operations offers a corporation increased power over its employees. For example, if workers in one country do not approve of the corporation's wage scale, then the business can threaten to move its operations to a country where workers will settle for lower wages. The corporation's workers are therefore rendered powerless and possibly subject to unemployment or unjust wages.
>
> Two possible changes can equalize the power of employers and employees. First, the workers might organize on an international level, in which case the workers of different countries would not be in competition with each other. Second, the workers might gain more say in the running of the corporation by buying its stock or negotiating for seats on its board of directors. As you can imagine, either of these changes might well threaten those who presently control the corporation.

Living in the Spirit of Justice

Recognizing Our Talents

According to an ancient Greek myth, Atlas was a god forced to carry the sky on his shoulders. The legend of Christopher represents an early attempt to Christianize the figure of Atlas. In the Christian version, Christopher accepts his unique strength and willingly puts it to use in service to God. In so doing he comes to realize the special Christian insight that serving people in need means serving Jesus as well.

> Christopher towered over others of his time. Strong, brave, and fearless, he was also a good and sensitive person who wanted to serve God. For that reason, he visited a monk to inquire how best to serve God.

"One can serve God through a life of fasting and self-denial," the monk told Christopher.

"Thank you, wise monk, but that would not be for me," replied Christopher, who was also an honest person.

"Then dedicate your life to constant prayer—that is also a way to serve God," suggested the monk.

Christopher thought about this and again told the monk, "That too would not be a method suitable for me."

The monk studied Christopher for some time and then said to him, "Nearby is a river. Many travelers come to this river but find the crossing treacherous. However, with your great strength and size, you could easily carry them across. In this way you could serve God."

Upon hearing this suggestion Christopher exclaimed, "That is a service that suits my talents."

For years Christopher helped people to cross the river. Then one evening, a small child appeared on the river bank.

"Can you carry me across?" asked the child.

"I will gladly do so, little one," answered Christopher. Christopher swept the child up into his massive arms and made his way into the water. However, as they reached the deepest part of the river, the child became heavier and heavier. Soon the child got so heavy that Christopher could just barely support him. Christopher needed every bit of his strength to carry this suddenly stupendous weight through the raging current. It took all of Christopher's dedication and prayers to make any progress through the treacherous water. At last Christopher was able to deposit the child safely on the banks of the river.

"You are truly a heavy passenger, little child," said Christopher.

"I am a great weight, sir, for I am the Child Jesus. Within me lie the sorrow, pain, and tribulations of all the people of the world. While transporting me across the river, you actually were carrying the weight of the world upon your shoulders." With these words, the child vanished.

Christopher knelt down and praised God because now he knew for certain that he was serving God with his talents.

This is the legend of Christopher, whose name means "Christ-bearer."

Like Christopher, each of us possesses unique talents. Each of us brings a particular personality, special abilities, and our own fund of knowledge to our task of serving God and neighbor. Some of us are outgoing and others reserved. Some of us can "get the job done" while others make sure that everybody is getting along. To varying degrees each of us can sing, write poetry, fix cars, work computers, play sports, tell stories, listen well, think things out, express the group's feelings, and so on.

From the day that we enter high school, we notice how different all of our classmates are. As we mature, we not only notice differences but we also come to appreciate them. When we place our own uniqueness at the service of justice and join with others who also contribute in their own unique ways, we supply the richness and diversity that a just world needs. In his analogy of the body, Saint Paul offers us an excellent portrait of the Christian vision of all people contributing their unique talents to the creation of a just world: "The body is one and has many members, but all the members, many though they are, are one body; and so it is with Christ. . . . If all the members were alike, where would the body be?" (1 Corinthians 12:12,19).

The message of Christopher—and of Christianity itself— is that we all can be Christ-bearers in our own unique fashions. Of course, we can also stretch ourselves by developing new talents or testing new dimensions of our personalities. Nonetheless, the first task in acting for justice remains, to "know thyself." The more we know ourselves, the more we can join our talents with others' talents to share the burdens and joys of working for justice. This work can be pursued in all the settings of our lives, including the personal, social, and spiritual settings. Let's look briefly at each of these settings.

Lifestyles and Justice

The term *lifestyle* simply refers to the usual way we live. In a spirit of justice, we want to live our life in such a way that we maintain an association with the poor and forgotten people of our world. Maintaining such a relationship does not mean that we must live like the poorest of poor people, even though some heroic Christians throughout history and in our present time have chosen to do so. It does mean that we question the style of life offered us by our culture: what does this lifestyle mean in terms of my relationship with the poor? The following story suggests how our lifestyle can affect our view of poverty.

Recently a Midwestern priest invited a Venezuelan priest to visit him. The North American priest picked up his South American visitor at the airport in a late-model Oldsmobile sedan and drove him to his rectory in a nearby suburban parish. They arrived close to the time for the evening meal, so they joined the other priests living there for a drink followed by a delightful meal. After eating they retired to an air-conditioned, carpeted lounge that contained a stereo system, a television set capable of receiving numerous cable channels, and large comfortable chairs.

At the end of the evening the North American priest asked his friend, "What do you think of our country so far?"

"So rich! So rich! I can't believe that you are so rich!" the Venezuelan replied.

"But we are not really rich," his friend laughed. "Everyone in our neighborhood lives as well as, if not better than, we do."

During their two-week visit together, the Midwestern priest tried to convince his friend that he was in fact not a wealthy person. For his part the South American priest always asked in amazement, "But living this way—how will you ever understand real poverty and those who are poor?"

Migrant workers camping on their job site

Before his South American friend visited him, this North American priest thought little about what comforts his car, his rectory, and his lifestyle afforded him. In his mind he simply lived the way that others lived. He considered his lifestyle ordinary and his possessions not excessive. Yet in the eyes of the visiting priest, he was living a life of great luxury.

In the spirit of justice, we need to avoid buying every new gadget just because we can afford it. We need to monitor our use of the car, the television, and other conveniences in order to determine whether they make us more in touch with our world and more alive or more insensitive to others and deadened within. We need to question the personal price we pay for the comforts available to us. (For example, "Now that I have a television, a stereo, and a telephone in my own room, I see very little of my family.") We need to consider how we can make special times such as Christmas and other holy days occasions for giving to those who are truly in need. In short, we need to live so that we remain attentive to the concerns of the world's dispossessed.

Two notes of caution regarding lifestyle must be made. First, examining our lifestyles in the spirit of justice does not imply heaping shame on ourselves. Justice is a virtue; shame is a vice. Justice and concern for others energizes us; shame saps our energy. Justice says, "Because of you I want to do this." Shame says, "I hate to do this, but I'd better do it anyway."

The second point of caution is that the spirit of justice suggests certain lifestyle directions but cannot easily be reduced to specific actions. For instance, to say "concern for justice implies no use of air-conditioning" is obviously too broad a statement. We respond to the call to justice through our lifestyles when we make any concrete changes in our habits out of consideration for poor people.

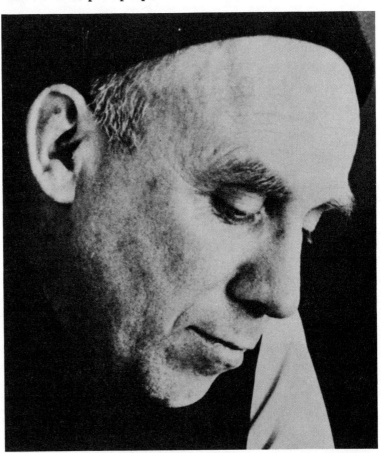

Thomas Merton

Community and Justice

Thomas Merton (1915–1968) was one of the most vocal advocates of justice in the U.S. Catholic Church. In a monastery in Kentucky, Merton spent most of his adult life as a solitary monk. Although such a setting lends itself more to a "me-and-God" spirituality than to a sense of involvement in world issues, Merton steadfastly linked his relationship with God to his concern for justice. He maintained a steady correspondence with others who were actively involved in creating a just world and regularly received visits from many of them. Paradoxically, from this solitary monk, we receive the message that "in working for justice, do not work alone."

Working for justice is best carried out in a community setting. Just as we are not meant to be Christian alone, so we are to seek out others with whom to overcome injustice. In the spirit of justice we are to include others, not to exclude them. A community setting reminds us that our concern is for real people with real needs and that we need others as they also need us. A community setting allows us to share our strengths, as well as our struggles. The presence of a community setting for justice stands in opposition to the selfishness and excessive competitiveness that mark an unjust world.

Prayer and Justice

> We all long for heaven where God is, but we have it in our power to be in heaven right now—to be happy at this very moment. But being with God now means
> loving as God loves,
> helping as God helps,
> giving as God gives,
> serving as God serves,
> rescuing as God rescues,
> being with God twenty-four hours,
> touching God in God's distressing disguise.
> (Adapted from Mother Teresa of Calcutta)

One of the early church leaders described prayer as "keeping company with God." Prayer is exactly that—spending time with God, allowing God to speak to us, speaking to God about our concerns. Yet, as Mother Teresa suggests in the above passage, caring for others is also keeping company with God. Therefore it is only natural that the proper setting for justice is a prayerful one.

Prayer helps us to see connections that we might otherwise miss. When we include prayer in our response to justice, we acknowledge that we are working hand in hand with God. By attending to prayer we create a rhythm of active involvement and rejuvenating inwardness that is similar to the rhythm of withdrawal and involvement that Jesus employed during his active years. Through prayer we place our concerns, our strengths and weaknesses, and our successes and failures in God's hands. Out of prayer we can emerge refreshed and filled with a new enthusiasm for the work of justice.

Celebration and Justice

> If I had only two loaves of bread, I would keep one and sell the other in order to buy flowers to feed my soul. (A Hindu proverb)

If we remained depressed until the world came around to the way we wanted it, we would be morbid for a long time. In working for justice we celebrate *what is* even while we pursue our vision of *what can be*. Celebration declares that although the struggle continues, the victory is already in sight.

Too often we think of justice as "serious business" that lacks a lighter side. Celebration reminds us of the lighter side of working for justice. Celebration recognizes that when people are actively involved with others, many humorous occurrences happen. It incorporates a sense of humor with a spirit of playfulness. Celebration allows us to joke about our fears and failures and unburdens us from overbearing responsibility. In short, celebration asks, Is our working for justice a drudgery or is it joyful? If at least an element of joy is not present, probably another strategy is called for.

Finally, the Hindu proverb mentioned above recalls the image of bread in the Gospel. The Last Supper especially suggests how celebration and justice are tightly linked in Christian faith and liturgy. Every time we go to Mass we are reminded that what we are to do in memory of Jesus is to enjoy the bread of life and to share it with others.

Conclusion: Choosing Our Responses

The needs of justice are great. When deciding how to respond to the call to justice we have many avenues open. When we assess our talents, the needs present in our community, possible actions that we can take to address problems, and our setting for working for justice, we realize that we *can* contribute to creating a just world. If we are faithful to the call, we will discover in surprising ways that we are indeed "keeping company with God."

For Review

1. In connection with works of mercy, explain what is meant by standing *with* and not *above* other people.
2. List the six differences between works of mercy and social action.
3. Explain what is meant by the phrases "power with" and "power over" in regard to social action.
4. Why is knowing ourselves the first task in action for justice?
5. Explain the two cautions in regard to justice and lifestyle.
6. Explain the connections between justice and community, justice and prayer, and justice and celebration.

For Reflection

1. Examine the characteristics of works of mercy and social action that are listed on page 80. For each characteristic, describe in writing an example of an activity that demonstrates that characteristic.
2. Complete one of the following exercises:
   a. Spend time working with an organization involved in caring for the needy people within your community. In writing, describe the experience.
   b. Interview someone who helps people in need in your community. Write a report on his or her comments about the experience.
3. Mother Teresa and Archbishop Tutu are models of mercy and social action. Name other people who you believe are models of mercy or social action. Explain your choices in writing.
4. Imagine that your school is forming a club to work on justice-related concerns in your school and community. Reflect on your personal talents, skills, and interests. Then list specific ways that you feel you could best contribute to such a group.
5. Reflect on your lifestyle in relation to concerns of justice and peace. List fifteen objects that you own personally. Comment on whether each object is necessary or merely nice.
6. List and describe the ways that your community—family, school, parish, and local community—helps you to respond to the call to justice.

7. Create a brief prayer on a justice-related issue that you have been thinking about.

8. Reread the Hindu proverb on page 88. Why is it important for us to be attentive to celebration, joy, and humor in our response to justice? List and describe some concrete examples of how these three qualities can help us serve the cause of justice.

Part B:
Justice
and Human Needs

5

Poverty: A Scandal, Not a Scourge

We Christians are fond of asking, If Jesus were alive today, what would he be like? Yet we already have an answer to that question from his own words when he said that whenever we help those in need, we are helping him. So if we wish to know Jesus, we can learn about him from those who are homeless and needy. To see Jesus in poor people and to join with them in overcoming their poverty are essential parts of our responses to the Christian call to justice.

Sultan the Beggar

Every day Sultan sat with the other beggars by the side of the road near the gates of a prosperous city.

"Give me your money," he cried. "Listen to the jingle of your coins. Don't they trouble you? Empty your pockets. Lighten your burden. Set yourself free."

Most passersby quickened their pace and pretended that Sultan was not even there. Some glared at him as if to say, "How dare you disturb my day with your begging!" Sometimes a poor street peddler stopped and chatted with Sultan, sharing some of her meager lunch with him. On occasion someone tossed a coin to him, and Sultan exclaimed, "Praise to Allah for lightening your burden!"

One day a traveler observed Sultan and was struck by his unusual style of begging. She was so curious that she asked him, "When you beg, why do you say, 'Set yourself free' and 'Lighten your burden'?"

"Let me explain it to you," Sultan replied, "since you obviously do not understand the ways of the world. I beg so that I can be of service to people with money. When they walk around with money in their pockets, their minds become preoccupied: 'What can I buy with my money? How can I get more money so that I can buy even more things?' They also walk around thinking, 'Look at that poor person. I'm glad I am not like him—I have money.' But at the same time they are thinking, 'Why can't I be like this other person—she has much more money than I do!'"

Sultan continued to instruct the stranger. "When people with money meet another person, they ask themselves: 'Is this person someone who wants to take my money? I'd better keep my distance for fear that he will steal from me. And I had better buy locks for my doors and perhaps a weapon to protect my money.'"

"But how do you fit in, beggar?" asked the stranger.

Sultan replied, "When some people with money see me, they feel guilty. Some feel angry or sad or perhaps moved to compassion. In any case, I invite them to think about the way that their money may trap them. By giving away some of their money, they may begin to see a way out of their trap."

The stranger thanked Sultan for informing her about "the ways of the world." She stepped aside, and Sultan resumed his peculiar cry: "Give me your money! Empty your pockets! Set yourself free!"

That night the stranger followed Sultan. As he walked over a bridge, Sultan stopped to examine the fruits of his day's begging. He kept a coin or two—enough for a modest meal—and tossed the rest into the river.

Examining Poverty: The Cries of Poor People

Just as during the time of the Exodus and the prophets, as during the time of Jesus and the early Church, and as during the time of Saint Francis of Assisi and Saint Vincent de Paul, poor people today are crying out for help. Yet their cries, like Sultan's, are also for our conversion because in order to help the needy we must change our values and priorities. So their cries can breathe new life into traditional notions about the human family and Christian community. Their cries also challenge the current world order, which offers poor people little hope of progress.

Sultan—who is a prophet, as well as a beggar—reminds us that homeless and helpless people can lead us to God. As Jesus also told us, it is not in our wealth that we meet God but in our poverty. For that reason, as seekers of God and followers of Jesus, we have much to learn from poor people.

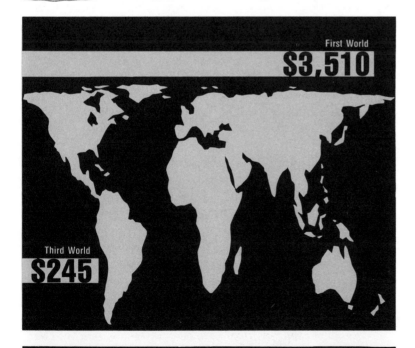

First World
$3,510

Third World
$245

Personal Income Worldwide

Who Are the Poor People?

Poor People in the Third World

The majority of the world's needy people are clustered in the poorest countries. In the Third World, the vast majority of the population is poor. Furthermore, although standards of living vary, more than one fifth of the Third World population exists in conditions termed *absolute poverty*—conditions of life so characterized by malnutrition, illiteracy, and disease as to be beneath any reasonable definition of human decency.

To illustrate what poverty in the Third World is like, economist Robert Heilbroner offers the following scenario:

> We begin by invading the house of our imaginary American family to strip it of its furniture. Everything goes: beds, chairs, tables, television sets, lamps. We will leave the family with a few old blankets, a kitchen table, a wooden chair. Along with the bureaus go the clothes. Each member of the family may keep in his "wardrobe" his oldest suit or dress, a shirt or blouse. We will permit a pair of shoes to the head of the family, but none for the wife or children.
>
> We move into the kitchen. The appliances have already been taken out, so we turn to the cupboards and larder. The box of matches may stay, a small bag of flour, some sugar and salt. A few moldy potatoes, already in the garbage can, must be hastily rescued, for they will provide much of tonight's meal. We will leave a handful of onions, and a dish of dried beans. All the rest we take away: the meat, the fresh vegetables, the canned goods, the crackers, the candy.
>
> Now we have stripped the house: the bathroom has been dismantled, the running water shut off, the electric wires taken out. Next we take away the house. The family can move to the toolshed. It is crowded, but much better than the situation in Hong Kong, where (a United Nations report tells us) "it is not uncommon for a family of four or more to live in a bedspace, that is, on a bunk bed and the space it occupies—sometimes in two or three tiers—their only privacy provided by curtains."
>
> But we have only begun. All the other houses in the neighborhood have also been removed; our suburb has become a shantytown. Still, our family is fortunate to have

a shelter; 250,000 people in Calcutta have none at all and simply live in the streets. Our family is now about on a par with the city of Cali in Colombia, where, an official of the World Bank writes, "on one hillside alone, the slum population is estimated at 40,000—without water, sanitation, or electric light. And not all the poor of Cali are as fortunate as that. Others have built their shacks near the city on land which lies beneath the flood mark. To these people the immediate environment is the open sewer of the city, a sewer which flows through their huts when the river rises."

And still we have not reduced our American family to the level at which life is lived in the greatest part of the globe. Communication must go next. No more newspapers, magazines, books—not that they are missed, since we must take away our family's literacy as well. Instead, in our shantytown we will allow one radio. In India the national average of radio ownership is one per 250 people, but since the majority of radios is owned by city dwellers, our allowance is fairly generous.

Now government services must go. No more postman, no more fireman. There is a school, but it is three miles away and consists of two classrooms. They are not too overcrowded since only half the children in the neighborhood go to school. There are, of course, no hospitals or doctors nearby. The nearest clinic is ten miles away and is tended by a midwife. It can be reached by bicycle, provided that the family has a bicycle, which is unlikely. Or one can go by bus—not always inside, but there is usually room on top.

Finally, money. We will allow our family a cash hoard of five dollars. This will prevent our breadwinner from experiencing the tragedy of an Iranian peasant who went blind because he could not raise the $3.94 which he mistakenly thought he needed to secure admission to a hospital where he could have been cured.

Meanwhile, the head of our family must earn his keep. As a peasant cultivator with three acres to tend, he may raise the equivalent of $100 to $300 worth of crops a year. If he is a tenant farmer, which is more than likely, a third or so of his crop will go to his landlord, and probably another ten percent to the local money lender. But there will be enough to eat. Or almost enough. The human body requires an input of at least 2,000 calories to replenish the energy consumed by its living cells. If our displaced American fares no better than an Indian peasant, he will average a replenishment of no more than 1,700–1,900 calories. His body, like any insufficiently fueled machine, will run down. That is one reason why life expectancy at birth in India today averages less than forty years.

But the children may help. If they are fortunate, they may find work and thus earn some cash to supplement the family's income. For example, they may be employed as are children in Hyderabad, Pakistan, sealing the ends of bangles over a small kerosene flame, a simple task which can be done at home. To be sure, the pay is small: eight annas—about ten cents—for sealing bangles. That is, eight annas per *gross* [144] of bangles. And if they cannot find work? Well, they can scavenge, as do the children in Iran who in times of hunger search for the undigested oats in the droppings of horses.

And so we have brought our typical American family down to the very bottom of the human scale. . . . (*The Great Ascent,* pp. 33–37)

Poor People in North America: "The Other America"

Citizens of the United States and Canada enjoy the highest standard of living in the world. If you are an "average" North American, you live in a home with more than five rooms that you share with only two or three other people. At least one member of your family holds a job. Unlike the average Third World family, your home has running water, electricity, a refrigerator, a telephone, and a host of other conveniences. Your family possesses at least one car. With an abundance of food available to you and given your country's efficient health-care establishment, you can expect to live into your seventies.

Yet, even in the midst of this overabundance, poverty exists. North American poverty is an invisible poverty because poor people usually live in rural areas or in densely populated inner cities that most people see only from a train or an expressway. The poor people of North America are also invisible because they usually dress the same as most others in society, because they do not necessarily speak a foreign language, and because they may actually own such things as a home, a television, or a car.

Nevertheless, these North Americans are poor: They are poorly educated, and so their opportunities for employment are severely limited. When they do work, as do the majority of poor people who are the heads of families, their income is inadequate. In addition, their families survive on a monotonous and inadequate diet. Their infant mortality rate and life expectancy are well below the national average.

Furthermore, the health care available to poor people is grossly inferior to what is available to the rest of the population. A health-care worker in a Philadelphia hospital serving a poor neighborhood observed that most of the other hospital workers were unseasoned apprentices: The medical technicians were students. Most of the doctors treating patients were interns or young residents. After gaining experience at the expense of poor people, typically these health-care workers moved on to other hospitals.

Who are these needy people who make up about 15 percent of the population of the United States?

Women: The most striking point of identification of North American poor people is their sex. According to an article in *Sojourners* magazine by Vicki Kemper "Two out of every three poor adults in this country are women." The same article quotes a 1981 government study that concluded that if current trends continued, "the poverty population would be composed solely of women and their children before the year 2000." This phenomenon is referred to as *the feminization of poverty* and will be discussed further in chapter 7.

Nonwhites: A second identifying mark of poor people in the United States is race. Although about 15 percent of all U.S. families fell below the poverty level in 1984, only 9 percent of the total white population is poor. By contrast, of the Native American population, over 40 percent is poor. Blacks and Hispanics also have high percentages of their number who are poor.

Young people: Besides sex and race, age is a factor in identifying the poor people. A disproportionate number of young children and young parents are poor. Recently the percentage of families headed by someone aged twenty-four or younger who were in poverty rose from 15 percent to over 25 percent. One institution that warehouses many poor young people (especially poor, uneducated young men) is the U.S. prison system.

What Are the Effects of Poverty on People?

The experience of being poor in North America is basically similar to being poor in the Third World. Along with the physical deprivation, poor people in North America experience a sense of powerlessness, of being locked into their poverty. Often they feel disheartened with an existence that aims at merely surviving more than at truly living. Moreover, when they observe the affluence around them, they question their own worth and dignity. As the U.S. bishops recently made clear in their pastoral letter on the economy, whether in the Third World or hidden within the underbelly of affluence, poverty is a scandal.

Poverty is more than physical deprivation; it affects the spirit as well. A Peruvian theologian, Gustavo Gutiérrez, echoes a truth shared by many who work with poor people:

> The real issue in this situation is becoming increasingly clear to us today: poverty means death. It means death due to hunger and sickness, or to the repressive methods used by those who see their privileged position being endangered by any effort to liberate the oppressed. It means physical death to which is added cultural death, inasmuch as those in power seek to do away with everything that gives unity and strength to the dispossessed of this world. In this way those in power hope to make the dispossessed an easier prey for the machinery of oppression. (*We Drink from Our Own Wells,* pp. 9–10)

Gustavo Gutiérrez

Gutiérrez is here describing the bind in which many of the world's poor find themselves. When they accept their fate, they die of hunger or sickness. However, when they join together and attempt to take charge of their lives in any significant way, they oftentimes encounter forces bent upon resisting any such change.

Gutiérrez's reference to "cultural death" is worth noting also. To be stripped of one's cultural heritage is a great loss. Culture serves an important function by uniting people and providing a common identity. For instance, through their art, religion, family life, and work patterns, the Native American cultures provided solid and vital identities for their members. Unfortunately, within the last few centuries, they have been overwhelmed by Europe's urban, industrialized culture.

By contrast, in places such as Poland and Latin America, where the Christian religion is part of the cultural heritage, Christianity has recently provided a rallying point for poor people. In response, the authorities in those countries have often tried to suppress religious expressions of culture.

Why Are People Poor?

Are Poor People Simply Lazy?

In the previous chapter, the notion of poor people's being merely lazy was briefly discussed. From its beginning Christianity has taught that we must help those in need without judging them. Let's look more closely at the situation today.

A preliminary caution in discussing poverty is to beware of blaming the victims in ways such as these:

- People on welfare don't want to work.
- Why can't they pull themselves up by their bootstraps like we did?
- It's their own fault they're so poor; they have too many children.
- If they had applied themselves more and taken advantage of the education offered them, they wouldn't be where they are today.
- Face it, they just don't have the talent, technology, or temperament that made us what we are.

Statements like these blame the victims of poverty for their own fate. Many studies have proven such claims to be false, yet the stereotypes persist. Blaming the victims, however, only creates inaction.

In our society, in which personal dignity is closely tied to status and possessions, we need to remind ourselves that persons in need are persons just like ourselves. That is to say, that given opportunities, poor people will help themselves. One movement in the Church that exemplifies poor people helping themselves and celebrating their own dignity is the **basic Christian community movement,** which began in Latin America. Here is one writer's account of his visit to such a community:

> To give the reader some idea of what a base community is, I would like to describe the experience Nancy and I had when we visited one in Santiago, Chile. To get there we took the subway to the end of the line and then traveled by a bus to the point where it turned around. We found ourselves in the middle of a very poor neighborhood, in which the majority of heads of families had no steady, full-time jobs, due to the high rate of unemployment. People began to gather in a one-room shack they had built themselves, which was used not only for their religious meetings but for a wide range of community activities. When about thirty people had assembled, they began talking about their experiences of the past week: their frustration with not finding work anywhere, the fact that the city was cutting off the water of those unable to pay, personal and family problems of various members of the group, all this culminating with a number of stories of police harassment.
>
> At this point a woman in the group stood up and said that she had found a biblical text she thought spoke to their discussion. With a great deal of difficulty – and helped by others – she read the words of St. Paul in 1 Corinthians about how God has chosen the weak to confound the strong and those who are "nobodies" to overthrow the existing order (1:27–28). Then a lively discussion began with many participating, including the priest and nun who were present. Several women spoke of how the community had given them a new sense of themselves and empowered them to speak and act. And then Maria, who had been an active member of the group since its beginning, told of her experience at the city market the previous Sunday. She was there selling a few items, as were hundreds of other jobless persons. Suddenly the police arrived, intending to arrest the men who were selling without a

license and confiscate their goods. [The police] began with a group near Maria. When they were about to haul them away, Maria decided she could not remain passive. With great fear, she stood up, placed herself between those men and the police, and declared: "If you're going to arrest them, you'll have to arrest me because I don't have a license either. Besides, you should be ashamed of yourselves taking away from us the only chance we have to keep our children from starving." Gradually a number of other women nearby joined Maria, and the police walked away. When Maria finished her story, everybody applauded.

Bible study was followed by a time for planning for the week ahead, deciding who would take responsibility for things that needed to be done to help others in the community, the program of religious activities, and work on a number of specific projects. This base community had initiated fourteen self-help projects in that *población*—for instance, soup kitchens, literacy classes, and child care— and for some of them they needed greater support than they were receiving. After these matters were settled, two new topics were raised for discussion: how to do something to stop the city from cutting off the water of those who could not pay their bills; and, whether or not the few who had regular jobs should run the risk of losing them by taking part in the demonstration being planned for the following Sunday by the base communities as a protest against unemployment. They all wanted to be part of this movement even though it might lead to beatings and arrests, but those who were employed needed the help of the community to decide where their responsibility lay.

The meeting ended with a time of prayer. As we mingled among the members and then walked toward the bus, we realized that we had witnessed a miracle. The rejects of society had discovered their own worth; people formerly isolated and abandoned had begun to share almost everything with each other. Together they were taking unusual initiatives in local self-reliance and were beginning to realize that they had power to bring about changes in their situation. And they had more vitality and energy and greater hope for the future than we had found anywhere else in Chile during our weeks there. (Richard Shaull, *Heralds of a New Reformation,* pp. 119–121)

The people in the base community described above prove that poverty is a scandal, not a scourge: In other words, no one is fated or condemned by God to be poor. Past and present *human* decisions have contributed to the current scandal of poverty. Consequently, human decisions can help to eliminate it.

Poverty and the Present World Order

When we think about Third World countries, we immediately picture scenes of poverty. We might ask, Haven't these countries always been poor? In fact, in the past the Third World has supported flourishing cultures. Africa, Asia, and Latin America have had periods of great prosperity. In some instances, the Third World was highly developed culturally when Europe was still developing.

The division of the world into the rich northern hemisphere and the poor southern half is a recent event, stemming from the period of European colonialism. It is not a coincidence that today's Third World represents former colonies of Western Europe. The relationship between First World countries and Third World countries has often been marked by exploitation, and a look at the current world order indicates that exploitation continues to exist. Here is an account of a Third World city's fall from prosperity due to exploitation:

> If we . . . tried to imagine what an underdeveloped area looks like, we would probably conjure up a town like Potosi, Bolivia. At an altitude of 15,000 feet above sea level, Potosi is difficult to reach. The roads leading to it are bad. The native Indian people who live there eke out a meagre living from the poor soil. The only other major source of employment is a tin mine in the mountain which overlooks the town. Housing is poor, and running water and electricity are a luxury in the area. . . .
>
> However . . . in the 1600s, in the heyday of Potosi, they say that even the horses were shod with silver. At the height of its boom, the town had a population equal to that of London and larger than that of European centres like Madrid, Rome, or Paris. Potosi attracted silks and fabrics from Canada and Flanders, the latest fashions from Paris and London, diamonds from India, crystal from Venice, and perfumes from Arabia. Something really valuable in the 17th Century was referred to commonly as being "worth a Potosi."
>
> . . . The entire economic and social life of Potosi was based on wealth from a single commodity—silver. This

silver was mined by the native Indian population and shipped directly to Spain. Potosi silver financed, in large measure, the development of the Spanish empire in the 17th Century. . . .

. . . The underdevelopment of Potosi, then, began with the abuse of its people and resources through the European colonial system. The Latin American economy was geared by the Europeans to meet their own needs, not those of the local people. . . .

The arrival of the Europeans in Asia, Africa, and Latin America—what is known today as the Third World—fundamentally altered the processes of development which were taking place at the time. In some cases, these societies were more advanced than others; and all, of course, had problems to surmount. But the people in these areas were constructing societies which, although not industrialized, were often highly sophisticated and complex. They were able to meet their physical and psychological needs through their own institutions. The military conquest of Third World people led to the plunder and destruction of some of the world's greatest civilizations. (Development Education Centre, "Development and Underdevelopment")

The world's economic order has not changed greatly since the time of Potosi because global economics continues to favor the First World. In recent years, those concerned about poverty have realized that charity to poor countries will not change the world order that keeps so many people poor and powerless. Only a restructuring of the world order will bring real change. The United Nations, which represents the community of nations, has come to realize that economic changes in the world order are especially necessary. Along with other international organizations, the United Nations has made a number of concrete proposals for change that are categorized under the heading **A New International Economic Order**. The following four U.N. proposals reveal causes of, as well as possible solutions to, Third World poverty.

1. Trade, Not Aid

The first proposal calls for trade agreements more favorable to poor countries. Generally speaking, the Third World supplies much of the First World's raw materials and simple manufactured goods. At the present time, trade agreements favor industrialized countries such as Japan, Great Britain, and the United States. A more just economic world order would include a move in the direction of strengthening the Third World's power in the international market.

Here is one example of such trade relationships:

■ The South American country of Colombia is a supplier of much of the world's coffee. Colombia exports raw coffee to be processed and packaged in industrialized countries such as the United States. If this coffee would be processed within its own borders, Colombia would reap a much greater income from it and would also gain desperately needed jobs for its people. Yet, because of U.S. trade restrictions prohibiting the importation of large quantities of processed coffee, Colombia must settle for exporting its coffee in raw form.

In addition, many Third World countries have **single-export economies,** meaning that they export one or just a few commodities. Raw coffee, for instance, comprises over 40 percent of Colombia's exports. Single-export countries have very unstable economies because, first, prices on a single commodity may fluctuate greatly and, second, these countries have little negotiating power concerning the prices that they receive. On the other hand, industrialized multiple-export countries have mixed economies with a great variety of exports, providing greater stability and negotiating power.

Therefore, proponents of a new economic order see trade, not aid, as the long-term solution to Third World poverty. Foreign aid from wealthy countries to poorer ones usually comes with stipulations that benefit the giving nation more than the receiving one. Changing the rules of international trade to better favor poor countries can lead to their greater self-sufficiency. Yet, along with this self-sufficiency comes a loss to the First World of "power over" or control, which can seem threatening.

A worker stacking sugar cane, a single-export commodity in many Central American countries

2. Appropriate Models of Development

The Third World is often labeled *underdeveloped,* but it would be just as true to say that the First World is *over-developed.* In other words, if the Third World were to develop in ways that make it more like the First World, disaster would occur because the earth's limited resources could not support the First World's level of consumption on a global scale. Moreover, models of development that are appropriate to one culture may not be appropriate to another. So the new economic order calls for types of development that make sense in each culture. For example:

■ Mexico City has an efficient and greatly used subway system. The charge for riding the metro is one peso (less than one cent). The United States, in contrast, has made a greater commitment to private transportation than to public transportation. If Mexico City, which is projected to become the most populous city in the world in the near future, would imitate the United States in its emphasis on private transportation, the consequences would be disastrous.

Third World countries must be granted the freedom to initiate types of development that are consistent with their unique national characters.

3. Greater Power to the Third World

The third principle of the New International Economic Order is to allow Third World countries more power within the international community. Specifically, it suggests that countries be given greater control over their own resources. Much as in the case of Potosi, today many of the Third World's resources are owned or controlled by First World companies.

4. Acceptance of Interdependence

Finally, the New International Economic Order calls for the recognition of and a commitment to interdependence. At the present time, nations are expending a great deal of their energy in competing against each other. Unbridled competition, however, is harmful to all nations. Only a spirit of cooperation among nations can lead to a hopeful and peaceful world future.

Students at the College of African Wildlife Management, in Tanzania

A New *National* Economic Order

The focus of justice is not poor countries but rather poor people. Therefore, restructuring on the international level must be accompanied by national economic policies that benefit the poor people of each country. Three of the principles of the New International Economic Order can be used to examine national economic structures as well.

The International Chocolate Recipe

- The *sugar* might be from the Caribbean island nations or from elsewhere in Latin America.

- The *corn syrup* might have been produced by a farmer in Iowa.

- The *cocoa beans* could have been grown in Ghana, the Ivory Coast, or Nigeria. These three West African countries account for over 55 percent of the world's cocoa bean production.

- The *nuts* that add crunch to the chocolate bar may have come from the Sudan in Africa.

- The *chocolate bar* itself might have been made in Switzerland, Great Britain, or the United States.

- The *wrapper* might be from Canada, the world's largest producer of wood pulp for paper.

- The *copper* for the boilers used for cooking the chocolate might have come from Chile in South America or from Zambia in Africa.

- The *trucks* that carry the chocolate bars to market might have come from Japan or Germany.

- The *fuel* needed for the production and transportation of the chocolate bar probably came from Third World nations, which provide the world with over 56 percent of its crude oil.

- People who have less education often have only a few simple skills with which to earn their livings. Unfortunately, as in the case of single-export countries, having only a few skills makes it much tougher to find adequate jobs.
- If wealthy people cannot set reasonable limits to their own needs for money and power, then poor people are likely to be exploited to feed the greed of the wealthy. In other words, just as nations can be overdeveloped, so can individuals. In the same way that countries are sometimes forced to accept prices that are too low for their goods and services, many individuals also must work for less than living wages.
- Cooperation, not only competition, has to have a larger role in the running of a society if people are to be treated justly.

Putting Poverty into a Christian Perspective

The Scriptures Offer Poor Persons as Models of Faith

As chapter 2 points out, God intervenes for poor people throughout the Scriptures. Mary especially is portrayed as a model of faith. In the *Magnificat*, the great hymn of praise, she refers to herself as poor—a servant or slave girl, whom God chooses. She numbers herself among the lowly whom God favors. Then Mary says:

> My being proclaims the greatness of the Lord,
>   my spirit finds joy in God my savior,
> For he has looked upon his servant in her lowliness;
>   all ages to come shall call me blessed.
> God who is mighty has done great things for me,
>   holy is his name;
> His mercy is from age to age
>   on those who fear him.
> He has shown might with his arm;
>   he has confused the proud in their inmost thoughts.
> He has deposed the mighty from their thrones
>   and raised the lowly to high places.
> The hungry he has given every good thing,
>   while the rich he has sent empty away.
>   (Luke 1:46–53)

Workers in Mexico City place a golden crown over the image of Our Lady of Guadalupe

Interestingly, throughout Latin America, stories are told of Mary appearing to poor people to offer a message of hope. The most famous of these, the appearance of Our Lady of Guadalupe, occurred in Mexico in 1531. In this story, Mary appeared to an Indian peasant named Juan Diego at a time when the once-proud Aztec Indians had been conquered and subjugated by the Spanish. Mary appeared as an Indian princess on a hill that had been a shrine dedicated to an Aztec goddess. Since that time Our Lady of Guadalupe has symbolized hope to the poor people of Mexico.

Born in a stable surrounded by shepherds and animals, Jesus himself models poverty. Indeed, he is God-become-poor:

> Though he was in the form of God,
> he did not deem equality with God
> something to be grasped at.
> Rather, he emptied himself
> and took the form of a slave,
> being born in the likeness of men. . . .
>
> (Philippians 2:6–7)

Does this mean that God loves poor people more than rich people, or that God desires salvation for poor people but not for rich people? Obviously not. Jesus proclaims a God who is God of all and who brings salvation to all. Still, like the humble shepherds who led the way to the stable at Bethlehem, poor people are our models of faith.

In the Scriptures, the rich are criticized not because they are rich but because they do not share with poor people. As Christians, we are called to respond to poor people as if they were God:

> He who has compassion on the poor
> lends to the LORD.
>
> (Proverbs 19:17)

In the paradoxical wisdom of Christianity, the treasure we seek comes from solidarity with poor people.

Today's Church and Poverty

Modern church documents are filled with statements proclaiming the Church's commitment to poor people. Throughout the world, church leaders have attempted to apply to their particular setting Jesus' message of Good News to poor people. In 1975, bishops from the Appalachian area of the United States issued a document addressing the poverty in their region. They produced a moving statement about local poverty:

> Appalachia makes us think
> of people who live in the hills,
> who love nature's freedom
> and beauty,
> who are alive with song
> and poetry.
> But many of these people are also poor
> and suffer oppression.
>
> Once they went to the mountains
> fighting to build a dream
> different from the injustice
> they knew before.
> Until this day,
> their struggle continues,
> a bitter fight
> whose sound still rumbles
> across the hills. . . .
>
> Besides the struggle in hollows,
> typical of the central region,
> there are struggles in industrial centers,
> grown gray with smoke and smog,
> blaring with the clank and crash
> of heavy machinery
> and urban congestion,
> where working people,
> and those who wish there was work,
> white and black,
> native and immigrant,
> speakers of one and many languages,
> battle for dignity and security,
> for themselves and for their children.
>
> So too there is the struggle in farmland,
> typical of rolling hills in the southern sector,
> where little farmers and sharecroppers,
> day laborers and migrant workers,
> who help the earth
> yield its food to the hungry,
> battle for that same dignity and security,
> for themselves and their children.
>
> (*This Land Is Home to Me*)

Similarly, in 1973 the bishops of northeast Brazil issued a strong statement calling for a radically different economic order to benefit poor people in their region:

> We want to see a world in which the fruits of work will belong to all. We want to see a world in which people will work, not in order to get rich, but in order that all should possess the necessities of life: enough to eat for their health, a house, education, clothes, shoes, water, and light. We want to see a world in which money is placed at the service of human beings and not human beings at the service of money. We want to see a world in which all will be able to work for all, not a divided world in which all persons work only for themselves. Therefore, we want to see a world in which there will be only one people with no division between rich and poor. (*The Marginalization of a People*)

The U.S. bishops call for the actions of individuals, government policies, and business decisions to reflect a "preferential option" for poor people. In other words, "Decisions must be judged in light of what they do *for* the poor, what they do *to* the poor, and what they enable the poor to do *for themselves.*" (*Economic Justice for All*, no. 24). The contemporary Church's preferential option for poor people affirms the traditional Christian belief that

> the living God,
> the Lord whom we worship,
> is the God of the poor.
>
> (*This Land Is Home to Me*)

Responding to Poverty

The Personal Level:
Asceticisms on Behalf of Poor People

Developing ourselves physically is hard work that requires a program of exercise and diligence in performing those exercises. Similarly, developing ourselves spiritually is also hard work that requires regular exercise. *Asceticism* is a term that means spiritual exercise. From the Church's beginning, Christians have practiced various asceticisms, or spiritual exercises. Three traditional dimensions of asceticism are prayer, fasting, and a compassionate spirituality.

Prayer

Lord, my God
today I have decided to love you
without beating my chest
without change in my pocket
without praying on my knees, down front, in the center
without daily visits to the church
without hypocritical hymns
without banal words
even without crying out Alleluia!

Lord, my God
together with the children of the market trash collectors
with the shouting children, the fruit vendors, car watchers
with the shoe shiners
with the farmers dispossessed of their lands
with workers who increase the capital of others
with mothers who sell their flesh to buy bread for their
children
with the old people left forgotten on the streets
with the mentally retarded
with the anonymous alcoholics of the neighborhoods
with all the helpless handicapped people
and through them I have decided to love you.

Lord, I have decided to love you
by giving to them that which I have
because what you have given me
is not for myself
but for them.

(Orlando Perez V.)

Like the prayer of the Nicaraguan poet above, our prayers can be related to poor people. In praying during a brief moment before class, at Mass on Sunday, during a retreat, or in time spent alone, we are taking time out to welcome God into our lives. In prayer we raise our minds and hearts to God, to our personal concerns, and to the concerns of our family and friends. In a spirit of hospitality, we also raise our minds and hearts to the concerns of poor people in our neighborhood and in distant lands. The prayer of hospitality, praying for and with poor people, is an asceticism that relates our personal spirituality to the problem of poverty.

Fasting

A second ascetical practice, fasting, can obviously be linked with concern for poor people. For example, Operation Rice Bowl combines the traditional Lenten fast with raising money for the hungry. Participants are encouraged to eat less during Lent. The money saved is then donated to organizations helping poor people. Some schools sponsor days of giving up lunch, Third World meals, and other creative uses of fasting in order to develop our awareness of poor people and to provide help for poor people.

A Compassionate Spirituality

A third ascetical practice to undertake on behalf of poor people involves a compassionate spirituality. Members of religious orders traditionally take a vow of poverty to minimize the lure of possessions in their lives. In our consumer-oriented society a lifestyle that shows concern for poor people certainly includes a de-emphasis on possessions. Given the fact that teenagers do more buying today than ever before, this spiritual lifestyle can be a challenging asceticism.

To practice this spirituality, some youth groups have sponsored children through one of the many agencies that work in the Third World. Each person in the group pledges a certain amount and meets to discuss the child's progress and to reflect on how the project has affected his or her thinking—as well as finances.

The Interpersonal Level: Solidarity with Poor People

Poor people are not statistics but persons. They are not strangers but sisters and brothers. Poor people are not "they," others, but "we," one of us. To see the human face of poverty, then, we need to listen to poor people and to spend time with them. Only when we arrive at a spirit of solidarity with poor people will we wholeheartedly take up the task of overcoming poverty.

> If the hunger of others is not my own
> if the anguish of my neighbor in all its forms
>   touches me not,
> if the nakedness of my brother
>   does not torment me,
>
> then I have no reason
>   to go to church and to live.
>
> Life is this: to love one's neighbor
>   as oneself;
> this is the commandment of God.
> Love means deeds, not good wishes.
> For this reason I commit myself to working
> for the necessities of my brothers.
>   (Javier Torres B., "The Hunger of Others")

We can begin to achieve solidarity with poor people by getting to know poor people. Explore your neighborhood to discover the existence of shelters for homeless people, tutoring programs for younger children, "meals-on-wheels" programs, or community centers. Try getting involved—to learn from poor people as much as to help them. A number of organizations provide opportunities to spend a week, a summer, or longer working with poor people. Through opportunities such as these you can encounter poverty close up and enjoy an educationally and socially enriching experience while doing so.

You might also consider learning about poor people indirectly. *Maryknoll Magazine* offers monthly accounts of ongoing work with poor people throughout the world. Reading fiction or nonfiction accounts of the experience of being poor can help you to appreciate what it means to be poor. Likewise, some movies and TV shows creatively describe the plight of poor people.

The Structural Level: Working Toward a New Economic Order

> We cannot segregate God's word
> from the historical reality
> in which it is proclaimed.
> That would not be God's word.
> The Bible would be just a pious history book
> in our library.
> It is God's word
> because it enlightens, contrasts,
> repudiates, praises
> what is going on today in this society.
> (Archbishop Oscar Romero)

One traditional U.S. myth suggests that what is good for big business is ultimately good for the United States. Recently many church leaders, economists, and other people have questioned this myth. They are pointing out that the present national and international economic structure that places profit above other considerations needs challenging. Where the economic order leads to larger numbers of poor people, no avenues of relief for poor people, and economic insecurity for much of the population, then justice calls for change.

If we are to affect changes in the economic order, we need to become knowledgeable about business and government policies. One helpful way to do this is to join organizations that work for positive social change. With the help of organizations such as Operation PUSH, Bread for the World, and NETWORK (a Catholic social justice lobby), we can be better informed voters and more active citizens. Surprisingly, we can make a difference. Once a group of five women who met after Mass every Sunday decided to write letters to their representatives and senators concerning local poverty. Within three weeks their congressman asked to meet with them.

Conclusion:
A Conversion to Helping Poor People

Sultan the beggar plays the prophet's role of disturbing the haves and of siding with the have-nots. Our Christian call to justice calls for a conversion to helping poor people. We have many options available to us for siding with poor people—lifestyle changes, works of charity, and political action. While our aim is to improve the lot of poor people, at the same time we can ourselves become—like Sultan and the followers of Christ—freer and more joyful.

For Review

1. What is the message behind the story about Sultan?
2. Define the term *absolute poverty*.
3. In what sense is North American poverty an invisible poverty?
4. List the groups who make up most of the poor people in North America.
5. The text refers to *cultural death* as a reality for many poor people. What does the term mean?
6. Give an example of what the text means when it says that we should avoid blaming the victims of poverty.
7. What is a basic Christian community?
8. What does the story of Potosi, Bolivia, point out about today's global economics?
9. List each of the four U.N. proposals for a New International Economic Order.
10. What would a new *national* economic order be like?
11. Describe the attitude toward poor people that is presented in the Scriptures.
12. What does the Church mean by operating with a "preferential option" for poor people?
13. What is asceticism? How can asceticism serve to alleviate poverty?
14. List two ways in which we can begin to achieve solidarity with poor people.

For Reflection

1. The story of Sultan the beggar suggests that poor people have something to say to us. Write a two-page essay describing what we can learn from the needy about the priorities in our lives, our relationship with God, our interdependence, and our happiness.

2. Reread the passage on blaming the victims of poverty, pages 101–102. The text suggests that North Americans are inclined to believe that poor people are needy because of something the poor people have or have not done.

   a. Do you agree with this contention? Explain in writing why or why not.

   b. Respond to each of the following statements with either *agree* (it is essentially true) or *disagree* (it falsely blames the victim):

      1) Anybody who wants work can find a job.
      2) Poor people don't take care of their money, their houses, their neighborhoods, or their other possessions.
      3) People on welfare don't want to work—why should they when the government supports them.
      4) Poor children have the same opportunities as rich children. If they do not do well in school it is because they are not as smart.
      5) Most poor people lack common sense. Otherwise, they would save their money and spend it more wisely.

   c. List other statements that can be viewed as blaming people for their own poverty.

3. Basic Christian communities are one way in which poor people have joined together to counteract powerlessness. List other ways in which poor people could gain power over their situation. (For instance, welfare-rights organizations have been formed by people on welfare to protect their interests.)

4. Describe in writing at least one possible change in our national or international policy that would reflect the spirit of each of the four elements of the New International Economic Order proposed by the United Nations.

5. Read the following passages in the Gospels:
   - Mark 10:17–25
   - Mark 12:38–44

■ Mark 14:3–9
■ Luke 4:14–19
■ Luke 6:20–25

For each passage, write a paragraph that answers these questions: What do you believe is the message for you in this passage? How do you feel about the passage?

6. Write a one-page essay that answers the following questions: What is success as prescribed by our culture? What is success as our Christian faith suggests it to us? What differences in our lifestyle does each imply?

7. In the pastoral letter quoted on page 112, the bishops of northeast Brazil say, "We want to see a world in which there will be only one people with no division between rich and poor." Do you share this world vision with the bishops? Write a one-page response to the statement, sharing both your thoughts and your feelings about it. Mention what changes it implies in your life and in society.

8. A Christian spirituality involves a response to the world's poor. Describe in writing what elements you would include in a personal spirituality that shows concern for the poor. Why would you include these elements?

9. This chapter suggests that buying by teenagers supports big businesses in our culture. Is spending important in your life? Explain in writing why or why not.

10. To achieve solidarity with the poor, it is helpful to recognize our own poverty. Other than financial, what are other ways that people can be poor? Make a list of these other types of poverty. Do these types of poverty share any characteristics in common with financial poverty? Write a one-page essay about possible similarities shared among all forms of poverty.

11. Interview a representative of your local government or your parish. Take notes on their answers to the following questions:

■ Are there poor people in your neighborhood?
■ If so, how would this person describe their situation? (For instance: Are they elderly, living alone, living with large families, unemployed? Has their poverty been long-term or recent?)
■ What attempts are being made to meet their needs?
■ What else might be done for them?

12. Write an imaginary autobiography as a poor person. You live in a city, a poor rural village, or a migrant workers' camp somewhere in the world. Let your imagination run free. Write about how you feel about your life—what your experience of being poor is like, how you and your family live, and what your prospects are for the future.

    Then read an article about what it is like to be poor. Compare your description with that of people who actually have experienced poverty firsthand.

13. A structural analysis of poverty attempts to find out *why* people are poor so that the causes can be eliminated.
    a. Make a list, as inclusive as possible, of causes that you believe explain why people are poor.
    b. Choose the causes that you believe are the most significant reasons (the *root* causes) that people are poor. State why you selected these reasons.
    c. Determine which causes could best be eliminated through the following approaches. (Some causes may be addressed in more than one way.)
       ■ the individual initiative of poor persons
       ■ assistance from wealthier individuals
       ■ government programs
       ■ a change in a society's structures, policies, or priorities
    d. Which way or combination of ways of addressing the problem of poverty do you believe to be the most effective?

6
Hunger: Poverty Can Be Fatal

This chapter continues the topic of poverty begun in the previous chapter. People are hungry for the same basic reasons that they are poor. The problem of hunger takes us to the cutting edge of poverty where being poor can be fatal. At its worst, hunger carries with it the scourges of diminished resistance to disease, poor physical and mental health, a lowered capacity to help oneself, and ultimately a desperate battle with death. When we meet hungry persons, we encounter the poorest of poor people. Likewise, by responding to hunger we are also responding to poverty.

Friday Night Pizza

"Friday night ★ Shrimp ★ Dancing" read the sign outside the roadside cafe. Always the first with the jokes, Gary said to no one in particular, "That sounds like fun, I've never seen shrimp dancing before."

As they pulled into Dino's Pizza next door, the others in the car shook their heads at Gary's remark. "Do you think we'll be able to enjoy our pizza after those talks today?" asked Troy.

"I never like those presentations," said Nancy. "I didn't like the one we had last month on abortion, and I didn't like the one today on hunger."

"Yeah, what are we supposed to do anyway?" chimed in Rich.

"I don't think Dino's delivers to Ethiopia," Gary couldn't resist adding.

"Today was Sister Joan's brainstorm, I'm sure," said Chrissy. "Remember in sophomore year when she showed us those slides about homeless people? After that my Dad and I made casseroles for the hospice program. At least I learned to cook some different dishes."

"But what good did that actually do?" questioned Rich. "Once I went to serve meals at the hospice. All I remember is that it was very depressing. I tried to be friendly, but all those people just wanted to eat. They were getting a free meal, and they weren't even grateful. They didn't even talk to each other."

"Sounds like dinner at my house," reflected Gary.

"Well, if Sister Joan wanted us to feel guilty, she's succeeded," responded Nancy exasperatedly. "Here we are about to eat pizza, and all we can think about is all those starving people we saw in the movie today. But the problem is so mind-boggling, what are we supposed to do? I'm trying to figure out how to write a book report for English this weekend without reading the book, and now I'm supposed to worry about world hunger, too? I can't do it."

"And the question is, why bother?" agreed Rich.

"This is getting depressing, guys," said Gary. "Forget about it. Let's eat."

Examining Hunger: Christians in a Hungry World

The response "Why bother?" is an admission of surrender. If while learning to drive, we said, "Why bother?" we would be giving up on ever learning to drive. If we say, "Why bother? I'll never understand chemistry," we are admitting that that subject has us beaten. Similarly, we pronounce the death sentence on friendships when we say, "Don't bother about Bill; he's just a jerk," or "Why try to be serious with Noreen? All she does is flirt."

Being Christian does not mean that we must avoid enjoying pizza on a Friday night. It does mean that we are to care about people who are hungry in our world. Sometimes we imagine that Jesus was above the problems that disturb the rest of us. For instance, we might picture him asleep in the boat while the merely mortal Apostles struggled with the storm on the Sea of Galilee.

In reality, Jesus was bothered by the pain and suffering around him. He was moved to tears; he became upset, angry, and frustrated. He did not give up on people, even when they were given up for dead. Recall the stories of the raising of Lazarus and of Jairus' daughter, both of whom had been taken to be dead before Jesus arrived.

Yet Jesus did not provide us with a clearly defined master plan for dealing with hunger and other problems. He left these choices and tasks up to us. What Jesus did give us was his Easter message of hope that life will triumph. Because we celebrate his triumph over death, we can join with him in bothering about people who suffer.

What Does It Mean to Be Hungry?

When you arrive home from school today, you will probably ask, What is there to eat? A trip to the refrigerator or to a kitchen cabinet will no doubt provide a quick and satisfactory answer to that question. For about one-fifth of the earth's people, however, trying to answer the question What is there to eat? consumes most of their day and a large part of their income.

Sadly, the answer that hungry people receive leaves them not only unsatisfied but also depleted of their health and strength. They end their day with gnawing, empty feelings and knowing that getting enough food to survive will be the principal task tomorrow. Because hungry persons have experienced many days of insufficient nourishment, they are more susceptible to sickness and disease than well-fed persons. Death is no stranger within the families and neighborhoods of hungry people: they live on the edge between life and death.

Of course, *hunger* is a relative term. Just before mealtime we might say, I'm hungry. Yet we all know that the hunger we feel is not what people concerned about "world hunger" are referring to. *Hunger* in this sense of world hunger refers to chronic malnutrition and undernutrition.

Chronic Malnutrition: A Lack of Necessary Nutrients

Malnutrition is a state resulting from a diet lacking the nutrients vital to proper health. When we were young we probably tried to read the strange-sounding words on the side panels of cereal boxes. They stated, "Satisfies the minimum daily requirements for the following vitamins and minerals . . ." Perhaps we were amazed that we could obtain our daily needs simply by eating a bowl of cereal. What about lunch, dinner, and snacks? Obviously we were enjoying very healthy diets! Probably we were—although we have been learning more and more about the dangers of the sugar, the salt, the processed foods, and the "junk food" that are usually a part of our diet.

By contrast, the one out of five people who are the world's hungry do not receive their minimum daily requirements of proteins, vitamins, and minerals. Because they can afford nothing else, the bulk of their diet consists of one type of food—usually rice, corn, or millet. For six out of ten people in the world, rice is the staple of their diet. Although nutritious in itself, rice alone cannot provide complete nourishment. Proper nutrition requires a diversified diet. Consequently, a poor diet leaves the world's

Deaths per hundred births

10 — Third World

8 —

6 —

4 —

2 —

First World

Infant Mortality

Infant mortality is much greater in the Third World than in the First World.

hungry people malnourished. When this condition persists, they are said to suffer from **chronic malnutrition.**

Chronic malnutrition leads to protein-deficiency diseases that eventually result in death. Lack of vitamin A causes blindness. Iron deficiency leads to anemia, producing fatigue and lethargy and reducing energy and motivation. Life expectancy among chronically malnourished people is in the forties, while well-nourished people can expect to live an average of seventy years. Naturally, chronic malnutrition is most damaging to young children and pregnant women. Young children are most likely to die or to become brain damaged from malnutrition.

Undernutrition: A Lack of Sufficient Calories

While malnutrition refers to the quality of a diet, **undernutrition** refers to the quantity. Undernutrition is a condition in which the quantity of food is inadequate. In recent years we North Americans have become very weight conscious. We fret about eating too many calories. We tend to forget that calories provide needed heat and energy for the human body. The undernourished of the world lack minimum caloric requirements. As a result, their bodies must feed on their own tissues. Here is a description of the physical results of undernutrition:

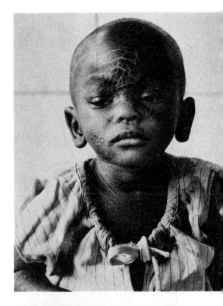

> When food intake drops below energy expenditure, the body must draw upon its own tissues for energy. When this energy drain continues too long, the person starves. The body burns up its own fats, muscles and tissues; kidneys, liver and endrocrine systems often cease to function properly; blood pressure and pulse fall drastically; edema [swelling from excess fluid] usually happens, skin acquires the consistency of paper; abnormal . . . hair grows on the forearms and backs of children; lassitude and confusion set in so that starvation victims often seem unaware of their plight . . . and the body's immunological defenses drop. . . . Once more than 40 percent of the body weight is lost, death is virtually inevitable.
>
> Adults can recover from near starvation. Children are permanently damaged. No amount of vitamin D can straighten bones damaged by rickets. Eighty percent of human brain growth occurs between conception and the age of two. Brain development cannot take place in the fetus if the mother is malnourished, nor can it take place if the infant is starving. Brain development that does not occur when it is supposed to will never take place. The

child is permanently damaged by physical deformity and mental retardation with no hope of recovery. (Medard Gabel, *Ho-Ping: Food for Everyone*)

Why Are People Hungry?

Imagine ten children at a table dividing up food. The three healthiest fill their plates with large portions, including most of the meat, fish, milk and eggs. They eat what they want and discard the leftovers. Five other children get just enough to meet their basic requirements. The remaining two are left wanting. One of them manages to stave off the feeling of hunger by reducing physical and mental output, though she is sickly, nervous and apathetic. The other dies from a virus which he is too weak to ward off. (Arthur Simon, *Bread for the World*, p. 18)

This bleak picture causes us to ask, Why are people in our world chronically malnourished and undernourished? The answer takes us back to our last chapter: people are hungry because they are poor. For example, peasants working on lush plantations are too poor to feed their families what they themselves are helping to harvest. Some countries with severe hunger problems export food to other nations because they need the revenue that these exports bring.

If people are hungry simply because they are poor, then steps taken to overcome poverty can also defeat hunger. As pointed out in the previous chapter, the present economic world order keeps people poor—and consequently hungry. International trade regulations that favor wealthy, industrialized nations force poor countries to make cruel choices between feeding their own hungry people or trying to pay national debts. One writer describes the dilemma in this way:

Because they dominate world trade, the affluent nations have been able to set to their own advantage the rate of exchange for products traded between themselves and the Third World. The net result is that the poor nations cannot generate enough capital from their exports to purchase more food or to invest in agricultural production so as to meet their domestic food needs. The ironic consequence is that the poor nations provide more protein (in the form of oilseeds, oilseed products, and fish meal) to the affluent world than they receive from the affluent in the form of cereals. (Suzanne C. Toton, *World Hunger*, p. 10)

The present global economic system too often places profit above people. This perverse priority was clearly seen in the decisions made during a major food crisis in the early 1970s. Even though drastic food shortages were predicted, the United States cut back its grain production in order to raise the price of wheat. Then, instead of providing grain for the masses of starving people in Bangladesh and other places, the United States sold large quantities of wheat to the USSR. Since the United States produces over half of the world's grain supply, many people were appalled at this apparent insensitivity in the midst of a major food crisis.

The Impact of Other Factors: Fact and Fiction

Isn't there too little food in the world? Aren't there too many people? Hasn't drought brought on starvation in Africa? Although economic factors are the most significant root causes of hunger, other factors do deserve comment. Experts do not completely agree on all of the reasons for hunger's existence, and the specific impact of various factors continues to be debated. Nevertheless, it is possible to shed some light on a number of popular misconceptions about hunger.

1. Scarcity: Too Little Food, Land, and Water

> If the present world food production were evenly divided among all the world's people, with minimal waste, everyone would have enough. Barely enough, perhaps, but enough. (Arthur Simon, *Bread for the World*, p. 18)

These words are hopeful yet not encouraging. Food cannot be evenly divided, and waste occurs in large proportions. So we can say yes, there is enough food in the world. But at the same time, we must accept that **scarcity of food** is a major problem.

A response to the reality of scarcity calls for increased food production, a reduction in waste, and attention to methods of food consumption. A practical response also requires attention to the *distribution* of the food that is currently available. A change in the distribution of the world's scarce food supply might have unwelcome effects on food-rich North America. It might result in higher food costs or perhaps in changes in some of our eating habits. Yet a more equitable redistribution of food would have a lifesaving impact on the hungry people of the Third World.

Concerning the **scarcity of land**, the authors of *World Hunger: Ten Myths* state that "only approximately 44 percent of the world's cultivable land is now being cropped." Furthermore, much of the arable land in the Third World countries is used to produce cash crops rather than food crops. *Cash crops*—for example, coffee, sugar cane, bananas, and cocoa—are grown to be exported in order to raise money. *Food crops* are grown to feed the people within the country itself. Farmland owned by large landowners as an investment is more likely to be used for cash crops or left unplanted than is land in the hands of farmers of smaller plots.

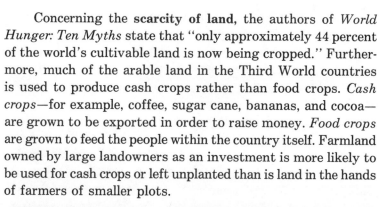

Scarcity of fresh water may cause more problems worldwide than scarcity of land. Water is used for drinking, cooking, bathing, and crop irrigation—uses that are essential in staving off hunger. For many Third World people, finding drinkable water is a daily struggle. Sometimes the solution to scarcity of water is as straightforward as digging a well, installing a community water tap, or devising a simple irrigation system. Of course, these and more elaborate endeavors require money, planning, and community cooperation.

Eighty percent of disease worldwide is water related.

2. Overpopulation: Too Many People

An old movie portrayed a lifeboat built for only eight people bearing twelve passengers. If all twelve persons remained aboard, the lifeboat was in danger of sinking. What could be done?

Some writers suggest that our earth is like that lifeboat. We have to make choices: either some people are left to die or else the entire boat will capsize. A model called *triage* (trē-ˈäzh) has been proposed as a way of deciding who will receive food from the earth's limited resources. **Triage**, a system first employed by the French during World War I, places wounded soldiers into three groups: (1) those who can survive with little or no attention, (2) those who can survive but need immediate attention, and (3) those who can survive only with intensive treatment. Under triage, the third group is left untreated until the first and second groups are cared for.

Applying the triage model to the hungry of the world suggests that some people be left to die. Those who advocate this method suggest that when we try to help the hungry, all we succeed in doing is creating an even greater strain on the earth's limited resources. So, they reason, people suffering from chronic malnutrition should not be helped because too many people mean not enough food for everyone.

Three points need to be made to clarify the relationship between overpopulation and hunger.

- In the first place, as already stated, enough resources exist to provide for the current world population.
- Second, the most crowded countries are not necessarily those with the greatest hunger problems.
- Third, population growth is a *result* of poverty and hunger, not a *cause* of them. In other words, when people face starvation conditions, many births help to ensure that at least some children will survive to adulthood. Children increase a family's income and often provide the sole support when parents are old. On the other hand, as the standard of living increases and greater economic security is assured, people tend to have fewer children.

3. Weather: Famine, Floods, and Drought

Some people think of natural disasters, such as famine and drought, as nature's way of controlling population. A drought causes poor crops. People strip the land of all food resources, and the entire ecological system is upset. Famine results, and many people die. Eventually the balance between people and nature is restored. The deaths due to hunger are viewed simply as nature's way of reasserting its balance with humanity.

For most of its history, drought and flooding have plagued humanity. However these natural occurrences need not lead to large-scale human suffering and death. Social systems can usually meet the challenges of nature. One example of organizing society to work with nature comes from our biblical history: In the story of Joseph, he advised the pharaoh to store up grain during the seven years of plenty to meet the needs of the seven years of drought (Genesis 41:28–36). Invariably, where modern famines have occurred, political and social conditions have contributed significantly to the problem. Famine is more often a by-product of war, social upheaval, and other human activity than it is of nature's wrath.

4. Technology: Is Bigger Better?

Haven't we made great strides in methods of food production? With more money and education, can't the Third World use the First World's advances in technology to become self-sufficient in food production?

Technology has assisted often in overcoming hunger. However, many recent examples serve to remind us that technology must be put to the service of people. Food technology makes a positive difference only insofar as it is appropriate to the social, political, economic, and environmental needs of the people it aims to help.

One recent revelation has been that in food production bigger is not always better. Large-scale farming is usually *energy-intensive*. That is, it depends heavily on machinery and on large doses of fertilizer, water, and pesticides. Small-scale farming is *labor-intensive*. That is, it depends more on people than on machines to do the work.

The *Green Revolution* demonstrated the pros and cons of energy-intensive food production. Begun in Mexico, this development project gained worldwide publicity in the 1960s by introducing high-yield strains of wheat and rice. Unfortunately, it also caused unemployment among the rural labor force because their work was no longer needed. Because this energy-intensive method relied heavily on machinery, fertilizer, and other products, the project was best suited to larger farms. As a result, many of the unemployed farmworkers migrated to already overcrowded cities, and large landowners displaced small farmers.

5. Overconsumption: Are We Responsible?

"Don't waste that food—think of the starving children in China!" In the recent past, parents used this stock response to cajole their children to finish eating their vegetables. In fact, however, modern China has been very successful in curbing hunger among its people. Yet the proposition is still worth considering: Does our waste help to cause others' hunger? Does overconsumption in the First World contribute to the hunger in the Third World? In addition, if we change our eating habits and alter our lifestyles in other ways, would those changes necessarily benefit the world's hungry?

Arthur Simon of the organization Bread for the World suggests that lifestyle changes have value only when they are combined with political action. Let's look at an example drawn from the previous chapter:

> If high school students throughout the United States decided to fast for a day and while doing so raised $1 million for the Third World poor, their sacrifice would have less of an impact than would even a slight increase in the price that the United States pays for coffee exported by the Third World. An increase of only one cent per pound in the price of raw coffee translates into more than $65 million a year for the coffee-exporting countries.

Simon does not see our attempts to simplify lifestyle and be more conscientious about consumption as unimportant. Rather, he reminds us that political action—what we have discussed as social action—must accompany those personal changes. Simon puts political action and personal responses to hunger in perspective:

> The appeal that is primarily needed is not for less personal consumption, but for a more positive national response to hunger. Therefore, the most important sacrifice that readers of this book can make is the sacrifice of their time and energy to change public policy. Life-style adjustments are sorely needed, but detached from attempts to influence government policy they tend to be ineffective gestures. (*Bread for the World*, p. 64)

6. Militarization: Guns or Food?

No discussion of hunger would be complete without mention of militarism. In a world of limited resources where choices have to be made, most countries have made a clear choice of guns over food. Many statistics, comparisons, and graphs could be cited to demonstrate the astronomical amount of money and resources that the nations of the world spend on armaments. For instance:

- One-half of one percent of the world's military expenditures in one year would pay for all the farm equipment needed for low-income countries to increase food production and approach self-sufficiency within ten years.
- A modern tank costs about $1 million, an amount that could improve storage facilities for rice and thus save over four thousand tons (8 billion pounds) of rice annually. A person can live on one pound of rice a day.

- Every minute the world's governments spend $1.3 million of their military budgets while thirty children die of starvation or from a lack of medications.

The argument can be made that national security is as important as national nutrition. Yet the fact is that hunger kills as certainly as war. Furthermore, the excessive amount spent on arms, once characteristic of the United States and the USSR, now has spread to the Third World. In 1980, thirty developing countries spent more on their military budgets than on health and education combined.

The flow of money and energy away from food production into weapons production—as well as the atmosphere of fear and mistrust that accompanies militarization—compounds the disheartening impact that the choice of guns over food has made. The ability to overkill the human population has been won at the price of underfeeding millions of people.

Putting Hunger into a Christian Perspective

Jesus, the Bread of Life

Anyone who has ever visited a Jewish delicatessen or attended a seder meal in a Jewish home knows the importance of food in the Jewish tradition. In that regard, Jesus was very much a product of his Jewish culture.

- Jesus' first public miracle took place at a wedding feast (John 2:1–11). Moreover, his most famous miracle involved feeding bread and fish to the crowds that had begun to follow him (John 6:1–13).
- Jesus compared his kingdom to a banquet (Luke 14:7–24).
- When he brought Jairus' daughter back to life, Jesus immediately told her parents to give her something to eat (Luke 8:55).
- Before his death Jesus shared a meal with his Apostles (Matthew 26:26).
- In Luke's Gospel, Jesus appeared twice after his Resurrection: once to the disciples on the road to Emmaus when he shared bread with them (Luke 24:13–35) and finally to the eleven Apostles, asking them, "Have you anything here to eat?" (Luke 24:41).
- In the last appearance of Jesus in John's Gospel, Jesus stood on the shore and asked the Apostles who had been out fishing, "Children, have you caught anything to eat?" (John

21:5). Jesus then enjoined them, "Come and eat your meal" (John 21:12).

Clearly, Jesus recognized hunger as a universal human experience. Just as clearly, Jesus had special compassion for those who suffered from hunger. Jesus viewed the emptiness of hunger and the joy of being fed as such deep human experiences that he related them to his message of salvation:

> I myself am the bread of life.
> No one who comes to me shall ever be hungry,
> no one who believes in me shall ever thirst.
>
> (John 6:35)

The Challenge of the Eucharist

Throughout the history of Christianity, the Eucharist has celebrated Christ's presence in the universal human experiences of sharing food and drink. Celebrated daily throughout the world, the Eucharist proclaims Jesus' continuing desire to nourish the hungry.

Yet we need to be cautious about the way we view the Eucharist. For example:

- If we *individualize* the Eucharist too much, we can forget that it is a community experience.
- If we *spiritualize* the Eucharist too much, we can separate its meaning from people's basic need for food and drink.
- If we *isolate* the Eucharist too much, we can forget that it is meant to be shared with others beyond the scope of the worshiping community.

As Christ present in the breaking of the bread and the sharing of the cup, the Eucharist holds rich significance. Most importantly for our discussion, the Eucharist challenges us to ask, How can we who are members of the Body of Christ help to feed those members of his Body who are crying out for food? During the Eucharist we give thanks that Jesus nourishes us in our own hunger, we pray that others who are hungry will be satisfied, and we humbly ask for the courage to work with Christ in feeding the hungry.

Today's Church and Hunger: The Right to Food

The Church declares that everyone has a right to sufficient food. Yet today many people throughout the world do not have this basic right met. This realization has been one of the most pressing concerns of church leaders in recent years.

. . . every [person] has the right to possess a sufficient amount of the earth's goods. . . . This has been the opinion of the Fathers and Doctors of the Church, who taught that [people] are bound to come to the aid of the poor and to do so not merely out of their superfluous goods. When a person is in extreme necessity he has the right to supply himself with what he needs out of the riches of others. Faced with a world today where so many people are suffering from want, the Council asks individuals and governments to remember the saying of the Fathers: "Feed the man dying of hunger, because if you do not feed him you are killing him." . . . (Vatican Council II, *The Church in the Modern World,* no. 69)

On this issue the Church has been performing the prophet's role—calling governments, civic leaders, individual Christians, and all people of goodwill to consider how the hungry can be fed and how a more just distribution of goods can be brought about. In many of its recent documents the Church addresses the urgency of the hunger problem.

The Church also recognizes that the existence of hungry people challenges in a special way those who are well fed. Concrete changes are called for:

While so many people are going hungry, while so many families are suffering destitution, while so many people spend their lives submerged in the darkness of ignorance, while so many schools, hospitals, homes worthy of the name, are needed, every public or private squandering, every expenditure either of nations or individuals made for the sake of pretentious parade, finally every financially depleting arms race—all these we say become a scandalous and intolerable crime. (Pope Paul VI, *On Promoting the Development of Peoples,* no. 53)

Catholic organizations, parishes, religious orders, and individual persons have responded to the Church's call to feed the hungry. Catholic Relief Services, the official overseas aid and development agency of the United States Catholic community, has effectively provided emergency food relief along with assistance for long-range development projects. Religious orders of sisters, priests, and brothers have committed their members to the task of alleviating hunger and related concerns. Many individual parish and school groups have been creative in providing various types of assistance to hungry people.

Responding to Hunger

Our Attitudes: A War on Hunger

Do you believe in miracles? Chapter 6 of John's Gospel tells of Jesus' feeding five thousand people with the bread and fish carried by one small boy. That is quite a miracle. To feed the hungry of our world requires an equally monumental miracle. This miracle demands the concerted effort of all humanity. How likely is it that this can happen?

During much of World War II, certain products were rationed and difficult to obtain in the United States. For the most part, citizens did not mind. They knew that priority had to be given to the soldiers and to the war effort. So they learned to waste less and to stretch their resources. They also reinstituted the practice of growing their own food in "victory gardens." People saved even small things such as aluminum gum wrappers so that these items could be put to service in the war effort. If sacrifices could hasten the war's end, people at that time were willing to endure them.

Wars cause a great deal of suffering, death, and destruction, but so does hunger. Catholic Relief Services reports that "every year 20 million people suffer hunger-related deaths and millions more experience the irreversible effects of childhood malnutrition: permanently impaired mental and physical development and diminished work performance." This means that on an annual basis, hunger is a greater killer than World War II, in which 17 million soldiers died worldwide. If drastic measures were called for during that war, then equally drastic measures are called for in our current war against hunger. If we see hunger as a war, then we need to reflect on our attitudes:

- We need to accept the seriousness of the problem: so many people dying of hunger on our rich earth is an intolerable situation.
- We also need to humanize the face of hunger: those suffering from hunger are just like us. Historical events, misguided policies, and other unfortunate circumstances have left them subject to suffering and deprivation.
- Finally, we need a spirit of energizing hopefulness. That is, we need to believe that the steps that we take can make a difference.

Our Actions:
The Recommendations of the U.S. Bishops

In the early 1970s the problem of hunger received a great deal of popular attention. The frightening extent of the problem reached the consciousness of many people for the first time. Church leaders worldwide addressed the problem. The U.S. bishops discussed the issue in a number of documents. In one, called *Statement on the World Food Crisis: A Pastoral Plan of Action*, they suggest specific responses to hunger. They identify both personal responses and structural changes that they see as helpful in addressing the problem. Their suggestions are still valid today.

Personal Responses
The U.S. bishops list three areas of response for individuals and communities of Christians: liturgy, lifestyle, and locating and feeding the hungry. In the words of the U.S. bishops, "The themes of life, bread, community, solidarity, and responsibility flow through the symbol and substance of the liturgical life of the Church." The Mass, the liturgical year, and various types of community prayer and worship experience can appropriately be related to the problem of hunger.

Lifestyle changes suggested by the bishops include these:
- responsible consumption—especially minimizing waste of food and energy
- regular days of fast and abstinence—fasting twice a week is encouraged
- intensified efforts to locate and minister to those in local communities who are suffering from hunger

Beef or Granola?

16 Beef
6 Pork
4 Turkey
3 Eggs
3 Chicken

Pounds of vegetable protein (from grains) needed to produce one pound of animal protein

The U.S. bishops' calls to fast and to abstain from meat on Fridays can take on meaning when viewed in light of global food resources. As a source of protein, meat is inefficient. That is, many pounds of perfectly nutritious vegetable protein are required to produce one pound of meat. The chart at left shows how much vegetable protein is needed to produce the meat products that are major items in our North American diet. By contrast, in Africa and Asia 90–95 percent of the grain produced is consumed by people.

Structural Changes

When addressing the hunger problem, the bishops recognize that it is important to provide immediate short-term relief, as well as "to work for long-term structural changes for human development." In their statement they list seven changes in public policy that Christians should work toward:

1. *Agricultural development:* to promote greater food production, especially in Third World countries
2. *Food aid:* to increase food aid and to divorce aid from political and military strategy
3. *International trade:* to modify U.S. trade policies to help Third World countries while making adjustments to ensure that U.S. workers are not adversely affected
4. *U.S. farming:* to maintain the viability and productivity of U.S. agriculture
5. *Social-welfare legislation:* to promote programs to help the poor in the United States, such as food stamps and school lunches
6. *Assistance for lower- and middle-income persons:* to protect family farmers and lower- and middle-income consumers
7. *The international marketplace:* to modify the operation of the free-market system, especially the impact of the large corporations, when it stands in the way of justice

Conclusion:
Hunger Is a Problem That Can Be Solved

The next time that you gather together with friends or your family to enjoy a meal, recall that hunger is a problem that can be solved. Although far too many people suffer from hunger, many people are dedicated to alleviating their suffering. Steps can be taken to eradicate hunger. Although the suffering of the hungry is theirs alone, in a caring and Christian world, their suffering is a problem for all of us.

For Review

1. Describe an example of the ways in which Jesus bothered about people who suffer.
2. Define the terms *chronic malnutrition* and *undernutrition.*
3. According to this chapter, what is the primary reason that people are hungry? What implications does this have for our work in alleviating hunger?
4. Outline the major points made in this chapter about each of the following factors in connection to world hunger:
   - scarcity
   - overpopulation
   - weather
   - technology
   - overconsumption
   - militarization
5. What was Jesus' attitude toward hunger? Give two examples from the Gospels that reveal Jesus' attitude.
6. What have the Church's declarations said about food as a basic right of all people?
7. What view of hunger can help to spur us on to attack the hunger problem?
8. List three suggestions that the U.S. bishops make for people who are interested in addressing the problem of hunger.

For Reflection

1. What feelings do the four characters in the opening story express toward the problem of hunger? Have you ever experienced similar feelings toward the problem? Write about your feelings toward hunger.

2. Write a two-page essay entitled "Being Christian Means to Bother."

3. Complete one of the following exercises:
   a. Research and write a report on the effects of hunger—malnutrition and undernutrition. If possible, include current statistics on the extent of world hunger.
   b. Write a poem, story, or creative essay whose theme is hunger or the alleviation of hunger.
   c. Create a drawing, painting, or collage related to hunger.

4. Read about the Russian grain deal of 1972 in magazine articles of the time. Write a report on the pros and cons of the U.S. action.

5. On one half of a sheet of paper, list the causes of our current hunger problem as they were mentioned in this chapter (pages 128–134). On the other half, comment on each of the causes as you understood them before you read this chapter.

   Then, having read this chapter and reflected on the causes of hunger, how would you answer if someone were to ask you what causes today's hunger problem?

6. List all of the food and beverages that you consume that have little or no nutritional value. Then, estimate the cost of one week's consumption of these. Write a report on your findings and on what they mean to you. If you were to change your eating habits to avoid so-called junk food, in what ways could you use your savings to help change public policy?

7. Read the section of Luke's Gospel about hospitality and the great feast (Luke 14:7–24). Imagine that you are visiting a very poor parish where hunger is no stranger and are invited to deliver a sermon based on this passage. What would you say? Outline the points that you would make in your sermon.

   Next imagine that you have been invited to deliver a sermon on the same passage to a wealthy parish. How would your sermon change in that setting?

8. As a sacrament, the Eucharist symbolizes hospitality to strangers, the sharing of goods, and the community of all people. Write a two-page essay entitled "The Eucharist: A Challenge to World Hunger."

9. Church leaders consider the existence of so much hunger in today's affluent world a scandal. From your experience, describe examples of hunger's being a scandal.

10. Find out what you can about organizations committed to addressing the problem of hunger. They may be local, national, or international; they may be church-related or secular. After reading their literature or speaking with their representatives, report in writing on what approach to solving the problem of hunger each organization follows. (You might consider becoming actively involved in one of them.)

11. If you declared a personal "war on hunger," what would you do differently? Make a list of specific changes that touch on all aspects of your life. (During World War II, people willingly made sacrifices for their loved ones who were going off to war. It might help you develop a fervor for your war on hunger if you would imagine that some people close to you were in danger of being victims of hunger.)

12. The structural changes recommended by the U.S. bishops include policies related to developing Third World farming, providing food aid to poor countries, modifying international trade relations, and supporting social programs. If you were part of an international task force on hunger, what programs, policies, or legislative action would you recommend to various government and private organizations as steps to eliminate hunger? List your steps.

13. No matter where we live, people complain about high food prices. Find out what percentage of the population's average income is spent on food in these places: (a) the United States and in two other First World countries, (b) the USSR and two other Second World countries, (c) Nigeria and two other Third World countries. Comment in writing on what these figures mean to you.

7
Sexism:
Equal Protection, Equal Opportunity

Seventy years ago women in the United States were still struggling to achieve the right to vote. Only thirty years ago the opinion "A woman's place is in the home" was considered accepted wisdom. Historically women have constituted an underclass in most cultures. With their fates and fortunes often in the hands of men, women have lacked protection, opportunity, and equality. The recent women's movement has sought to change that, and in so doing, it has affected the way both women and men perceive themselves.

Portraits of Sexism Today

■ Ann Marie likes Mike and wants to go out with him. She agonizes over whether to ask him out directly or to coyly let him know that she's interested. Ann Marie wonders if it is appropriate for a girl to ask a boy for a date, and she fears hurting Mike's feelings or scaring him off. She decides on the direct approach and asks him out. Mike gladly accepts, but just before their date he agonizes over whether he should drive, open doors for her, pay her way, and perform all the other traditional, masculine roles. Both Ann Marie and Mike agree that it is not easy being a girl or a boy today.

■ While watching his younger brother's soccer game, Scott notices one boy get hit with the ball. He appears to have the wind knocked out of him and starts to cry. The game stops. A coach runs out onto the field and tells the boy: "You're okay. Shake it off and play like a man."

■ Stephanie is spending the evening watching an old Western movie on television. She is amazed that in all the fight scenes, the women stand by helplessly as men battle each other. She wonders if that really represents the way it was in the days of the Old West or in any past era. Then she recalls that even today young men are subject to the military draft while young women are not. Stephanie wonders if the fact that men are usually bigger than women will always make them assume that they are better than women.

■ Joan is in her mid-twenties and has worked her way up the corporate business ladder to become her company's personnel director. She applies for the lucrative position as director of public relations, only to be turned down for the promotion. She finds out indirectly that in the eyes of her company's leaders, "a woman in that position does not present the strong image that the company is seeking to project."

■ Bill and Mary have been married for four years. All during that time both have been working. Mary is offered an excellent promotion that would require moving to another city. Bill says that even though in this new position Mary would be making twice as much as he does, she should refuse the promotion because he would have to leave his job. Mary asks Bill if he would make the same suggestion if it were his job promotion. In the end she refuses the job for fear that, in her words, "it would crush Bill's self-image as the family breadwinner."

■ While attending Mass recently, John has noticed that the new priest substitutes "men and women" or "people" when the readings say "men." He also has noticed that the music director changes some words of songs to make the language inclusive: instead of "We are all brothers," she has people sing, "We are all brothers and sisters." John is not sure if this is really important or if it is being done simply for the sake of a few overly sensitive women.

■ Brian has always enjoyed dance. He is grateful that his mother enrolled him in the ballet school when he was very young. He struggled through his early years of high school when boys were expected to play sports, and only girls and so-called feminine guys danced ballet. By his senior year Brian was comfortable with his chosen interest. In fact, it seemed ironic to him that football and wrestling are regarded as especially "masculine" when they involve men grabbing each other, while his embracing a woman in ballet is considered "feminine." Brian was pleased that a number of his friends seemed to sincerely enjoy the recital that marked his graduation from ballet school.

Examining Sexism: Sex Roles and Social Justice

Many more incidents relating sex roles to social justice could be mentioned in addition to the portraits described above. Such incidents ring true for many of us. You could make your own list of injustices based on sex discrimination, that is, *sexism.* The basic, justice-related questions here are these: (1) Are men oppressed in any way because of society's attitude toward and treatment of men? (2) Are women oppressed in any way because of society's attitude toward and treatment of women? These same questions can be stated in a more positive way: In the face of traditional customs and current circumstances, how can men and women achieve the freedom and dignity that is their right as human persons?

The Recent Roots of the New Consciousness

The struggle for justice in the face of sexual oppression is often called women's (or men's) liberation. The modern impetus for this liberation began in the 1960s and centered around the **women's liberation movement.** This movement involved the recognition that women were unjustly denied certain types of employment, social status, and even leisure activities. Because of such denials of jobs and power, early women's liberationists declared that women were treated as second-class citizens, robbed of their human rights. These leaders saw that traditional customs (such as "a woman's place is in the home" and "the husband should be head of the family") too often contributed to economic hardship for women. Furthermore, they saw that the stereotypes and resulting role limitations were products of cultural adaptation—not biological necessity—and therefore were open to criticism and improvement.

Many North Americans viewed the early women's liberation movement as a passing fad only of concern to a fringe group. But soon it became clear that the valid questions about what it means to be a woman or a man needed to be addressed. Courses on women's studies became popular at many universities. Women's organizations that centered on political action and other concerns were formed. Small groups of women and, eventually, men met for consciousness-raising—that is, to share their personal stories and their ideas about what being a man or a woman meant.

In 1966 an author named Betty Friedan founded the National Organization for Women (NOW), which ever since has been at the forefront in dealing with women's issues. In 1972 Gloria Steinem and others decided to take a chance on publishing a magazine strictly concerned with women's issues. The magazine met with immediate success: the three hundred thousand copies of the first issue of *Ms.* sold out in a matter of days. In fact, other traditional women's magazines have since joined *Ms.* in voicing concerns for women's rights and issues of justice. Today we frequently find women's magazines containing articles on new images of fatherhood and on women who are successful in various professions. Even men's magazines, TV talk shows, and other forms of popular media address the changing image of women.

Top: Betty Friedan
Bottom: Gloria Steinem

Men's Liberation
Must Accompany Women's Liberation

During its early years, some people believed that the women's liberation movement was basically antimale. In fact, women were not trying to take over from men or to become men or to treat men as the enemy or to eradicate all differences between the sexes. On the contrary, they were genuinely interested in tackling the many problems that both men and women face on their way to becoming whole persons with the rights, the protections, and the opportunities due to them as persons.

One popular statement of the new men's consciousness was the 1979 movie *Kramer vs. Kramer*. The film broke new ground in popular entertainment by portraying a father who struggles with raising his son alone and then battles his ex-wife for custody of the child. At the start of the movie, the father is an absentee father—busy about his work outside of the home, leaving the homemaking and child rearing to his wife. When his wife leaves him with child and home, he finds himself completely inept in caring for both. By the end of the film, however, he has developed into a dedicated and competent parent and clearly has reached a level of parenting not usually achieved by fathers.

Sex Roles and Economic Issues

The following questions relate sex roles and social justice to the key area of economics:

- Do inequities still exist between men's and women's salaries for comparable work?
- Are traditional women's jobs—nursing, teaching, and secretarial work, for example—still largely the domain of women, and are they still comparatively low-paying?
- Are homemakers and mothers who do not work outside of the home jeopardizing their future financial security by working for no pay and with no Social Security insurance?
- Are women more or less likely than men to be hired for prestigious and lucrative positions? Do men provide the primary income for most North American families?

When we examine differences between women and men related to economic concerns, we can begin with two observations: (1) women generally earn less than men, and (2) today's changing social structures place new economic burdens on women.

Women Constitute a Majority of Poor People

In response to the question about inequities in pay for comparable work, statistics reveal continuing economic injustices against women today. Even though more women are working outside of the home than ever before, a clear gap exists between what women and men earn. According to government statistics, in 1983, U.S. women earned only sixty-six cents for every dollar

$1.00

$0.66

Women's Wages

During the early 1980s, women continued to earn about sixty-six cents for every dollar earned by men for full-time, comparable jobs.

that men earned for comparable work. A difference in women's salaries compared to men's occurred in all categories of professions.

A gap also exists in the types of jobs occupied by women as compared to those held by men. That is, men hold a large majority of the highest-paying jobs while a proportionately larger number of women than men are found in the lowest-paying jobs. Managerial, union, and skilled trade jobs are still overwhelmingly the domain of men. Also, the low-paying jobs occupied by women offer limited potential for advancement.

Such statistics reveal that women make up a majority of North America's poor people. Specifically, the majority of North Americans living below the official poverty line are women. Because of the rising number of families maintained by single women (divorced, widowed, separated, and unmarried), women and their children constitute a growing number of the poor persons in the United States.

In other words, a representative portrait of North America's impoverished would include these categories of women:

- mothers of young children who are trying to support their families on minimal incomes
- working women whose salaries do not match those of their male counterparts
- elderly widows who had spent their lives working as non-salaried homemakers or in low-paying jobs

Women's Economic Needs Are Changing

Most of us share a similar mental portrait of the traditional, ideal North American family: the father works from nine to five, the mother stays at home to take care of the house and the children except for the time she spends volunteering at the neighborhood school, and the two or three children depend on Mom's being home whenever they need her. Although this picture may be perceived as an ideal, it does not describe the reality of family life for most of us.

Today nearly 67 percent of all women with children over six years of age hold jobs outside of the home. Fifty percent of the married women with children under six years of age work outside the home (compared to only 19 percent who did in 1960). For most of these families, having both parents working is not viewed as an extra income for luxuries but as an economic necessity. Many families today find themselves one paycheck away from poverty. The mother's income is as essential as the father's.

In addition, an ever-increasing number of women are supporting themselves or their families with only their paychecks. The traditional image of women—economically dependent on their parents, then on their husbands, and finally on their adult children—is further and further from the present experience of most women. Women need opportunities for economic self-sufficiency as much or more than men.

Sex Roles and Positions of Power

When we look at the positions of power in our communities, schools, businesses, Church, and government, we arrive at one overwhelming conclusion: men run the world. In the U.S. political sphere, for example, no woman has been president and only a few women are cabinet members. In 1984, two of the one hundred U.S. senators were women, less than 5 percent of the members of the House of Representatives were women, and only one woman served as governor of a state. This imbalance exists despite the fact that women have had the right to vote since 1920 and presently make up a majority of potential voters.

Statistics reveal a similar absence of women in key power positions in all other areas of life. For instance, in education the majority of less prestigious elementary school teaching positions are held by women while the majority of college professorships are held by men. In medicine most doctors are men while most nurses are women. In business most executives are men; most office workers are women.

The Question of Sexual Stereotypes

So far we have presented the issue of sex roles and social justice as primarily a women's issue. But earlier we stated that men suffer oppression and are in need of liberation as much as women. The fact is that even though men are economically more secure and politically and socially more powerful, they must pay a price for that power and security. That price involves a lessening of freedom and maturity.

If we would stop right now and think about them, we could probably list many **sexual stereotypes**—that is, oversimplified, unreasonable statements that we apply to all men or all women:

- Women should be placed on a pedestal.
- Men are more logical than women.
- Men should wear the pants in the family.
- Women want men to take care of them.
- Women are more sensitive and romantic than men.
- Men don't cry.

Some of us might hasten to modify the above list by saying, "Men don't have to exhibit so-called masculine qualities to be a man, and women don't have to fit into a feminine stereotype." Others of us might state the opposing view: "Men and women are biologically different; so naturally they exhibit different qualities." Whatever our position, it is clear that sexual stereotyping holds important implications for justice. Let's look briefly at two of these sexual stereotypes.

Sexual Stereotyping

Be

yielding
compliant
gentle
conciliatory
childlike
excitable
cooperative
sympathetic

Don't Be

strong
enterprising
forceful
confrontational
adult
calm
competitive
objective

Are Boys More Aggressive?
Are Girls More Sensitive?

A basic sexual stereotype is that boys are better at expressing aggression while girls are better at expressing feelings. The cases at the beginning of this chapter included one about Scott, who observed a young boy being discouraged from crying. In another case Stephanie wondered about the old movies' portrayal of men as aggressive and women as passive. To the extent that this stereotype is accepted and fostered in our culture, men and women are not free to develop as whole persons—with both feelings of tenderness and aggression and with the ability to express both care and anger.

This cultural stereotype is especially harmful because it ignores the fact that all people share the same set of emotions. Maturing, moreover, is learning to enjoy and deal with all our emotions. Thus our cultural behavior conflicts with our natural development. As a result, the guy who is "all man" is only half human.

Is a Woman's Place in the Home?

Another sexual stereotype present in our society is that men are better suited to the world of business and politics outside the home whereas women are better suited to matters of home management and child care. As we noted earlier, one problem with this notion is the resulting inequity in pay and status between men and women. Also, women lose touch with the workings of the commercial world, and men lose touch with intimate family concerns.

Counteracting the stereotype in recent years, many men have discovered the beauty and wonder of nurturing their children and also the challenge of maintaining a home—not just the house. The *Kramer vs. Kramer* story is not one for divorced men only. Men's liberation has freed husbands to choose to be parents, as well as breadwinners, so that their wives can choose to be breadwinners, as well as parents.

The above sexual stereotypes create unjust obstacles to both women and men in their lives and careers. Other sexual stereotypes are even more sinister because they present physical dangers to women. For instance, violence is often linked with women in popular films. Such films can even be seen on television because violence is not considered pornographic in our society. As a result, these media foster the perverse stereotypes that women expect physical abuse as part of courtship or marriage and that women enjoy rape and even encourage it. Nothing could be further from the truth.

Signs of Hope: Changing Images, Changing Roles

The goal is now to complete ourselves. Progress for women lies in becoming more assertive, more ambitious, more able to deal with conflict, and becoming more active outside the home. Progress for men will lie in becoming more empathetic, more compassionate, more comfortable working inside the home, and better able to admit failure or defeat. We're not trading places. We're just completing ourselves. In the long term I can think of no movement that has more to offer. We can all be allies. (Gloria Steinem)

The modern movement for women's and men's liberation has had an impact. We have models of successful women and men in varying capacities, comfortable with expressing a rainbow assortment of roles and emotions, interacting with each other as equals, and learning from each other. Young women today *expect* equal opportunities and equal treatment. No longer is being a doctor, a lawyer, a business executive, or even a president a role to which women cannot aspire. On the other hand, young men today are realizing more and more that home and family are shared responsibilities and that career goals need to be tempered with concerns for a wife's and a family's needs and wishes. Beyond that, many young men now accept that a liberated woman, who is aware of her own strengths and goals, is not someone threatening to their manhood. A generation of men and women who struggled with changing roles can be thanked for these brighter perspectives and broader opportunities.

On a social level, some businesses now provide day-care centers in their offices for employees with children. Approved time off from work for child care is becoming more common for men, as well as for women. Although the Equal Rights Amendment in the United States has not been passed and child-custody cases still favor the mother, numerous other laws and

court rulings have been enacted, protecting the rights of both men and women.

The present picture of social justice for all and of liberation for both sexes is not a completely rosy one. In some ways the changes that have occurred define more problem areas. For instance, the shared custody of children does not always prove to be to the benefit of the children, who can wind up shuttling between parents or being expected to continually choose between them. Nevertheless, sexual equality has become a top item on our social agenda, not to be ignored.

Putting Sexism into a Christian Perspective

A Look at the Scriptures

Historically, the Scriptures have been used to support both the equality and inequality of men's and women's roles. The creation stories in Genesis are used to support beliefs both in the oneness and the equality of women and men and in their essential differences and inequality.

In his Epistles, the words of Saint Paul seem quite definite:

> Wives should be submissive to their husbands as if to the Lord because the husband is head of his wife just as Christ is head of his body the church, as well as its savior. As the Church submits to Christ, so wives should submit to their husbands in everything. (Ephesians 5:22–24)

Yet elsewhere Paul says,

> There does not exist among you Jew or Greek, slave or freeman, male or female. All are one in Christ Jesus. (Galatians 3:28)

Biblical scholars remind us that in interpreting such passages, we must read them in light of the culture of that time. Given the attitudes toward women in biblical society, it is not surprising to find that wives were told to be submissive to their husbands or that women were denied certain privileges and roles. In the ancient Near East, women generally had no rights as free persons. They were always subject to men, either fathers or husbands. This low status defined the place of women in Greek society as well. Given this cultural background, what stands out as surprising and significant is Paul's statement suggesting that no distinctions are to be made between women and men.

Jesus, Women, and Men

When we examine Jesus' attitude toward people generally, one fact stands out strongly: Jesus lived the message that Paul expressed in his Letter to the Galatians. He treated Jews and Gentiles, the upright and sinners, men and women all alike. In chapter 4 of John's Gospel, for example, Jesus spoke to the Samaritan woman freely. Thus, he broke two cultural taboos in that he spoke to a Samaritan who was also a woman. Not only did he speak to her, but he asked her to proclaim the news of his presence to her townspeople. Jesus also counted both women and men among his friends. In short, Jesus ushered in the reign of God that was to be marked by an emphasis on the oneness of all people rather than on differences and separateness.

As the early church communities developed, they adopted the attitudes toward women's and men's roles present in their cultural setting. (Remember that the Church also borrowed its organizational structure, many of its ceremonies, and other elements from the various cultural settings in which it found itself.) Yet the Church of the Middle Ages still provided women with positions of power through its monasteries for women.

Some monastic writers even referred to God in feminine images. Several Cistercian monks of the twelfth century, for instance, spoke of "Mother Jesus," referring to Christ's tenderness and supportive love. This feminine image of Jesus has biblical roots in his own words. Jesus once referred to himself as a mother hen: "How often have I yearned to gather your children, as a mother bird gathers her young under her wings, but you refused me" (Matthew 23:37).

Today's Church and Sexism

In its teachings on justice, the Church today recognizes the need to include concern for justice for women. For example:

- Pope John XXIII in his 1963 encyclical *Peace on Earth* stated that "since women are becoming ever more conscious of their human dignity, they will . . . demand rights befitting a human person both in domestic and public life" (no. 41). He described this as one of the "three distinctive characteristics" of our age.
- The Second Vatican Council called on humanity to "develop the dignity proper to individuals and to societies" (*The Church in the Modern World,* no. 9) and used as an example of that dignity women's claim for "parity with men in fact," as well as before the law.
- Later, in 1971, the international Synod of Bishops declared that "women should have their own share of responsibility and participation in the community life of society and likewise of the Church" (*Justice in the World*).

Many individuals and groups within the Church are seeking to live out these church statements calling for justice for women. One focus of their concern has been reexamining the role of women in the Church itself; another focus centers on applying the Church's concern for women to all women in society. The first focus involves discussion of the role of women in ministry and of its relationship to the role of the male leadership in the Church. The second focus seeks to involve the Church in working with non-Catholic groups to alleviate oppression and discriminating practices in political, domestic, and work-related settings.

Responding to Sexism

Examining Our Attitudes

Living as we do in an environment filled with the virus called *sexism*, we are not likely to be immune to the disease. By battling the sickness, however, we can begin to turn our own infection into an immunization.

Spend some time reflecting on the following sets of questions:

- What does it mean to you to be a male? What does it mean to you to be a female? Do your responses to these questions limit men or women to certain roles or functions?
- Compare the way you relate to members of the same sex with the way you relate to members of the opposite sex. What do the differences or similarities tell you about your attitudes toward women and men?
- Are you free of sexual stereotypes? What are the stereotypes that affect your thinking? Can you accept others who do not fit the stereotypic images of a man or a woman?
- Do you seek to understand problems that are unique to women? to men?
- Do you treat women's struggle for equality and justice seriously, or do you treat it as something trivial?

Working for Structural Change

Upon hearing of the ratification of the Nineteenth Amendment to the U.S. Constitution, which granted women the right to vote, the Democratic presidential candidate at the time exclaimed: "The civilization of the world is saved. The mothers of America will stay the hand of war." Of course, wars did not end in 1920, but the candidate was making an interesting point: if women achieve power, they can make some crucial contributions to the way the world is run.

Studies indicate that women's patterns of voting and leadership do tend to reflect values and concerns different from those of men. Structural changes that create more power for women would not simply place control in the hands of different people. Women as leaders might well introduce new values and perspectives.

For instance, the traditionally masculine emphasis on competition influences many decisions in the political and business world. While men have tended to prove their manhood by competing with others, women have shown themselves more often motivated by a spirit of cooperation and care for others. This valuable "nurturing spirit" does not suddenly dissolve when women gain power outside the home. In other words, if the values traditionally assigned to women's roles are allowed to have greater force in our society, they will provide a balance to the masculine role values already present.

So the primary aim of structural change in response to sexism is to allow women to be a more powerful force in the workings of our communities, our businesses, our governments, and our Church. The accompanying influx of new attitudes, values, and perspectives may bring a better balance, a new vitality, and greater justice to our world.

Conclusion

> God created man in his image:
>   in the divine image he created him;
>   male and female he created them.
>   (Genesis 1:27)

According to the Scriptures, when we look within ourselves or outward toward others—women and men—we are seeing the image of the divine. When we limit the scope of expression—our own or others—to cultural stereotypes, we are limiting God. Likewise, so long as our society is structured in such a way that half of the population is relegated to secondary roles due to their sex, we limit full expression of the God who found a home within humanity.

For Review

1. In what sense is sexism a justice-related issue?
2. What did the leaders of the modern women's liberation movement see that was unjust about traditional sexual customs?
3. Men's liberation must accompany women's liberation. Explain.
4. Choose two key economic issues that are related to women. Describe an example of how each issue may create economic hardships for women.
5. What do statistics reveal concerning men, women, and positions of power in our culture?
6. List two sexual stereotypes and describe how each stereotype can limit or harm either men or women.
7. What is the message of the Scriptures regarding the equality of women and men?
8. How was Jesus' treatment of women different from the cultural standards of the time?
9. What reason does Pope John XXIII give for women's calling for rights in domestic and public life?
10. Structural changes are a necessary part of our response to sexism. What is the primary aim of structural change as stressed in this chapter?

For Reflection

1. Look at the brief cases that open this chapter. Write four scenarios portraying sexual discrimination—two portraits of discrimination against women and two portraits of discrimination against men.

2. The idea of women's and men's liberation often evokes a variety of strong emotional responses—for example, anger, amusement, embarrassment, or fear. Consider the following images and think about the immediate feeling that each evokes in you. Then, choose two images that bring on the strongest response and comment in writing about why you believe they evoke such a response.
   - a girl trying out for an all-boy baseball team
   - a girls' athletics program receiving only half of what the boys' program receives
   - women as ministers, rabbis, and priests
   - a male ballet dancer

- a wife working to support the family while her husband takes care of the house and children
- a girl directly asking a boy for a date
- a family choosing to send their son but not their daughter to college because they expect the daughter to marry and be cared for by her husband
- "I pray to God often, and she always listens to my prayers."

3. If you were asked to be on an editorial board for a magazine designed to promote greater consciousness of women's and men's issues among teenagers, what topics would you like to see written about in the magazine? Suggest at least six topics.

   Then write titles and brief summaries for three of your suggested articles. Complete one of these topics as a two-page article.

4. Statistics indicate that on the average, working women earn only sixty-six cents to every dollar that men earn for comparable jobs. Two programs that seek to overcome this disparity are listed here:
   - *Affirmative-action programs for women* support preferential hiring of women over men in traditionally male-dominated professions.
   - *Pay-equity programs* allow people in traditionally female-dominated professions to receive a salary equal to comparable positions in traditionally male-dominated professions. (For example, a skilled nurse or secretary would receive pay equal to a skilled machinist or service repair worker.)

   Interview a group of men and women, asking them if they would vote to make such programs official policy. Write about the results of your interview.

5. Look for statistics on the highest-paying and most-powerful positions in society to discover the percentages of women and men who hold these positions. Then, look for statistics about the lowest-paying and least-powerful positions to discover who occupies those positions. Report in writing on your findings.

6. Without first thinking about it at any length, write a description of your image of an "ideal family." Then answer the following questions:
   - Do you assign roles to men or women that could be performed by either?

- To what degree does your ideal family reflect cultural stereotypes?
- Do you personally know of families that either come close to your ideal or are far removed from it? How successful are they as family units? To what factors do you attribute their success or failure?
- How close is your family to your ideal?

7. Think about the following occupations. Describe the image that comes to mind for each one. (Do you imagine a woman or a man, a young or older person, a person of a particular race?)
   - doctor
   - lawyer
   - secretary
   - police officer
   - fire fighter
   - nurse
   - soldier
   - government official
   - housekeeper
   - factory worker

   Write a report about your impressions and your conclusions.

8. List the following:
   - qualities I most admire in a man
   - qualities I most admire in a woman

   Then respond to these questions in writing:
   - Which of these qualities are actually "human" qualities, that is, worth developing by both men and women?
   - Which of these qualities are sexual stereotypes created and sustained by society?
   - In terms of your list of qualities, describe a liberated man or woman. Is there a difference?

9. Do you believe that discrimination against men is as serious a problem as discrimination against women? Briefly describe in writing why one is more serious than the other or why they are equally serious.

10. Sensitivity to sexist language has caused many writers to substitute the word *humanity* for *mankind, ancestors* for *forefathers, chairperson* for *chairman,* and so on. List other examples of what might be considered sexist language. Then suggest alternative nonsexist, or inclusive, expressions for each example.

Survey a group of women, asking them if nonsexist language is an important concern for them. Survey a group of men, asking them the same question. Tabulate your results.

11. Look through the Gospels for incidents of Jesus' interacting with others. Based on these incidents, what do you think would be Jesus' message regarding women's and men's liberation today? Record your thoughts in writing.

12. What role do you think the Church should play in the movement for men's and women's liberation? List some practical ways that the Church could perform such a role.

13. Researchers have found that women tend to hold opinions on various issues that are different from the opinions typically held by their male counterparts. Women's views tend to differ from men's on the following issues:
   - war and peace
   - equal rights
   - economic issues, such as concern for poor and unemployed persons
   - the environment

   Write down your answers to these questions: How do you think women's views typically differ from men's on these issues? Why do you think this is so? Do you find differences of opinion on these issues among your own male and female acquaintances?

14. Liberation from sexual discrimination and oppression calls for changes on the personal, interpersonal, and social levels.
   a. Name one change in your attitude toward what it means to be a man or a woman that would help you toward greater liberation.
   b. Name one change in the way that you relate to others that would reflect a spirit of liberation.
   c. Name one area of sexual discrimination on a social level that you would like to take steps to overcome.

   Practice each of these changes in some way at least for a day. Then write about the experience.

8
Racial Prejudice: Many Races, One Human Race

"The body is one and has many members, but all the members, many though they are, are one body; and so it is with Christ . . ." (1 Corinthians 12:12–13). We live on a rainbow earth, rich in myriad colors, and in a rainbow world, rich in diverse cultures and races. Yet the human rainbow is not a smooth blending of differences but a harsh mix marred by discrimination and oppression. We live in a country and a world in which vast numbers of people are victimized because of race. This chapter looks at the negative attitude toward other races, which is known as *prejudice,* and at how it leads to racism, that is, the oppression of racial groups.

Portraits of Racial Prejudice

■ Kathy is reading the comics section of her local Sunday paper. In one cartoon she notices an Arab sheik portrayed with sneaky eyes and with a large purse of money bulging under his robes. In a political cartoon she finds a young Arab portrayed as a terrorist. Kathy assumes that many Arabs are like this, and so she is not disturbed by these portraits. In fact, she has never met anyone of Arab descent.

■ Tony and Glenn, black students in a predominantly white school, spend most of their time with other black students. Every day they eat their lunches at the same cafeteria tables and afterward join other black students by the soccer field. The other students accept this arrangement. Occasionally a white student asks, "Why do the black students stick together so much?"

■ Anita, who is from Puerto Rico, speaks English pretty well—considering that at home her family speaks Spanish. Yet she finds school a struggle because in addition to studying the subject material for each class she must constantly work on improving her English. As a result, Anita does not get good grades. When she has a good day, it is only because she has worked harder than usual. On bad days she tells herself that she is just stupid and will never get ahead.

■ John, who is three-fourths Native American, misses his reservation even though he has been away from it for many years. Since his family moved to the city, he has taken kidding about being a Native American. Most of the time he laughs it off, but inside he is angry that people do not treat seriously the glory and pain of his heritage. John gets angry at himself for allowing the joking to occur as frequently as it does.

■ Caroline, a white girl, has had two dates with Michael, who is black. She has known Michael for a few years, and they have been friendly for all of that time. When he asked her out, it did not surprise her. She liked him. The first time they went out, however, Caroline was self-conscious about the way many people stared at them. Her father, who is liberal about most things, did not say much about her dating Michael. Yet she feels that her father didn't say anything because he thought it would be a short-lived relationship. Caroline is not sure where the relationship is going or what it might mean. For the moment she is happy simply to be seeing someone as nice as Michael.

■ Ed, who is white and a college senior majoring in marketing, applies at a local business for a job after graduation. He notices that some other students—notably a Hispanic student and an Asian student—are applying to the same company. After his interview he goes home and tells his parents, "I don't have a chance for the job. You know they have to hire a minority person over me."

Examining Racism: Prejudice and Race

In the situations portrayed above, people may be hurt because of their race. When we are honest with ourselves, all of us admit that we have prejudices. We have any number of likes and dislikes about things such as foods, styles of dress, speech patterns, ways of spending a summer vacation, and methods of relating to others. Often our likes and dislikes are based on limited experiences. We might say "I don't like Chinese food" because we had one tiny bite of egg roll as children. We might say "People who wear expensive clothes are snobs" without anything resembling a fair survey to back it up.

If we hold prejudices about food and clothing, obviously we can have prejudices about racial, religious, and ethnic groups as well. But how is *racism* different from other prejudices? Beyond that, how does racism manifest itself in our particular culture? These are the questions to be addressed in this chapter.

The Characteristics of Prejudice

As the word itself indicates, *prejudice* means "prejudging," that is, making a decision about someone or something before the basic facts are known. When directed toward groups of people, it is related to stereotyping, in which we make judgments about an entire group of people based on limited, untested, often unjust assumptions. (For example: "Football players are all brawn and no brains. All fat people are happy. Blonds are flighty.") A look at four characteristics associated with prejudging can help us understand prejudice in action.

1. Generalizations: Individual Traits Applied to a Group

Making generalizations is both a natural and a helpful use of human intelligence: If we are bitten by a snake and that is our only experience of snakes, naturally we become fearful of snakes generally. Likewise, a near-drowning incident might keep us from going near water for the rest of our lives.

In a similar fashion, we make generalizations about the people whom we meet. If you attended your first Native American festival and found people selling imported souvenirs, you might conclude wrongly that Native Americans have little pride in their heritage. Or, if you were traveling with your family and you passed through a predominantly Polish section of a large city for the first time, you might form an opinion based merely on the few streets and the few people whom you saw.

Generalizing is natural, but it is also dangerous when we fail to recognize its limitations and leave no room for new and better information. Generalizations can reduce reality to simple, orderly packages, but they do not offer us the true picture of life in all its richness and complexity.

2. Irrationality: Illogical Judgment

Prejudiced opinions are often held without any basis in reality. This is often the situation with children who declare that they hate some food, even though they have never tasted it.

Prejudiced people usually appeal to experience or reason to defend their positions in order to make their positions *appear* rational. For example:

- Prior to World War II, Nazi propaganda offered so-called scientific proof that Jews were racially inferior to Germans.
- During the last century, some British caricatures portrayed Irish people as closely resembling monkeys to support discriminatory practices against the Irish.
- Before the Civil War, some advocates of slavery in the United

The ovens used for murdering prisoners in the Nazi death camp at Weimar. During World War II, the Nazis attempted to exterminate the Jewish people and other groups in these death camps.

States argued that Africans enslaved and brought to America were fortunate to receive civilization and that slavery was actually beneficial for them.

- Often during wars, enemy soldiers and civilians are considered less than human, thereby justifying taking their lives.

In short, prejudicial thinking is warped thinking that can result in warped behavior toward others.

3. Closemindedness: The Inability to Change

If we were to say "People on welfare are lazy" and hold firmly to that belief in the face of all the studies and statistics that prove otherwise, then we would be closeminded. For example: A white woman was watching television one evening, and after an hour of viewing a show with a completely Caucasian cast, a one-minute commercial that included a black couple came on. When it was over, she remarked, "All you see on TV anymore is black people." In fact, her mind was closed to the presence of all the white people she viewed for fifty-nine minutes and perceived only what was different for her—the one-minute portrayal of a black couple.

While we must work from our own experiences of other people, it is also important to realize that our base of experience is limited. We practice prejudicial thinking when we "jump to conclusions" that are based on a small set of experiences. We also practice prejudice when we hang on to opinions in spite of solid information that contradicts them.

4. Strong Feelings: Anger Toward or Fear of Others

When our opinions about other groups are accompanied by anger and fear, then we are likely to think or behave prejudicially. For example, we may dismiss acts of violence committed by members of our own social group but react strongly to similar acts by members of a different group. This often happens with events that concern the government: On the one hand, military acts with only the remotest of connections with Communists are quickly reported as terrorism by the national media. On the other hand, U.S. military operations—such as the invasion of Grenada, the bombing of Libya, and the mining of Nicaragua's harbor—are not considered terrorist activities, even when creating terror is their stated purpose.

Because we all have prejudices—that is, generalizing, irrational, closeminded, emotional opinions—we need to examine them continually. If we are playful and humble enough, then we can transform unjust prejudices into profound insights.

Racism Is More Than Prejudice

Although prejudice is a commonplace human experience, some groups of people have suffered greatly because of **racial prejudice**. The stereotypes and strong feelings associated with racial prejudice have often resulted in unfair treatment inflicted on individual races or cultures. Throughout history, people have been denied basic rights and enslaved because of their race. Attempts called *genocide* have even been made to annihilate all the members of certain races.

Racial prejudice becomes racism when one group has control over another group. In other words, *racism combines prejudice with the abuse of power.* Although prejudice can be directed toward any group, racism is directed toward less-powerful groups and is intended to keep them relatively powerless.

Often minority groups suffer from racist practices. In the United States, black, Hispanic, and Native American minorities are victimized by racism. South Africa is infamous for a policy called *apartheid* (ə-'pär-tāt) that keeps power in the hands of a small minority of ruling whites and denies rights and freedoms to the black majority.

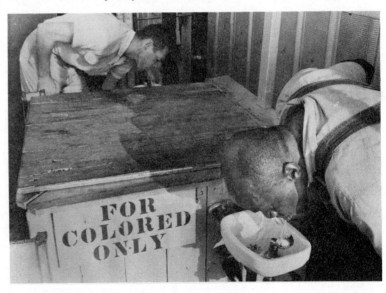

Institutional Racism

Racism is especially insidious when it is part of the fabric of a society. This is termed *institutional racism* because the institutions of a society are structured so as to subordinate a particular group of people. Apartheid is an obvious example: South African blacks are by law forbidden to vote, to live in certain areas, and to travel freely even within their own country.

The U.S. civil-rights legislation for the past twenty-five years has moved in the direction of eliminating racism from all U.S. institutions. Summarized below is one famous example of these legal changes from an early court case known as *Brown* v. *Board of Education:*

> In 1950 a seven-year-old black girl named Linda Brown wanted to attend a nearby school with her white and Hispanic playmates. Because she was black, she was directed to attend the "Negro" school two miles away. Angered by the injustice of this separation of schools by race, Linda's father filed a suit against the local school board.
>
> Four years later, this suit led to the U.S. Supreme Court's landmark decision: "Does segregation of children in public schools solely on the basis of race, even though the physical facilities and other 'tangible' factors may be equal, deprive the children of the minority group of equal educational opportunities? We believe that it does."
>
> In other words, separate but equal schools affect black and other minority children negatively because to separate them "from others of similar age and qualifications solely because of their race generates a feeling of inferiority as to their status in the community that may affect their hearts and minds in a way unlikely ever to be undone."

Affirmative Action

In its famous *Brown* v. *Board of Education* judgment described above, the U.S. Supreme Court found racially segregated schools discriminatory to minorities. Since the 1950s, laws discriminating against blacks and other minorities have gradually been eliminated. Most leaders felt that when all people received equal treatment under the law, equality of the races would be assured. But the Supreme Court justices and other concerned leaders soon realized a significant flaw in this hopeful reasoning. Because of centuries of discrimination, blacks and other minorities made up a small percentage of professional groups, decision-makers, the wealthy, and leaders in general. In other words, the major institutions of U.S. society were racist not because of present laws but because of a long history of discriminatory practices.

For instance, how could a black person receive equal treatment under a criminal justice system in which the vast majority of judges, jurors, lawyers, police officials, prison guards, and

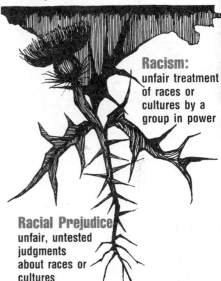

The Poisonous Weed of Prejudice

Institutional Racism: policies and traditions of unfair treatment of races or cultures that have become part of the institutions of a society

Racism: unfair treatment of races or cultures by a group in power

Racial Prejudice: unfair, untested judgments about races or cultures

Prejudice: making a decision about someone or something before the basic facts are known

wardens were white? In the area of jobs, the leadership of most companies and labor unions was white. In education, few teachers and fewer principals and school board members were nonwhite. Thus, in every important social and political arena, leadership resided in the hands of the controlling white majority. Consequently, changes in this racial imbalance would be very slow in coming if they were made only through natural developments.

To address this problem of long-standing institutional racism, a policy known as **affirmative action** was proposed. Rather than a passive, hands-off approach to end racism, this policy called for more active and positive measures. Specifically, affirmative action called for controversial measures such as having *racial quotas* in hiring practices. For example, in order for a city to receive federal funds, a certain percentage of minority persons would have to be hired in the city's police and fire departments. Schools and industries also needed to meet required levels of minority employment. In addition, minority-owned companies received preferential treatment in being awarded government contracts.

The U.S. Supreme Court addressed the legality of affirmative action most directly in its 1978 *Bakke* decision.

> In this case a young white man named Allan Bakke sought admission to the medical school at the University of California at Davis. He knew that only one hundred positions were available in the medical school program, and that sixteen of those positions were reserved for minority students under the school's affirmative-action policy. He sued the university for denying him equal treatment regardless of race. The case made its way to the Supreme Court, which attempted to reach a compromise position on what the justices considered a complex issue. In the end the court ruled that in certain circumstances race could legitimately be used as an element in judging students for admission to universities.

The controversial nature of affirmative action is easy to see. It seems to contradict the U.S. Constitution's ideal that all people are created equal and the First Amendment prohibition against laws based on "race, creed, or color." At the same time, the deep scars left by institutional racism clearly require practical measures if they are to be healed. Advocates of affirmative action recognize that this policy veers from the ideal precisely because of the less-than-ideal condition of our contemporary society.

Putting Racism into a Christian Perspective

The Story of Jonah

In the Scriptures there is a short story called the Book of Jonah. In it the prophet Jonah was asked by God to go to the city of Nineveh to preach to its citizens. Jonah disliked this idea intensely: Nineveh happened to be the capital city of the Assyrians, who were at the time hated enemies of the Jews. Instead of making his way to Nineveh, Jonah set sail in the exact opposite direction. In the incident with which we are all familiar, Jonah was tossed overboard and swallowed by a large fish.

Three days later Jonah was spat up onto the shores of Nineveh. Reluctantly he preached God's threat of destruction for the past wickedness of the people of Nineveh and called them to repentance. Then Jonah adjourned to the side of a hill, confident that God would heap destruction upon the sinful Ninevites. But Jonah observed a very different outcome:

> . . . the people of Nineveh believed God; they proclaimed a fast and all of them, great and small, put on sackcloth. . . . When God saw by their actions how they turned from their evil way, he repented of the evil that he had threatened to do to them; he did not carry it out. (Jonah 3:5,10)

But God's forgiving these non-Jews "was greatly displeasing to Jonah, and he became angry" (Jonah 4:1). Rather than destroying Jonah's enemies, God saved them. Despite Jonah's loud complaints about God's compassion toward the Ninevites, God made a shady gourd plant grow up to ease Jonah's despair as he sat on the hillside. But the next morning, God caused the plant in whose shade Jonah was resting to wither and die.

> . . . and the sun beat upon Jonah's head till he became faint. Then he asked for death, saying, "I would be better off dead than alive."
>
> But God said to Jonah, "Have you reason to be angry over the plant?" "I have reason to be angry," Jonah answered, "angry enough to die." Then the LORD said, "You are concerned over the plant which cost you no labor and which you did not raise; it came up in one night and in one night it perished. And should I not be concerned over Nineveh, the great city, in which there are more than a hundred and twenty thousand persons who cannot distinguish their right hand from their left, not to mention the many cattle?" (Jonah 4:8–11)

Through the story of Jonah, the Scriptures show us some important lessons:

- God does not lovingly create any people in order to destroy them.
- God's vision is broader and more inclusive than our narrow and limited vision.
- God is not a God only of one group but of everyone.
- All people are sisters and brothers under God.

Jesus Teaches a Radical Love

> "If you love those who love you, what merit is there in that? Do not tax collectors do as much? And if you greet your brothers only, what is so praiseworthy about that? Do not pagans do as much?" (Matthew 5:46–47)

A noted theologian once remarked rather cynically that in Western society love occurs only within the family and at Christmas. The above words of Jesus—like the story of Jonah—call us to love more than our families and friends. Throughout the Gospels, Jesus not only preached this radical love but also lived it. He baffled his fellow Jews by deliberately treating Jews and non-Jews alike. When he met people in need, he concerned himself with their pain rather than with their nationality, religion, or color. Today Jesus asks us to look beyond such superficialities as skin color, speech patterns, and styles of dress, and to see others ultimately as being as human as ourselves.

The Church and Racism

As a product of its culture, the Church has not been immune from racism. Yet throughout most of its history the Church's enthusiasm for spreading the gospel message has led it to seek communion with others. For example, even though he lived in a Roman culture that looked down on barbarians and enslaved them, Pope Saint Gregory the Great (died 604) called for their conversion. When he saw a boy—one of the pagan, English people called *Angles*—about to be sold into slavery, Gregory remarked, "I will not call them Angles, but angels."

The history of the European conquest of America is a ruthless and bloody one, and the Church of the time must share the blame because it was so much a part of the culture. Yet many French and Spanish missionaries risked torture and death to introduce Native Americans to God's love for them. In light of their struggles and those of other missionaries, any racist tendencies within Christianity are aberrations.

Today's Church and Racism

Today in our land the face of Catholicism is the face of all humanity—a face of many colors, a countenance of many cultural forms. (National Conference of Catholic Bishops, *Brothers and Sisters to Us*, p. 8)

In their 1979 pastoral letter on racism, the U.S. bishops refer to racism as both a "fact" and a "sin." By calling racism a fact, the bishops are pointing out that racism clearly continues to exist "when we look beneath the surface of our national life." By calling it a sin, the bishops are reminding us that we need to respond to the harmfulness of racism with the same fervor that we would any other sinful condition.

The Church today stands as an important voice against racism not only because of its mission from Jesus but also because of its present makeup. Few worldwide organizations transcend national and racial barriers to the degree that the Catholic Church does. Papal statements, as well as the actions of individual Catholics and local organizations in many countries, disclose the Church's commitment to achieving racial justice. For example, many religious and laypersons are involved in the struggles against apartheid in South Africa and on behalf of Hispanic migrant workers.

Responding to Racism

1. Learning from Other Races

All good people agree,
and all good people say,
All nice people like Us are We
And everyone else is They:

But if you cross over the sea,
Instead of over the way,
You may end by (think of it!)
    looking on We
As only a sort of They!

(Rudyard Kipling)

Did you know that within certain Native American cultures, competition is frowned upon and looking someone directly in the eye is considered impolite? Did you know that major types of specifically U.S. music—such as jazz, rhythm and blues, and rock and roll—trace their origins to black culture? Did you know that Chinese and other Asians possess rich

A bilingual classroom

cultural heritages that predate the white, Western culture by thousands of years? Did you know that every major, living world religion began in Asia? Even though our society is a "cultural stew" that has many ingredients contributed by different groups, we continue to think of these groups as "They," not "We."

Interesting bits of cultural information help remind us that we have much to learn from all races and cultures. Too often we think of racial differences as problems. In fact, the many races found in our country make it a beautiful mosaic. As we outgrow an "us and them" mentality and cultivate a spirit of learning from other races, we will know more about our world and about ourselves.

2. Recognizing the Victims

Certainly we realize that there are individual members of every race (including one's own) whom we would not want to live near or sit next to in a restaurant or become best friends with. However, unpleasant experiences with individuals of other races and personal dislikes that we hold toward other cultural styles and values do not justify the fact that in our society people are oppressed simply because of their races. Statistics related to all areas of U.S. life reveal that such racial discrimination still exists:

- When unemployment among young people rises, unemployment among black youths becomes substantially greater than the average increase.
- The studies indicating that women in the United States are paid less than men also reveal that minority women are paid even less than their white sisters.
- When prison overcrowding is a problem or hunger reaches epidemic proportions or older people must struggle to keep up with rising costs due to inflation—then blacks, Native Americans, and Hispanics suffer to a disproportionate degree.

Recognizing the victims of racism, then, means knowing that members of certain races are denied rights and privileges not denied those of another race and that they must seek to survive and function in a society in which power lies in the hands of others. We can respond to the victims of racism through works of mercy and through social action that aims to shift power into the hands of all races equally.

3. Celebrating Our Differences

Even though we humans are much more similar than different, differences still exist. Along with the obvious color differences, cultures and races also have developed unique languages and speech patterns, lifestyles, various ethnic foods and ways of preparing food, and even different fundamental values. To say that we are all one does not mean that we cannot also glory in our rich diversity.

Note that differences among us are not deviances. The term *deviance* implies a value judgment. Something is deviant when it deviates from a *norm*. For instance, if blond hair, blue eyes, and light skin are considered the cultural norm for beauty, then dark-haired and dark-skinned people are looked upon as deviant or inferior. Similarly, if speaking English is considered normal, then those who speak another language may be viewed—or even view themselves—as not just different but deviant.

Prior to the mid-1960s many U.S. blacks tried to make themselves look like whites. The image of beauty presented to them by the dominant culture was the white image. Then a movement emerged that encouraged blacks to glory in their own style of beauty, their own culture, and their own personal sense of worth and dignity. At times this movement, often referred to as "the black power movement," was considered antiwhite. In fact, it was problack but not antiwhite. It was also antiracist. Quite rightly, proponents of black power would not accept one culture as the norm for all the subcultures existing in the United States.

Soon others joined the cry, calling for their own affirmation of dignity and power, and groups came into existence advocating "gray power" for older people, "Chicano power" for Mexican Americans, "red power" for Native Americans, and so forth. Underlying each movement was the genuine need to affirm and celebrate distinctive qualities, the many facets of our common humanity.

4. Affirming Our Common Humanity

Astronauts are granted a unique view of our world. In relating their experiences while in space, astronauts often mention that they sense a "oneness" not only of the planet itself but of all the passengers on "spaceship earth" as well. Because of their special perspective, astronauts often realize what important religious figures throughout the ages have proclaimed: we are all one.

During our own moments of insight into life, we too can experience that the world is one and that we are all members of one family. Perhaps deep down we know that when one person suffers we all suffer and that the universal good of all people is also good for us. If we focus too much on differences, we can lose our perspective on this underlying truth.

When we participate in the Eucharist, we are reminded of this vision of the one human family—a vision that can become blurred in our day-to-day encounters with others. In fact, all prayer draws us out of our limited view of things and leads us to the truth that "there is one Lord, one faith, one baptism; one God . . . of all, who is over all, and works through all, and is in all" (Ephesians 4:5–6).

Conclusion

Racism is a continuing evil in our world. We naturally want to do all that we can to change society so that it reflects the values of equal rights and racial justice. In this way we will be helping those who are victimized by racism, as Jesus wishes. Also, we will be making the world a richer, more diverse and exciting place for all of us.

For Review

1. List the four characteristics of prejudice and give an example of each.
2. How is racism different from prejudice?
3. Define and give an example of institutional racism.
4. What resulted from the U.S. Supreme Court's landmark decision *Brown* v. *Board of Education?*
5. What are affirmative-action programs? What did the U.S. Supreme Court decide about affirmative action in its 1978 *Bakke* decision?
6. What does the story of Jonah reveal about God's message to us concerning our attitude toward people of different races or ethnic groups?
7. If we used Jesus as our model, how would we respond to people whose race or ethnic background is different from ours?
8. What does it mean to say that the Church has often been "a product of its culture" in regard to racism?
9. Why is today's Church an important voice against racism?
10. List the four major ways in which we can respond to racism.
11. Who are the victims of racism in our society?

For Reflection

1. Respond in writing to the following question: How do you try to become personally acquainted with and appreciative of people from ethnic and racial backgrounds different from your own?

2. Reread the cases found at the beginning of this chapter. Do all of them strike you as examples of racial prejudice? What specific images come to mind when you think about racial prejudice? Have you ever personally encountered racial prejudice toward yourself or toward people you know? Write a portrait of racial prejudice based on your own experience.

3. Choose the opinion below that comes closest to your position on racial prejudice. Write an explanation of your position.
   a. Racial prejudice is as natural as breathing and eating. We are born into a particular race, and by nature we are more comfortable with our own kind and mistrustful of those who are different.

      b. Racial prejudice is unnatural. We are born without pre-conceived attitudes toward others. Unfortunately we often pick up prejudicial attitudes from society or other people. Hate is learned.

4. Prejudice becomes racism when, as members of a racial group, people are denied rights accorded to others.

      a. List three examples of racial stereotyping. Which of these examples describes both racism and prejudice?

      b. Based on your examples, describe some characteristics that distinguish racism from prejudice.

5. Research and write a report on one of the following topics:
   - Apartheid in South Africa
   - The Treatment of Native Americans
   - The Sanctuary Movement—endangered Latin Americans illegally seeking refuge in the United States

6. Choose three examples of institutional racism. In writing, outline changes that could be made in our society to help alleviate these examples of racism.

   List the pros and cons of affirmative-action programs as described in this chapter. State your position on this remedy for racism.

7. Read the Book of Jonah found in the Bible. Draw a cartoon or comic strip depicting a segment of the story.

   Jonah's attitude toward the people of Nineveh was typical of the Israelites' narrow view of foreigners, and it continues to accurately portray the modern-day attitude of many people toward foreigners. Describe Jonah's attitude toward the Ninevites.

8. Write a two-page essay entitled "Jesus and Racism" or "The Sin of Racism."

9. Describe in writing some ways in which the sacraments of Baptism, Confirmation, and the Eucharist are aimed against racism and racial prejudice.

10. Write a report on your cultural heritage. Describe some of the unique characteristics of your heritage and the contributions of some of those who share your ethnic background.

11. An important question regarding racism is, What racial groups suffer because of their race? Use almanacs and statistical abstracts to gather current statistics pertinent to race. What is the racial makeup of the unemployed? the homeless? the prison population? various professions such as government officials, doctors, and lawyers?

12. Reread the section on difference and deviance (page 177). List three examples of cultural differences that are often viewed by people as deviances. (For example, the Scottish custom of men wearing kilts is a cultural difference that North Americans might consider deviant.)

13. Complete one of the following exercises:
    a. Create an art project that depicts one or both of these two responses to racism: *affirming our common humanity* and *celebrating our differences.*
    b. Create a visual image or write a poem using a rainbow as a symbol of unity in diversity.

9
Older Persons: A New Look at Old Friends

The pain of social injustice weighs heavily on many older people. Our society is quick to label the difficulties faced by these persons as merely part of the aging process. This view implies that nothing can be done to change the prevailing unfair attitudes, practices, or social structures that affect older persons. Seeing the situation from the perspective of justice, on the other hand, reveals that most problems faced by older people result from society's attitudes and practices rather than from the aging process itself.

The Future Is Now: Portraits of Older Persons

■ At age sixty-six Anna Berger is the oldest worker in her sewing factory. Although her hands ache with the constant pain of arthritis, she has continued at her sewing machine beyond retirement age. She fears that Social Security and her husband's pension will not adequately meet the spiraling costs of daily living. Anna would like to retire and feels that she has plenty around the house to keep her busy. Because her work production no longer matches the output of the younger women, her bosses are also anxious for her to retire. But for now Anna continues to work. At sixty-six she feels that she must still "save for the future."

■ Mr. and Mrs. Boyle are preparing for a trip to Italy— their third such vacation since retirement. Both are physically healthy, mentally alert, financially sound, and blessed with two children who now maintain families of their own. Although a number of their friends have died in recent years, the Boyles have never lacked for companions or activities. They find their lives full and rich and look forward to many active years together.

■ Betty never seemed to recover from her husband's death. With some relief, a great deal of fear, and a deep sense of despair, Betty accepted the moves from her own home to her daughter's home and now to the nursing home. She feels continually anxious over the most basic concerns: When will she eat? Who will help her to the bathroom? Will her medication make her more comfortable? Because she frequently voices her concerns about these elementary matters, Betty frustrates those family members who find time to visit. Whether she suffers from senility or simply a broken heart, Betty is clearly the shell of the person that she was in her younger years.

■ At eighty-five years of age, Sister Peterson has been officially retired for many years. Fifteen years ago, "just to keep busy," she became involved in volunteer work at the prison near her convent. Since then she has helped to establish the city's most successful program for aiding ex-offenders. Sister Peterson also serves on a number of committees concerned about prisoners' rights and is a frequent speaker on behalf of prison reform. She is often asked, "How do you do all this at your age?" She has no readily satisfying answers: she is too busy helping the needy.

Examining the Problems That Older Persons Face

The Graying of America

In the United States, women and men over the age of sixty-five are the fastest-growing age-group. At the turn of the century the average life expectancy was forty-seven years; today it is about seventy-five. Reaching the age of one hundred is becoming more and more commonplace. According to the best estimates, by the year 2000, people over the age of sixty-five will comprise 15 percent of the U.S. population. That means that approximately one in six citizens will be what is now considered an older person.

This trend, sometimes referred to as *the graying of America,* holds implications for justice. As the above portraits indicate, not all older people are presently suffering from age discrimination or burdened by society's mistreatment. Nevertheless, older people are a unique group: Because an increased life span is a relatively recent phenomenon, the need to address the concerns of older people has never had the importance that it does today. These increasing numbers—one thousand people reach age sixty-five each day—mean that the problems associated with old age are growing ones and that better solutions must be found.

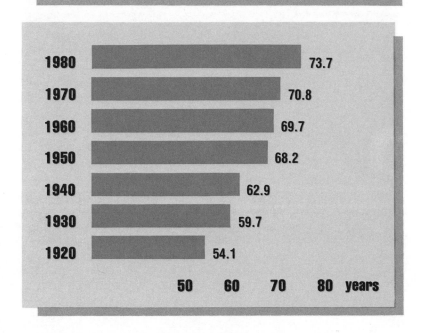

Life Expectancy in the United States

Year	Years
1980	73.7
1970	70.8
1960	69.7
1950	68.2
1940	62.9
1930	59.7
1920	54.1

50   60   70   80   years

When Is "Old"?

Sixty-five—the traditional age of retirement—generally marks the beginning of what we call *old age*. Yet today more than ever before, there are people in their sixties who still go home to visit their own parents, who are a generation older. Often presidents, Supreme Court justices, doctors, corporate executives, and many others remain active in their work into their seventies and beyond.

On the other end of the scale of chronological age, professional athletes who turn thirty-three must seriously consider what their lives will be like after retirement. Similarly, many people upon reaching their thirtieth birthday are struck with the realization that they no longer belong to the younger generation.

So, although the reality of aging faces all of us, no single birthday initiates people into old age.

Golden Years or Natural Disaster?

Our current stereotypes of older people are both positive and negative. On the positive side we find the commonly held belief that older people lead a relatively comfortable, secure, and trouble-free life. According to this view, thanks to government programs like Social Security and medicare and to numerous employment benefits, our senior citizens can relax and enjoy their retirement while younger people work to support them.

If this is the rosy picture in our heads of older people, it is not an accurate picture. Nor are the darker stereotypes

true, however. Here is one writer's summary of these negative images:

> An older person thinks and moves slowly. He does not think as he used to or as creatively. He is bound to himself and to his past and can no longer change or grow. He can learn neither well nor swiftly and, even if he could, he would not wish to. Tied to his personal traditions and growing conservatism, he dislikes innovations and is not disposed to new ideas. Not only can he not move forward, he often moves backward. He enters a second childhood, caught up in increasing egocentricity and demanding more from his environment than he is willing to give to it. Sometimes he becomes an intensification of himself, a caricature of a lifelong personality. He becomes irritable and cantankerous, yet shallow and enfeebled. He lives in his past; he is behind the times. He is aimless and wandering of mind, reminiscing and garrulous. Indeed, he is a study in decline, the picture of mental and physical failure. He has lost and cannot replace friends, spouse, job, status, power, influence, income. He is often stricken by diseases which, in turn, restrict his movement, his enjoyment of food, the pleasures of well-being. He has lost his desire and capacity for sex. His body shrinks, and so too does the flow of blood to his brain. His mind does not utilize oxygen and sugar at the same rate as formerly. Feeble, uninteresting, he awaits his death, a burden to society, to his family and to himself. (Robert N. Butler, *Why Survive?* pp. 6–7)

This sad description approximates the picture of old age held by many younger people. In fact, numerous studies confirm that most people in our Western culture view aging in a negative light. Even experts in the study of aging emphasize old age as a period of decline. Earlier in this century some doctors even classified old age as a disease.

Most unfortunately, this negative view has given rise to a fear of old age. This is an unnecessary fear and indeed does not exist in all cultures. The U.S. Catholic bishops describe the problem well:

> America today faces a great paradox: It is an aging nation which worships the culture, values, and appearance of youth. Instead of viewing old age as an achievement

and a natural stage of life with its own merits, wisdom, and beauty, American society all too often ignores, rejects, and isolates the elderly. (*Society and the Aged,* no. 1)

Good information can go a long way toward building a less fearful, fairer view of the aging process. So let's look at some facts regarding aging, physical and mental decline, senility, and retirement.

The Question of Aging

A person who is ninety years old obviously has lived longer than someone age fifty. But although peoples' chronological ages might be the same, studies indicate that great differences in the rates of *biological aging* are found from person to person. In fact, the variation in rates of biological aging is greater in old age than in any other age-group.

Yet, while the accumulation of years leaves its scars, it also produces its unique charms. In fact, people from ages sixty to ninety also exhibit more personality differences from each other than can be observed in any other age-group:

- Older people have had many years in which to develop distinct personalities.
- They also experience different degrees of health and wealth.
- They possess different needs and interests.
- They spend their time at a great variety of activities, shaped over a lifetime of choices.

In short, aside from their shared chronological age, older people are more distinct from each other than are individuals in the rest of the population.

In addition to biological aging, we can speak of *sociological aging,* that is, how society views older persons. Our focus here is on sociological aging because older persons frequently view themselves in terms of the roles and the stereotypes assigned to them by society.

A writer turning age forty was told by an interviewer in an attempted compliment, "You don't look forty." The writer responded, "On me this is how forty looks." The interviewer had a stereotyped notion of what age forty looks like. As did the interviewer, we each have images of what ages fifty, seventy, and ninety look like. We also have a sense of what those ages feel like and how people at those ages act. What we do not realize is that older people suffer from the pressure generated by these popular stereotypes. For instance:

While attending her fiftieth high school reunion, Martha sees former classmates whom she hasn't seen for many years. Upon entering the room she is immediately struck by how old they are. When she looks at them, she sees senior citizens, the elderly, people who are "over the hill."

When Martha pictures herself, however, she doesn't think of herself as "old." Instead she remembers the time she and her best friend caused an uproar in their high school senior year when they were caught smoking in the girls' bathroom. Martha pictures herself as the young woman who had many good times with friends and could always be counted on to join in a dance or a song. She also sees herself as a wife and mother, raising three children and keeping house while working full-time. In her mind's eye she is not "old." Inside she knows that she has more in common with herself at earlier ages than she does with any "old people."

While Martha sees herself as the unique individual that she is, she nevertheless views her former classmates as stereotypes of older people. Unfortunately, she has difficulty looking beyond her stereotyped images of old age. If Martha would look more closely at her classmates, she might stop seeing them as stereotypes. Then perhaps she would see that John, Alice, Margaret, and Bill remain as playful, passionate, thoughtful, satirical, and sensible as ever.

The Question of Mental and Physical Decline

The assumption is widely held that intelligence decreases from early adulthood through old age. Indeed, many people treat older persons as if they are in a "second childhood" and possess the intelligence and emotional stability of children. Recent studies indicate, on the contrary, that intelligence continues to improve right into old age. Certainly, illness and other factors can alter a person's intelligence level dramatically. But intellectual decline is not a necessary occurrence for older people, nor is it a characteristic of aging. When a person is willing to learn, researchers say, the ability to learn may be as high at the age of eighty as it was at twelve.

Physical problems, on the other hand, *are* an important concern for older people. A clear link exists between old age and the incidence of serious illness. Degeneration of the circulatory and other body systems does occur in older people, though not at the same rate for all.

Being sick is frightening. Being old and sick is doubly frightening because every illness or physical problem is a reminder of overall physical decline. But a rigid, stereotyped association of old age with ill health creates psychological factors that can actually help bring on illness.

The Question of Senility

Isn't it true that many older people suffer from senility? Like the term *aging*, **senility** refers to a wide variety of symptoms and conditions, and therefore it is an imprecise term in its popular usage. When medical science speaks about senility, it usually refers to irreversible brain damage—a condition that can affect older people and is due to a number of causes.

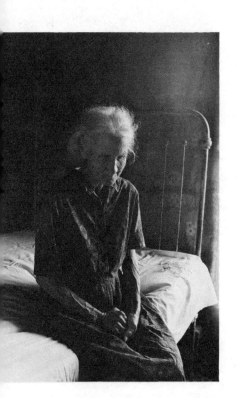

Senility in this medical sense probably affects as few as 3 percent of all older persons. Yet other people who are not suffering brain damage are often diagnosed or judged as senile. One interesting study revealed that a group of young people who were treated as "senile" for a period of time actually began to manifest the symptoms associated with senility. Other studies indicate that in societies where older people are highly respected, senility is seldom evident among their older population.

So society's attitudes and social pressures clearly contribute to the so-called senility among older persons. As a teenager, if you are forgetful or misplace things or fail to hear what your teacher says to you, you and your friends can laugh it off. Yet if your grandmother exhibits any of these traits, they may be attributed to her age.

When we attribute problems to age or senility, we are suggesting that nothing can be done to reverse them. One expert calls senility a *wastebasket label.* Such a label says in effect: "There is nothing we can do. It's to be expected. It's all downhill from now on." In other words, from this viewpoint a person labeled *senile* is beyond help and therefore can be discarded.

The Question of Retirement

The "Eskimo way" regarding older persons holds a strangely romantic appeal: older members of the community, rather than burden the rest of the tribe, steal off into the wilderness to die. This custom may sound natural, heroic, dignified, perhaps even Christlike. We might even say that in a community struggling for survival, perhaps this custom makes sense. Yet it raises some tough questions: Who determines when someone is ready to go into the wilderness? What combination of factors indicates that it is time to die? Should a fixed time of death exist for all members of society? Does a modern, affluent community gain or lose with the death of an elder member?

Of course, retirement is not synonymous with wandering off into the wilderness to die. Nevertheless, for many older persons retirement marks a time of entering, usually unprepared and often unwilling, an untracked territory. In the eyes of society and of retirees themselves, retirement can signal an end to purposeful activity and to meaningful contributions. The experience of retirement can be devastating for older people, so we need to share some basic information about it.

In the first place, **retirement** is a relatively recent phenomenon. It began in Germany toward the end of the last century as a means to better the conditions of older people. In many areas of the world today retirement still remains meaningless: where life expectancy is only in the fifties or early sixties (as it is even in the United States among Native Americans and Mexican Americans), retirement at age sixty-five holds little significance.

On the other hand, in Western countries in which life expectancies continue to increase, many people could spend up to one-third of their lives retired. If no changes are made, a greater and greater percentage of the population will be retired. This would have devastating effects on the economic and other dimensions of society.

Some older persons welcome retirement willingly and gratefully; others retire only after being forced to do so. Many companies continue to have mandatory retirement provisions; that is, persons are required to retire when they reach a certain age. Some other companies, without a policy of mandatory retirement, nevertheless pressure older workers to retire. People over age forty-five who seek employment often find that companies consider their age an impediment to their being hired. In reality, many unemployed older persons wish to work and can work well. According to studies, older workers often have better work records than have younger ones—as marked by less absenteeism, greater stability, a steadier rate of production, and higher quality work.

Finally, contrary to the rosy picture of carefree leisure that we often have of retired people, the price of retirement is typically the loss of more than one-half of one's income. Unless greater freedom occurs regarding retirement, our society may be condemning many older persons to a wilderness of poverty and rejection while depriving itself of a valuable resource.

Putting Old Age into a Christian Perspective

Old Age in the Jewish Scriptures

> The whole span of Abraham's life was one hundred and seventy-five years. Then he breathed his last, dying at a ripe old age, grown old after a full life; and then he was taken to his kinsmen. (Genesis 25:7–8)

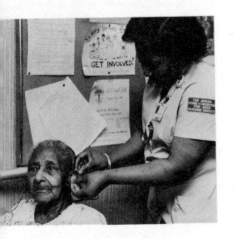

When we read the first book of the Bible, we are struck by the longevity attributed to the Hebrew patriarchs and their wives: Genesis records that Adam lived to the age of 930, and Methuselah reached the age of 969. Biblical scholars do not suggest that the ancients actually lived to such great ages. Rather they believe that portraying ancestors as extremely old showed the high degree of respect for and reverence of them. A long and full life was a blessing from God. In the Scriptures, the gradual reduction in life spans after those attributed to the earliest figures indicates a sense of increasing distance between people and God.

An examination of the Jewish Scriptures reveals no fear of old age. On the contrary, aging is associated with wisdom and understanding, and older people are described with widows and orphans as people deserving our special care. The commandment "Honor your father and your mother" (Deuteronomy 5:16) clearly states the Scriptures' call to respect and cherish our older people.

Jesus: A Man for All Seasons of Life

Jesus is unique among the key figures of the world's great religions: he alone died relatively young. All of the other founders of major religious traditions lived long lives. Indeed, their ages marked them as persevering and trustworthy prophets of faith and truth. For example, Chinese religion portrays both Confucius and Lao-tzu as well advanced in years: the name *Lao-tzu* actually means "grand old teacher." A central principle of Confucianism is respect for elders. The Buddha lived to around age eighty, and Muhammad lived to age sixty-two. Both founders remained active until their deaths.

What message about old age do we receive from Jesus, who died at age thirty-three? Jesus offers us a vision of people that speaks directly to our attitude toward older people. Jesus did not measure a person's worth in terms of usefulness, age, or positions of power. Jesus envisioned a world in which all people would be reverenced regardless of wealth, health, power, or any other apparent distinctions. As do all of the Scriptures, Jesus proclaimed that *life means relatedness:* that is, to divorce ourselves from any group would be to lessen our connection to life itself. In that sense Jesus saw through age differences and was truly a man for all the seasons of life.

Jesus also affirmed the triumph of life over death. Through his death and Resurrection, Jesus declared that no one is rightly given up for dead or discarded on a scrap heap. Everyone shares in the life of Christ—a life that does not end with death. Through the vision and hope of Jesus, we recognize older people as one with us; they are as indispensable to us as we are to them.

Today's Church and Older Persons: A Call for Reconciliation

Healing the rupture between society and its elderly members requires a major effort to change attitudes as well as social structures. In undertaking this task, we are not simply meeting the demands of charity and justice. We are accepting our own humanity, our link with past and future and, thereby, our link with the Creator. . . . (National Conference of Catholic Bishops, *Society and the Aged,* no. 52)

In recent times the Church has been calling constantly for basic human rights: the right to life, a decent income, employment, proper health care, sufficient food, adequate housing, and equal treatment. The Church views these as rights due everyone. It also recognizes that in modern society older people face unique challenges in having these basic rights met.

The U.S. Catholic bishops believe that our society requires, first, a change in attitudes if the unique needs of older people are to be met. If older people are viewed—or view themselves—

as noncontributing burdens on society, then providing adequately for them will be perceived negatively. In difficult times older people themselves may question the purpose of their existence and wonder, Why does God keep me alive?

Second, the U.S. bishops realize that the structure of our society needs altering. How our government spends money must be examined to see if it reflects a concern for older people who are in need. We must seriously consider passing laws that eliminate discriminatory practices against older people and ensure that their basic rights are met. In short, the Church is calling for a restructuring of society that reflects the respect for all age-groups underlying Jesus' life-affirming message.

Responding to Older Persons

Our Attitudes Toward Older Persons

Reluctantly, Sally joined the volunteers from her school who would be visiting the nursing home once every week for ten weeks. Sally had been to a nursing home only once before, when she had accompanied a friend who was visiting her grandmother. Sally found that visit completely depressing, and she was anticipating a similar experience this time.

Initially Sally's expectations were realized. Entering the home she found the facilities clean and pleasant enough, but the "hospital smell" and the moaning sounds coming occasionally from rooms brought back her earlier, depressed feelings. One woman sitting in a wheelchair in the hallway grabbed Sally's arm as she walked by. In a raspy voice the woman said, "Help me! Help me!" Sally didn't know what to do; so when the woman loosened her grip, Sally kept going and tried to hide among the others in her group.

Once in the hall where many residents were assembled, Sally was given the name of Mrs. Ruth Lewis, the woman who was to be her special friend during her visits. Sally first eyed her from a distance. She saw the woman sitting on a bench holding a cane by her side and watching the activity around her with an absent look in her eyes. Getting closer, Sally could see that her hair was disheveled and that her clothing bunched together uncomfortably. Mrs. Lewis leaned slightly to one side as if a gentle push could topple her. Sally was not looking forward to spending time with this being of blank eyes and aged skin.

In fact, however, after a few visits, hearing about Mrs. Lewis' life and telling Ruth about her own, Sally came to look forward to their visits. Sally became more and more comfortable holding Ruth's hands and even kissing her good-bye. By the time her volunteer period was completed, Sally forgot that initially she had been repulsed at the sight of Mrs. Lewis. In the end Sally felt that she had made a good friend and could honestly say, "Ruth is a beautiful person, inside and out."

Often we forget that our view of older people is heavily conditioned by our culture. Not every culture looks upon old age in so negative a light. For example, in Asian countries, older people typically are shown great respect. Even during the early years of U.S. history, older people were considered distinguished and worthy of respect. (Early Americans actually wore white wigs to make themselves appear older and thereby more dignified!)

Perhaps if we could spend time with older people, as Sally did, we would see them as people and not merely as "old." If we just want to help those "less-fortunate older people," however, we may end up treating them in a condescending way. We need to ask ourselves, How do I like to be treated by other people? We do not like to be treated like children or as "less-fortunate"—neither do older people. Instead we should approach older people with openness, respect, and readiness. Then they can share their wisdom and affection, and we can share our energy and affection. Valuable friendships can result, and we can become more comfortable with our own inevitable aging.

Society's Role in the Problems of Older Persons

If older people are more similar to than different from the rest of us, it follows that their needs are also basically similar to our own. Not all older people share the same problems, but two problem areas affecting many older people are economic concerns and health concerns. Many older people exist on what is termed a *fixed income*. That is, they depend on Social Security and other pension monies as their sole source of income. This income remains more or less the same in the face of increasing costs for goods and services.

Although some older people are well-off financially, most older people state that economic concerns are their biggest worry. Consequently, during times of increased poverty, older people suffer more than other age-groups. Upon retirement, most older people find their financial needs equal to or greater than they previously were—while their income is slashed.

Maintaining good health is a primary concern for all ages. Yet health problems—or the threat of them—increase with age. Assurance that health problems will be dealt with provides a great sense of security to older people.

Society plays an important role in these two concerns of older people. While it is true that people should seek to provide for their own basic needs and that family and friends are responsible for one another, at the same time we need to examine society's role: Is our society structured in such a way that the burdens of our older members are lessened? Do Social Security, medicare, and other services provide security for older people? Will those who cannot provide for themselves be cared for or become lost among the many other pressing concerns of our society? In summary, do the structures of society reflect concern for the needs of all members of our society, including our older people?

Learning from Older Persons

The eminent psychologist Carl G. Jung believed that only people who have experienced loss can be religious. Older people have experienced loss—of their youth, of jobs, perhaps of children raised and gone, oftentimes of parents and friends through death. Because of their many life experiences, older persons can serve as our "elders," as our guides through the life changes marked by the aging process.

Some older persons become bitter at the losses in their lives; others attempt to be untouched by their losses. However, many people who reach old age develop a sense of basic trust in the face of their gains and losses, their accomplishments and disappointments. For that reason, members of our older generation can serve as models of faith for the younger generation. Older persons have taken what life had to offer, and they have given themselves to life. They have experienced the waning of control over their own lives and have learned to place their trust in others and in God. Often the older person with failing eyesight, diminished hearing, and arms and legs that no longer function as well as they once did can nevertheless share with a younger generation a joyful and wisdom-filled faith. Because we too must travel the road of our own aging, we would do well to receive that powerful gift.

Conclusion: Being Older and Belonging

Is the complexion of our communities merely graying—or is it truer to say that today our crowd has a larger "silver lining"? As more people reach old age, we need to ensure that they are not merely an increasing minority but a welcome minority. To do that we need to examine our attitudes toward aging and society's treatment of older people. If our older people feel wanted and valued, they will more readily join Simeon in his prayer upon meeting Jesus after a long and full life:

> Now, Master, you can dismiss your servant in peace; you have fulfilled your word.
>
> (Luke 2:29)

For Review

1. What is meant by "the graying of America"?
2. What are the current Western stereotypes regarding old age?
3. What is the difference between biological and sociological aging? Why is this distinction helpful?
4. What is the popular conception about intelligence and old age? What has recent research indicated about intellectual decline in old age?
5. What does it mean to say that senility is a "wastebasket label"?
6. What is the popular perception about retirement? In what ways does the reality of retirement often differ from the popular image?
7. What view of old age is found in the Jewish Scriptures?
8. How can Jesus' basic message of love and reverence for life be applied to concern for older people?
9. What two changes do the U.S. Catholic bishops believe are needed in order to heal the rupture between older people and the rest of society?
10. What can we as individuals do in order to learn more about and from older persons?
11. List two problem areas that affect many older people.
12. What can we learn from older people?

For Reflection

1. Write down your responses to these questions: Who has been the most influential model for you of an older person—either someone you know personally or a public figure over the age of sixty? Why? What image of old age has that person conveyed?

2. Find and read several current articles on "the graying of America." Then, write a two-page essay on what old age might be like for your parent(s).

3. In writing, describe some specific examples of the media's treatment of older people. What image of older people is most frequently presented by the media? Is old age portrayed in a positive or a negative light? Are older people usually portrayed as stereotypes?

4. Which of the following phrases comes closest to describing our society's views of older people? Which comes closest to your views of older persons? Explain.
   - dried up
   - settled down
   - still flowing

5. Reread the passage on page 187 about negative images of older people. Explain your reaction in writing. Then, reflect on the passage again as a description of your own grandparents. Explain how this changes your view—if it does.

6. List five disadvantages of old age and five advantages of old age. Then record your answers to the following questions:
   - What steps could you personally take *now* to minimize these disadvantages? to enhance these advantages?
   - What changes in society would help to minimize these disadvantages and enhance these advantages?
   - How could you help older people today to minimize the disadvantages and enhance the advantages of their old age?

7. Write a position paper that states your opinion on retirement. Include in your paper any laws governing retirement that you would like to see enacted, as well as any other policy procedures related to retirement.

8. **Ageism** refers to discriminatory attitudes and practices toward people based on their age. Describe in writing some

examples of ageism. Which age-group in our society do you believe suffers the most from ageism?

9. The United Nations has promulgated a "Declaration of the Rights of the Child" that lists ten rights that all children should have. (For example, "the right to free education" is one.) Compose a "Bill of Rights for Older People," naming ten rights. Then, compose a "Bill of Rights for Teenagers," naming ten rights. In writing, compare and contrast the two statements.

10. List as many stereotypes about older people or aging as you possibly can. Do your stereotypes present a positive or a negative impression of older people? Try to name exceptions to these stereotypes among older people you personally know or among public figures.

11. Visit a nursing home. Is the general situation positive or negative? How are residents treated? Write a report of your impressions and observations. Would you like to work in a nursing home? Why? Would you, as an older person, willingly live in a nursing home? Explain.

12. Imagine that you are an older person. Write about how you would like younger people to relate to you and to treat you. Do you believe that the older people you presently know would like the same treatment as you?

13. Interview someone who is over age sixty-five. Ask the older person, "If you could convey a message to young people, what would it be?" Take notes or (with the interviewee's permission) record the interview on tape.

14. Write a prayer, a poem, or a short story, or draw a picture that conveys your attitude toward aging or toward older people.

15. Many older people are financially better off than those in other age-groups. Should senior citizen discounts and special government services for older people such as medicare be eliminated in favor of services made available to all people based solely on need and not on age? Write a defense of your position.

16. Write an essay entitled "The Spirituality of Aging."

10
The Earth: Nurturing Nature

The Christian call to justice expresses a concern for the victims of our world. Although we tend to limit our concern to the human realm, a closer look at our world reveals that nature itself is being victimized. The modern assault on nature has endangered the earth, and consequently, it has endangered humanity.

The Message of Chief Seattle

Chief Seattle, leader of the Suquamish tribe in the Washington territory, delivered the following speech in 1854 to mark the transfer of ancestral Native American lands to the federal government. As you read this passage, reflect on the ways in which Chief Seattle's message speaks to us today.

The Great Chief in Washington sends word that he wishes to buy our land.

The Great Chief also sends us words of friendship and good will. This is kind of him, since we know he has little need of our friendship in return. But we will consider your offer. For we know that if we do not sell, the white man may come with guns and take our land.

How can you buy or sell the sky, the warmth of the land? The idea is strange to us.

If we do not own the freshness of the air and the sparkle of the water, how can you buy them?

Every part of this earth is sacred to my people. Every shining pine needle, every sandy shore, every mist in the dark woods, every clearing and humming insect is holy in the memory and experience of my people. The sap which courses through the trees carries the memories of the red man.

The white man's dead forget the country of their birth when they go to walk among the stars. Our dead never forget this beautiful earth, for it is the mother of the red man. We are part of the earth and it is part of us. The perfumed flowers are our sisters; the deer, the horse, the great eagle, these are our brothers. The rocky crests, the juices in the meadows, the body heat of the pony, and man—all belong to the same family.

So, when the Great Chief in Washington sends word that he wishes to buy our land, he asks much of us. . . .

The rivers are our brothers, they quench our thirst. The rivers carry our canoes, and feed our children. If we sell you our land, you must remember, and teach your children, that the rivers are our brothers, and yours, and you must henceforth give the rivers the kindness you would give any brother.

The red man has always retreated before the advancing white man, as the mist of the mountain runs before the morning sun. But the ashes of our fathers are sacred. Their graves are holy ground, and so these hills, these trees, this portion of earth is consecrated to us. We know that the white man does not understand our ways. One portion of land is the same to him as the next, for he is a stranger who comes in the night and takes from the land whatever he needs. The earth is not his brother, but his enemy, and when he has conquered it, he moves on. He leaves his father's graves behind, and he does not care. He kidnaps the earth from his children. He does not care. His father's graves and his children's birthright are forgotten. He treats his mother, the earth, and his brother, the sky, as things to be bought, plundered, sold like sheep or bright beads. His appetite will devour the earth and leave behind only a desert.

I do not know. Our ways are different from your ways. The sight of your cities pains the eyes of the red man. But perhaps it is because the red man is a savage and does not understand.

There is no quiet place in the white man's cities. No place to hear the unfurling of leaves in the spring or the rustle of insect's wings. But perhaps it is because I am a savage and do not understand. The clatter only seems to insult the ears. And what is there to life if a man cannot hear the lonely cry of the whippoorwill or the arguments of the frogs around a pond at night? I am a red man and do not understand. The Indian prefers the soft sound of the wind darting over the face of a pond, and the smell of wind itself cleansed by a midday rain, or scented with the piñon pine.

The air is precious to the red man, for all things share the same breath—the beast, the tree, the man, they all share the same breath. The white man does not seem to notice the air he breathes. Like a man dying for many days, he is numb to the stench. . . .

I am a savage and do not understand any other way. I have seen a thousand rotting buffaloes on the prairie, left by the white man who shot them from a passing train. I am a savage and I do not understand how the smoking iron horse can be more important than the buffalo that we kill only to stay alive.

What is man without the beasts? If all the beasts were gone, men would die from a great loneliness of spirit. For whatever happens to the beasts soon happens to man. All things are connected. . . .

Teach your children what we have taught our children, that the earth is our mother. Whatever befalls the earth, befalls the sons of the earth. If men spit upon the ground they spit upon themselves.

This we know. The earth does not belong to man; man belongs to the earth. This we know. All things are connected like the blood which unites one family. All things are connected. . . .

One thing we know, which the white man may one day discover—our God is the same God. You may think now that you own him as you wish to own our land; but you cannot. He is the God of man, and his compassion is equal for the red man and the white. This earth is precious to him, and to harm the earth is to heap contempt on its Creator. The white too shall pass; perhaps sooner than all other tribes. Continue to contaminate your bed, and you will one night suffocate in your own waste. . . .

When the last red man has vanished from this earth, and his memory is only the shadow of a cloud moving across the prairie, these shores and forests will still hold the spirits of my people. For they love this earth as the newborn loves its mother's heartbeat. So if we sell you our land, love it as we've loved it. Care for it as we've cared for it. Hold in your mind the memory of the land as it is when you take it. And with all your strength, with all your mind, with all your heart, preserve it for your children, and love it . . . as God loves us all. . . .

Ecology: Caring for Our Home

When we read news stories about poisons seeping up from the ground near chemical waste dumps, about the poor air quality in many communities, about lakes and streams that are official-ly declared dead because of pollutants, about the numerous

Teenage volunteers in France cleaning up a beach ruined by an oil spill

species of animals in danger of extinction, and about land that no longer can support crops because of misuse, we realize the frightening truth of Chief Seattle's message. Modern society has treated nature as limitless and durable, thinking that it can handle any mistreatment. We consider earth, air, and water to be available for our unlimited and indiscriminate use. We believe that our waste is easily and safely disposed of: so long as our waste products are out of sight under the earth, far out into the sea, or invisible in the air, they are of no concern to us.

In his haunting prophecy spoken over one hundred and thirty years ago, Chief Seattle reminds us that the fate of the earth is humanity's fate and that our life is totally dependent upon the life of the air, the water, and the land around us. Chief Seattle cautioned those of us new to the North American continent to respect and cherish our country's resources as his people had.

In that sense, long before the term became popular, Chief Seattle preached the message of *ecology*. **Ecology** is the study of our environment, of the relationships among all the elements of nature. The Greek word *oikos* from which *ecology* is derived means "house." In fact, nature is our house, the dwelling place that we share with others. Chief Seattle also realized that only by treating the rest of creation as family can we make our house the home that it is meant to be.

Barges hauling garbage on their way to landfill sites

As defined so far in this course, justice is concerned with basic rights, a sense of dignity, a spirit of solidarity, and social structures. Thus understood, justice refers to humanity's treatment of other human beings. By adopting a broader view, we can also apply these four characteristics of justice to our understanding and treatment of nature. When we do, we recognize the injustice suffered by nature at the hands of humanity.

Nature's Basic Rights

- Does a redwood tree have rights?
- Should the whale and the condor be protected from extinction?
- If no-smoking laws are enacted to protect people in restaurants and trains, should similar laws be enacted to protect the atmosphere from contamination?
- If the owner of a plot of land perfectly suited for farming wishes to turn it into a shopping mall, should the life of the land be considered?

We Westerners are very **anthropocentric;** that is, we center on the *human* (in Greek, *anthropos*). We tend to consider nonhuman things like redwoods and whales important only insofar as they serve us. For example, redwoods and whales are creatures beautiful for us to look at, interesting for us to study, valuable for us to learn from, and profitable for our use. From an anthropocentric perspective, the nonhuman members of the world lack the inherent rights that humans assume—such as the rights to life and liberty.

Certainly we humans play a unique role in the natural order: like no other creature we can either destroy the earth and everyone on it or nurture it for everyone's benefit. However, when we do not consider the basic rights of all creatures and give them their due, we play a dangerous game that is hazardous to nonhumans and humans alike. A respect for all of nature—land, air, and water, as well as plants and animals—calls for recognizing its basic right to protection from abuse.

Respect for Nature

> No more cars in national parks. Let the people walk. Or ride horses, bicycles, mules, wild pigs—anything—but keep the automobiles and the motorcycles and all their motorized relatives out. We have agreed not to drive our automobiles into cathedrals, concert halls, art museums, legislative assemblies, private bedrooms and the other sanctums of our culture; we should treat our national parks with the same deference, for they, too, are holy places. (Edward Abbey, *Desert Solitaire,* p. 60)

Concern for people's dignity is an important element of justice. Yet Chief Seattle might suggest that if we do not treat our four-legged sisters and brothers with dignity, then we are unlikely to respect our two-legged ones either. Exploitation of people is a too-frequent occurrence: many people work long hours for little pay doing menial jobs. Similarly, nature is often victimized.

Exploiters see nature as only a commodity to be bought and sold, used and used up: "I own it; therefore I can do with it whatever I want." They are blind to what is sacred and beautiful in nature and care only about what can be gained from it: "What is the most that I can earn from this resource for the least investment of work and money on my part?"

Exploitation seeks to exert power over nature rather than to work with nature. This domination often leads to abuse:

"Growing the same crops every year is killing the land, but I'll keep adding chemical fertilizer to get from it whatever I can." In short, exploitation is a "care-less" treatment of nature.

Treating nature with dignity requires a "care-filled" attitude of respect, not domination. Respect flows from a spirit of nurturing, rather than of abusing. Nurturing people view the land and natural resources as trusts given to us to tend and to care for. Also, nurturing does not rule out the *use* of nature but seeks to eliminate its *abuse*. Finally, nurturing caretakers live in harmony with the earth rather than in domination over it.

Erosion due to poor farming practices ruined this farmland in Indonesia.

Solidarity with Nature

Taking a cue from Chief Seattle, we can begin our examination of nature and justice with the questions that center on solidarity:

- How do we envision our relationship with the rest of nature?
- Are we humans separate from and above the rest of nature?
- Do the other elements of nature exist primarily for our use?

We share our existence with the soil, the air, the water, the animals, the trees, the flowers, and the insects. Yesterday's soil, water, and plants are today's human tissue. In turn, our bodies replenish the soil and nourish plant life. The air that we pollute is the same air that plants purify and recirculate so that we can breathe it.

Yet most of us in our modern, technological society are more at home in artificial environments than in natural ones. We eat foods far removed from their natural sources. We control light, heat, and water with the flick of a switch or the turn of a faucet. In artificial and controlled environments, we can lose our sense of solidarity with nature. We can forget that cows, chickens, fruits, and vegetables are our "brothers and sisters"—especially when our only encounter with them is with a prepackaged form on a supermarket shelf or sliced and fried in a fast-food restaurant.

In addition, science has been both friend and foe to the spirit of solidarity with nature. Traditional science would discount Chief Seattle's words as mere poetry or romantic superstition. This lack of respect for nature stems from traditional science's perception of nature as a machine consisting of separate and individual parts. Although these parts interact—as do gears, for instance—they were seen as retaining their separate identities. As a result, scientists felt quite free to tinker with any element in nature without concern for how nature as a whole might be harmed.

More recently, some scientists have moved toward a less mechanical, more fluid model of nature. Matter and life forms that once appeared solid and separate to the naked eye were revealed under microscopes or through telescopes as more fluid and united. Nature's parts do not simply interact; rather, they change and grow in response to these interactions. So recent scientific insights can help us appreciate intellectually what Chief Seattle lived and preached—that all of nature, humanity included, is a dynamic unity.

Concerns for Structural Change

When people care for the earth, they seek to influence public policies and practices in ways that suggest that the earth matters. Our work of justice calls for the consideration of all dimensions of nature. Below is a sampling of justice-related concerns that are connected to specific elements of the earth.

1. Land

Every year the United States loses at least three million acres of farmland because they are being absorbed by urban developments—including shopping malls, parking lots, streets, and highways. One million acres equals a half-mile-wide strip of land extending from New York to California. According to the U.S. Department of Agriculture's own estimates, by the year 2000 the state of Florida will be one of a number of states in which agricultural land will disappear entirely. When that happens, Florida oranges will disappear from our supermarkets.

Preserving farmland in North America and throughout the world requires changes not only in priorities and policies, but also in our whole notion of property: ownership cannot continue to be a license for abuse of our soil resources. In recent years *inorganic farming*—that is, farming that is dependent on chemical fertilizers and pesticides—has been shown to deplete valuable topsoil. On the other hand, *organic farming* methods—which avoid toxic fertilizers, growth stimulants, and pesticides—can actually create topsoil. Also, how crops are planted and which crops are planted can make the difference between conserving and enriching the land or destroying its productivity for future generations.

2. Air

Air molecules breathed at the time of Jesus are breathed by us today. What we add to the air today will stay with us long into the future. The greatest polluters of the air today are

Top: Poor soil management combined with a drought in the 1930s created the Dust Bowl in the U.S. Southwest.
Bottom: A center in North Carolina where farmers are trained in organic methods

the gasoline engines in our cars. Every day U.S. drivers alone use 313 million gallons of fuel—enough to drain twenty-six tank trucks every minute. During the 1973 gasoline shortage, gasoline suddenly became very expensive and difficult to obtain. Naturally, public policies and practices quickly changed. People's prime motivator was their pocketbooks, but the environment benefited even so. People started demanding smaller, fuel-efficient cars. They became more conscious of their energy use. A national, maximum speed limit of 55 MPH was set—which has conserved human life, as well as energy and air. Experiments with new energy sources received a boost. Nevertheless, automobiles continue to pollute the air, and additional changes are required if our air is to remain breathable.

In addition to automobiles, factories, power plants, and waste-disposal units pollute the air. The haze that covers our major industrial cities on most days gives ample evidence of air pollution.

Apparently, the increased amount of carbon dioxide in our atmosphere may create increased temperatures worldwide, a condition termed the *greenhouse effect.* In the past fifteen years the public outcry for cleaner air has caused stricter antipollution regulations to be enforced, but often the ecology still loses out to the economy.

3. Water

Rivers so polluted that they catch on fire, oil spills in the ocean, fish infected with mercury poisoning, and streams devoid of plant life and fish—these are the most obvious forms of water pollution. Even in the United States, the demand for fresh water is beginning to exceed its availability. Used for irrigation, for drinking, and for supplying food indirectly in the form of fish and seafood, clean water is necessary for humans, animals, and plants.

Water is such a vast resource on our planet that we may find it difficult to imagine its scarcity. Yet experts agree that the lack of clean, drinkable water creates more problems worldwide than the lack of farmable land. Those of us who are used to water that is available at the turn of a faucet can be blind to the value of this endangered resource. The spreading problem of *acid rain,* which makes lakes lifeless, is an urgent reminder of the need to care for our water supplies.

4. Waste

Every day the United States produces 1.5 billion pounds of hazardous waste. If the waste was shared out equally, every adult in the United States would have to figure out what to do with nine pounds daily. Most seriously, the plutonium waste from nuclear power plants will remain radioactive for half a million years. Every day we also throw away this staggering amount of waste:

- 150,000 tons of boxes, bags, and wrappers
- one million bushels of litter from our car and truck windows
- 200,000 tons of edible food

In short, we are surrounding ourselves with our own garbage. Our earth is choking from its overdose of human waste. Community recycling programs and other creative uses of our waste products are attempts to lessen the burden of our waste on the environment. Disposing of waste in ecologically sound ways is essential. Of course, devising ways to diminish the amount of waste that we create in the first place is equally necessary.

Author Tom Parker compiled these statistics to show the amazing number of materials used to support the population of the United States.

Every Day . . .

Every day we bring 364,000 live wild animals into the United States. Of these wild animals, 2,000 are exotic birds, 500 of which die before being sold.

Every day we throw out 20,000 cars and 4,000 trucks and buses. Twenty thousand cars would form a line of traffic more than fifty miles long.

Every day we gobble up seventy-five acres of pizza. That's enough pizza to cover sixty football fields.

Every day we lay down about 2,750 acres of pavement. That's enough concrete and asphalt to make a bicycle path seven feet wide stretching from the Atlantic coast to the Pacific coast.

Every day we manufacture enough artificial Christmas trees to artificially reforest eight acres of land.

5. Animals, Plants, and the Natural Habitat

Wilderness and wild animals and plants have a unique beauty. If we tame and domesticate much more of our earth, we will lose the wild, natural places and creatures. As our human grasp on the planet becomes tighter, we easily forget that God's touch created the earth. The preservation of public lands and the protection of endangered species serve a spiritual purpose.

Many people today are calling into question our inhumane treatment of animals. Cruel practices such as *vivisection*—that is, operating on live animals—is done in the name of scientific research. Few people demand the curtailment of all animal experimentation, but many people realize that stricter guidelines are necessary.

Furthermore, modern farm practices are much different from the idyllic image of farm life presented to us in our first-grade reading books. Today's farms are more often "farm factories" in which cattle, pigs, chickens, and other animals are treated like mere products. For instance: Most egg-laying chickens spend their lives confined to small cages and never see the light of day. Their eggs are carried away on conveyor belts, and food and water is provided by automatic machinery. The production of veal—which is the flesh of young calves—requires similar confinement. Groups promoting animal rights are calling for an end to cruelty to animals.

Injustice Toward Nature and Other Justice-Related Issues

Our ecological crisis parallels our crisis in other justice-related areas: (1) the way we view nature often mirrors the way we view people, and (2) those who suffer most from the human maltreatment of nature are the poor people and the victimized.

1. To illustrate the first point, recollect the treatment of Native Americans. Traditionally white Americans looked upon them as wild, as a part of untamed nature. Although admired by some white people as "noble savages," Native Americans were nevertheless removed from their lands whenever their presence inconvenienced whites. Native Americans were not viewed as sisters and brothers to the white Americans, but as nuisances or, at best, as curiosities from exotic cultures.

All that can be said about the way that white Americans have viewed Native Americans also can be said about the way that they viewed nature. An inability to cherish nature often accompanies an inability to cherish people. In the same way that so-called wild Indians were forced to live on reservations, our wilderness has also been fenced in—that is, where it has not been eliminated outright. In justice, we are called to respond to the cry of the needy and the hungry and also to the cry of the wilderness.

2. Concerning the second point, one writer relates environmental justice with justice for poor people in this way:

> In a world with unlimited demand, finite resources, and enormous inequities in economic and political power, the question of who gets what and why—the historic problem of distributive justice—is at the heart of any system of resource planning. (Alan S. Miller, "The Environmental and Other Bioethical Challenges")

In other words, people who are needy and deprived suffer the most from nature's misuse. When crop production decreases because of a reduction in available farmland or because of land misuse, poor people are the ones who go hungry. Likewise, increased unavailability of clean water hits hardest those who already must struggle for water. Very often poor people live in areas most subject to air pollution or work where toxic chemicals or pesticides are a hazard.

Sometimes, however, the needs of the environment and human needs are considered at odds. For example:

- When people are starving, it may be more important to produce as much food as possible than it is to worry about long-term effects on the soil.
- When a country is poor, it may be more important to increase industrial production than it is to worry about air and water pollution resulting from those industries.
- When energy is not readily available, it may become more important to produce energy cheaply than to be concerned about whether or not energy production harms the environment.

These are hard issues for the world to address. Clearly, the way we treat the environment today is borrowing from the future. Yet in a crisis it is difficult to think about future consequences. A balance must be found: we must eliminate the human problems of hunger, poverty, and the unequal distribution of resources; and at the same time we must work to preserve the environment.

Nature and Militarism

Riding through Kansas, you may marvel at the unending fields of wheat. On occasion you will notice an uncultivated section.

This is probably government property that is housing underground missile silos. Using this productive land for a missile site symbolizes the principle that when military and environmental concerns conflict, the environment nearly always loses.

We are accustomed to thinking of wars as violence between people. But modern warfare and even the preparations for warfare have wreaked havoc on nature as well. Nuclear weapons especially drive home the point that warfare is violence against nature. Nuclear weapons represent the ultimate environmental crisis. They make this biblical injunction starkly relevant: "I have set before you life and death, the blessing and the curse. Choose life, then, that you and your descendants may live" (Deuteronomy 30:19). Later on, when you read the chapters on war and on nuclear weapons, remember that all of nature, as well as humanity, exists as a potential victim of militarism.

Putting the Earth into a Christian Perspective

The Earth Is the Lord's: Handle with Care

> [The LORD said:]
> Where were you when I founded the earth?
>> Tell me, if you have understanding.
> Who determined its size; do you know?
>> Who stretched out the measuring line for it?
> Into what were its pedestals sunk,
>> and who laid the cornerstone,
> While the morning stars sang in chorus . . . ?
>> (Job 38:4–7)

The psalmist proclaims:

> The LORD's are the earth and its fullness;
>> the world and those who dwell in it.
>> (Psalms 24:1)

In the Scriptures the earth is described as God's good Creation, whose purpose is to give glory to God. Human beings are part of the Creation, not separate from it. In the Noah story, for instance, the ark is home to Noah's family and to all of the animals. After the Flood, God makes a covenant with all of the creatures.

As we noted earlier, human beings have a special role to play in caring for nature. Sometimes the Scriptures are interpreted as saying that nature is for human use and that therefore people can do with it whatever they wish. Actually, the meaning of "cultivate and care for" the earth in Genesis 2:15 is that human beings are to be servants to nature. Nature is a gift from God for people, but the earth benefits people only if they handle it with care. In the Bible, misuse of the earth results in the earth's rebelling against human domination.

> [The LORD said to Moses,] "Be careful to observe all my statutes and all my decrees; otherwise the land where I am bringing you to dwell will vomit you out." (Leviticus 20:22)

U.S. planes spraying combat zones with plant killer during the Vietnam war

Jesus and Nature: A Message of Hope

A look at the words of Jesus reveals his appreciation for nature. He enlivens his sayings and stories with constant references to animals, plants, and other things of the earth. Nevertheless, because of his deep concern for the neighbor in need, Jesus is often considered strongly anthropocentric. Actually, Jesus is *theocentric*—that is, God-centered—in that he draws all things to the loving God who embraces all of Creation.

Most importantly, Jesus offers us a message of hope. Saint Paul realizes that "all creation groans and is in agony even until now" (Romans 8:22). Yet Paul affirms that the entire world is saved through Jesus Christ:

> Creation was made subject to futility, not of its own accord but by him who once subjected it; yet not without hope, because the world itself will be freed from its slavery to corruption and share in the glorious freedom of the children of God. (Romans 8:20-21)

Certainly the complexity of the ecological problem is enormous. It is overwhelming to ponder that every time we drive a car we are polluting the air, every time we throw a bottle or can into the trash we are adding to the garbage that the earth must absorb, and every use of electricity uses up limited energy resources. Saint Paul brings the message of hope to this disheartening situation when he asks:

> Who will separate us from the love of Christ? Trial, or distress, or persecution, or hunger, or nakedness, or danger, or the sword? . . . I am certain that neither death nor life, neither angels nor principalities, neither the present nor the future, nor powers, neither height nor depth nor any other creature, will be able to separate us from the love of God that comes to us in Christ Jesus, our Lord. (Romans 8:35,38-39)

Two Views of Nature in the Christian Tradition

Christianity has been profoundly influenced by two views of nature, one dualistic and the other sacramental.

Dualism splits reality into the two realms of matter and spirit (also called the *natural* realm and the *supernatural* realm). These two dimensions are separate, and the supernatural is valued much more highly than the natural. According to this view, human beings are blessed with a spiritual soul but cursed with a material body. The goal of human life is to build up the spirit and to leave behind the matter. Dualism, which dominates Western Christianity, can lead to a negative view of nature as inferior or even evil.

The other view of nature, dominant in Eastern Christianity, understands nature as a revealer of God. From this perspective, which is termed *sacramental,* nature is sacred. The world is the place where God is to be found, and it is the result of God's outpouring of love. The sacramental perspective leads to an attitude of appreciation for nature.

Both views of nature are present within the Christian tradition. Saint Francis of Assisi is offered as a model of the sacramental view of nature. The statues of Francis that are frequently found in gardens and in birdbaths attest to his association with nature in the eyes of Christians. Another Christian model of ecology is Saint Benedict, who established monasteries throughout Europe based on sensible practices of land use. Francis portrays the nature lover; Benedict models the respectful nature user. To love and to work with nature are both Christian virtues that need to be cultivated today.

Church Teaching Today: The Call to Stewardship

> Probably no other Pope has addressed land issues as much as the current Pontiff, John Paul II. In his travels throughout the world, he has usually made it a point to address the rural constituency of the regions or nations that he visits. Several themes recur in his addresses, themes that relate back to the teachings of his predecessors. He declares that we must care for the land, that we are its stewards for the well-being of future generations as well as our own; he affirms the dignity and worth of all of the land's workers; he laments farmers' forced exodus to the city and the consequent exacerbation of urban problems; he urges farmers to organize to change their conditions; and he advocates changes in laws and structures so that a more just society can be developed. (John Hart, *The Spirit of the Earth,* p. 109)

During his many pilgrimages to the countries of the world, one of the most-striking scenes has been that of Pope John Paul II descending a plane and kneeling down to kiss the ground. Along with other recent popes, Pope John Paul II recognizes that care for the land and its responsible use are essential elements of justice. He links stewardship of the earth and just land policies with the issues of poverty and hunger.

The Catholic bishops in two predominantly rural areas of the United States have written statements in which they call for responsible stewardship of the land. The Appalachian bishops' document, *This Land Is Home to Me,* has already been mentioned in connection with poverty. The U.S. Midwestern bishops' statement, issued in 1980, called *Strangers and Guests* makes ten points concerning the land that are worth pondering:

1. The land is God's.
2. People are God's stewards on the land.
3. The land's benefits are for everyone.
4. The land should be distributed equitably.
5. The land should be conserved and restored.
6. Land-use planning must consider social and environmental impacts.
7. Land use should be appropriate to land quality.
8. The land should provide a moderate livelihood.
9. The land's workers should be able to become the land's owners.
10. The land's mineral wealth should be shared.

In this document, the bishops present a new understanding of the meaning of land ownership. Most especially, they echo other recent church teachings linking ownership to stewardship in the care and distribution of the land.

In addition to official documents, the U.S. Church has also witnessed the growth of grassroots organizations concerned about land-use issues. The National Catholic Rural Life Conference began in 1923 to address issues of the just use and the stewardship of land. In 1933 the Catholic Worker Movement recognized the link between rural farm life and both urban unemployment and poverty. Dorothy Day and Peter Maurin, co-founders of the movement, proposed a unity between city and country. They opened houses of hospitality in New York City and at the same time began a communal farm in rural New York State.

Dorothy Day, co-founder of the Catholic Worker Movement

Responding to Nature

Developing a Spirituality of the Earth

> Before you can love a person you have to start with simpler things and gradually build up your skill—start with a rock, a cloud, a tree. (Carson McCullers)

This chapter began with a statement by a Native American. Chief Seattle voiced a spirituality that is sorely needed today. We Christians need to be humble enough to accept that we can learn much from other traditions about a spirituality of the earth. Along with the Native American tradition, Hinduism from India, Taoism from China, Japanese Shintoism, and even some of the so-called pagan religious traditions can teach us about cherishing the earth and relating to nature as mother, sister, and brother. Likewise, as mentioned, modern science can enhance our appreciation of nature.

In our world today we can too easily forget that we are children of the earth, the sea, and the sky. We cannot live apart from the earth's goodness; we are nourished and sheltered by it. The earth is our home; without it we are homeless. If we view the earth merely as property to be used, we do harm to our physical and spiritual environment.

Before we can change our personal behavior and our society's practices in regard to the things of nature, we need to renew our vision of the earth. We need to get to know our nonhuman neighbors and cherish them. The dominant Western

tradition has been indifferent to or even hostile to the environment. Creating a new vision of the earth and of our relationship to it will put us at odds with our present culture. However, a rich spirituality of the earth can be the basis of a more profound culture to include us all, humankind and "otherkind."

Working with the Earth

To cherish nature does not mean that we should avoid changing it. We are called to be cocreators, technicians, artists, and lovers in our work with nature. Sometimes we consider technology to be hostile to the way of nature. Although technology has been glorified for the past century, sometimes to the detriment of nature, it need not be destructive of nature. To be effective, technology must work with nature. We need to learn from nature and yet be bold enough to take a creative role in its continuing development.

Living As If the Earth Matters, As If the Future Matters

The way we manufacture and use energy affects nature. The foods we eat have an impact on nature. What we build and where we build implicate land, air, water, plant life, and animal life. Our use of the automobile affects the quality of life of all the other elements of nature. Our penchant for easily accessible driving and parking facilities, labor-saving devices, fast foods, packages wrapped in multiple layers of plastic and paper, disposable containers, and other modern conveniences reflect priorities that are detrimental to nature. For example:

- Our family just purchased a home in the Whispering Pines development outside of town where the Snyder's farm used to be. It has a large enough garage for our two cars and is convenient to the new expressway.
- Our community can now boast of the largest shopping mall in the vicinity and an enlarged industrial plant with prospects for more businesses to be built.
- Thanks to increased sales and industrial production, our nation's gross national product for the past year has been the best ever.

In old Western movies a scout might be shown putting his ear to the ground to listen for approaching danger in the form of distant hoofbeats. Today we need to put our ear to the ground to listen to what it says about impending danger. With conscientious changes in our lifestyles, we can lessen the

Top: Windmills generating electric power
Bottom: The world's largest solar energy cooling system, on a hotel in the Virgin Islands

amount of waste, pollution, and destruction of nature that we require future generations to cope with. We might also pass on to them the will and the spirit to lead ecologically sound lives.

Working for Changes in Social Priorities

Perhaps more than any other justice-related issue, our society says "We'll worry about that tomorrow" in regard to nature. We feel secure that lush forests and bountiful farmlands exist— even though we see them more frequently on television than in reality. We breathe the air freely, and only occasionally do the fumes it carries cause us discomfort. We drink water from our taps, but we trust fewer and fewer sources of untreated water. We encounter various exotic animals and plants, although almost always in a zoo or in some other specially protected environment. We continue to create waste and dispose of it unthinkingly, even though we hear of communities that are dying due to waste problems.

In our working for changes in social priorities, when we petition our government leaders and representatives, we need to ask of them: consider the earth. The environmental crisis is a human crisis, a national and an international crisis. When we call for changes to help the earth, we are also helping ourselves.

Conclusion: Nature, the Silent Victim

We face an ecological crisis. Unlike other victims of injustice, the immediate victims of nature's misuse are silent ones. In its silent rage the earth is crying out to us to show concern for our nonhuman sisters and brothers. They seek our friendship. Only by responding in justice to the earth and its inhabitants will our natural family prosper and our God-given home be preserved.

For Review

1. Describe Chief Seattle's attitude toward nature.
2. What is the root meaning of the word *ecology?* How can this word serve as a reminder of our relationship to nature?
3. What does it mean to say that Western society is anthropocentric?
4. To what does the "exploitation of nature" refer? What is the opposite of exploiting nature?

5. How can our modern, highly technological society hinder a spirit of solidarity with nature? How can recent scientific thought help us to appreciate Chief Seattle's message?
6. List a justice-related concern in each of the following areas: land, air, water, waste, and natural habitat.
7. Describe two ways in which our ecological crisis parallels our crises in other areas of justice.
8. In what sense does militarism create an ecological crisis?
9. What do the Scriptures say is the role that human beings are to play in relation to the rest of nature?
10. What do the words of Jesus indicate about his attitude toward nature?
11. What two conflicting views toward nature are present in the Christian tradition?
12. How does Pope John Paul II's view of nature affect other justice-related issues?
13. How did the Catholic Worker Movement propose to address land-use issues along with other justice-related issues?
14. Briefly explain and give an example of each of the four personal responses to nature that are suggested in this chapter.

For Reflection

1. Write a report comparing the Native American attitude toward nature with the white American attitude.

2. Books such as *The Giving Tree,* by Shel Silverstein, and *Watership Down,* by Richard Adams, have been written from a nonhuman point of view. Compose a story or essay about justice and the earth as if written by a nonhuman creature or a part of nature (for instance, a river that originates as a mountain stream and then flows through a city, a cloud passing over a nuclear power plant, or a forest animal who watches its home being turned into a housing development).

3. Compose a slogan that could be used in a national campaign calling for concern for nature (for example, "The Earth— Love It or Leave It"). Create a poster to illustrate your slogan.

4. Research one of the following elements of nature: land, air, water, plant life, or animal life. In writing, describe ways in which that element is being endangered or mistreated.

Then describe steps that can be taken to preserve and protect that element of nature.

Based on your research, write a bill of rights for one of these elements or for nature in general.

5. Write a report on the pros and cons of nuclear power, including possible alternative sources of energy. In the conclusion, state your opinion on the use of nuclear power.

6. Write a one-page essay entitled "When Nature Suffers, Everyone Suffers."

7. From the following statements, choose the one that comes closest to your position. Write a defense of that position.
   a. Pollution is evil, but it is a necessary evil. The days of cave dwellers are over. In order to enjoy our present standard of living we must accept that some pollution will occur. When a healthy economy and a healthy environment conflict, we need to set aside some environmental concerns to preserve jobs, manufacturing, convenient transportation, and other advantages that we now enjoy.
   b. Pollution is evil and must be curtailed to whatever degree possible. We must make radical changes in our lifestyles and priorities if the earth is to survive. No concerns should take precedence over concern for the environment. The earth is our home and the only one we have. We must protect it at all cost.

8. Nuclear weapons have been called "the ultimate environmental crisis." In writing, explain what that phrase means to you. List five environmental problems that you consider to be the most serious.

9. Write a response to the following opinion: Our Christian tradition does not value the earth and nature to the degree that other religious traditions do. For that reason, Christianity has not inspired humanity to take adequate care of the earth and has actually contributed to our current environmental crisis.

10. Write an essay explaining how the Church's sacramental vision can foster care for nature. Refer to specific elements associated with the sacraments, such as community, water, bread, oil, wine, and hands.

11. Review the ten points concerning the land that are presented in the Midwestern bishops' statement *Strangers and*

Guests. List any points that you do not agree with and explain your reasons for disagreeing, or list three points that you strongly agree with and explain your reasons.

12. List five ways that we could renew our friendship with nature, leading to a spirituality of the earth.

13. Imagine that you have been asked to create a "sacrament of communion with the earth." Outline an appropriate ceremony, including the rituals, symbols, songs, readings, and prayers that you would use.

14. List five specific ways that you could be more attentive to the spirit of ecology in your daily living. Practice these activities for a week, and write a report about the experience.

15. Outline five laws to protect nature that you would like to see enacted by our government.

Part C:
Peace
and Christian Faith

11
The Christian Call to Peacemaking

No true peace exists without justice, so peacemaking is intimately connected to our Christian call to justice. Although peace is essential to Christianity—and to the preservation of humankind—disagreement remains about what peace is. This chapter presents peacemaking as an activity involving strength, courage, and intelligence.

A World of Conflict

▪ A group of small islands lying off the coast of Argentina are called the Falklands by England and the Malvinas by Argentina. Although at present England controls the islands, both countries claim sovereignty. In 1982 the Argentine military invaded the islands and briefly held them before England sent a naval force to reclaim them.

Was Argentina or England justified in using violence to establish control over the islands? What factors determine the type and degree of violence acceptable in conflicts like this one? What alternatives to violence existed for either Argentina or England?

▪ For many years, Northern Ireland has suffered violence perpetrated by militant factions of Catholics and Protestants. The Catholic groups that have employed violence believe that the Protestant government violates their human rights. Certain Protestant groups retaliate with violence of their own. Decades of bloodshed have brought no end to the conflict, only bitterness and weariness.

Are the conditions in Northern Ireland such that Catholics are justified in using violence? Are there acceptable and unacceptable uses of violence in this conflict?

▪ In 1968, Czechoslovakia was enjoying a degree of freedom and prosperity untypical of eastern European Communist countries. Threatened by the Czechs' independence, the USSR invaded their country with nearly five hundred thousand Warsaw Pact troops. The Czechs countered using nonviolent tactics: For example, crowds of people sat in the paths of oncoming tanks, airport workers refused to supply Soviet planes with fuel, and citizens organized work stoppages and demonstrations. Other Czechs distributed leaflets explaining their position, and young people engaged the soldiers in spirited discussions about their actions. Bewildered and defensive, the young soldiers from other Communist countries found it hard to fight. By the fourth day of the invasion, Soviet leaders had to replace these troops with new ones because too many soldiers were being won over by the persistent and persuasive Czechoslovak citizens.

Would violence by the Czechs have been more effective or more destructive than their nonviolent methods? Could the tactics used in Czechoslovakia in 1968 be useful in other international conflicts?

■ In 1979 a leftist government gained control of the Caribbean nation of Grenada. In October of 1983, the leaders of the U.S. government decided that a leftist government was not permissible in what it termed "our own backyard." In addition, the U.S. leaders feared for the safety of a number of U.S. citizens who were attending medical school in Grenada. So the U.S. government used its military forces to invade Grenada and to replace the leftist government with one more favorable to the United States.

Was the United States justified in using violent means to resolve its disagreement with Grenada?

Examining Conflict:
Three Positions on Resolving Conflict

In our imperfect world, conflicts abound. We could easily expand the above list of international conflicts with examples of conflicts from within our society and our personal lives.

Sometimes the dimensions of a conflict are clear: there is a right side and a wrong side. Sometimes solutions to conflicts are simple. Yet ordinarily the simple, clear-cut scenarios of "good guys" and "bad guys" exist only in childhood games. More frequently, solutions result from a process of domination and submission or of negotiation and bargaining. Just how we handle conflicts depends on how we compare the effectiveness of nonviolent versus violent solutions:

■ What shape does peaceful resolution take in the minor day-to-day conflicts we all experience? in the very dangerous conflicts existing in our society and the world?

- Is there a rightful place for violence in resolving conflicts?
- Can peace become a reality? Or is it doomed to be an unattainable ideal or a sugary sentimentality?

A helpful way to view peace and violence is to visualize them at opposite ends of a line. At one end of the line, violent tactics may be used in resolving any conflict. On the other end, only nonviolent ways are employed to resolve conflicts. In between these two extremes, the acceptance of violent or nonviolent methods varies. Let's look at three prominent standpoints on this line, which we might term *the continuum of conflict.*

1. Militarism: The Glorification of Violence

- By nature, human beings are aggressive, warlike, violent creatures. Throughout human history they have killed one another, and the strong have dominated the weak. Human nature is not going to change. Therefore, the use of violence in conflict is necessary and natural. Furthermore, violence is often good and can bring about positive results.

The opinion expressed above suggests that using violence to resolve conflicts is natural and acceptable. If someone sees wrong being done, then that person should employ whatever means are necessary to resolve the conflict, including violence. When one nation considers itself in any way threatened by another nation, then it is justified in going to war.

Militarism not only accepts violence but often glorifies it: fighting for one's country or cause is seen as a noble act worthy of commemoration in monuments and on national holidays. Indiscriminate violence is abhorred, but violence for a righteous or patriotic cause is a courageous act. On the other hand, militarism views as cowardice any refusal of violence when a conflict arises.

Logically in the militarist view, preparedness is seen as sensible. Inventing and stockpiling weapons makes sense in a violence-prone world. The militarist believes that unfortunately but realistically, "might makes right."

2. The Just-War Theory: Limited Violence as a Last Resort

- Violence is evil in itself. Yet, the use of violence is acceptable in order to eliminate a greater evil. Violence is not to be valued on a level with other means of resolving conflicts, and it certainly should not be glorified. Violence is a last resort, subject to definite restrictions.

Toward the middle of the continuum of conflict is the **just-war theory**. With militarism it shares an acceptance of violence in resolving conflicts. Its acceptance of violence, however, is grudging and subject to many restrictions.

The just-war theory emerged in response to a specific conflict in history. In the fourth and fifth centuries, Roman civilization was being destroyed by European tribes that were invading the empire from the west and north. Saint Augustine of Hippo (354–430), a leading theologian of the time, suggested that violence is acceptable if certain conditions are met. His principles regulating the use of violence became refined into the just-war theory. This theory has provided the guiding principles for the Church's teaching on the use of violence since Saint Augustine's time.

The just-war theory includes three principles regulating *when* violence is acceptable and four others regulating *how* violence is used during a conflict.

Top: A terrorist hiding in the Iranian Embassy in London in 1980 *Bottom:* Five U.S. hostages attending a press conference during an incident in Beirut in 1985

The Basic Principles of the Just-War Theory

Regulating when violence is morally acceptable
1. Just cause: Does a real and certain danger exist?
2. Right intention: Is justice clearly being served?
3. Legitimate authority: Who is responsible?

revolution - ity issue

Regulating how violence is used
4. Proportionality: Will the good outweigh the damage?
5. Reasonable hope of success: Is there a reasonable hope of success?
6. Noncombatant immunity: Who will be involved?
7. Last resort: Have all other means been tried?

Applying the Principles of the Just-War Theory

A plane carrying five citizens of country *A* is hijacked by a group from country *B*. It is taken to country *B* where all of the travelers are held hostage. Demands are made for money by officials of country *B*.

According to the just-war theory, is country *A* justified in using violence to resolve this conflict?

1. Just cause: According to the U.S. Catholic bishops, "War is permissible only to confront 'a real and certain danger,' i.e., to protect innocent life, to preserve conditions necessary for decent human existence, and to secure basic human rights" (*The Challenge of Peace,* no. 86). In other words, before considering the use of violence, an individual or country must be involved in a conflict that is related to concerns of life and justice.

In the hijacking situation described above, one can argue that the taking of innocent hostages is a cause justifying the use of violence. Just-war theorists applying this principle likely would consider freeing hostages whose lives are endangered to be a just cause.

2. **Right intention:** Even if the cause is considered just, one's intentions must also be examined. For instance, if country *A* intends not only to free the hostages but also to overthrow country *B's* government or to take advantage of the other country in any other way, the use of violence is not justified.

The original cause for the use of violence in a conflict can become lost or blurred as a conflict escalates. The principle of right intention requires that throughout a conflict, violence is used only to serve the concerns of life and justice.

3. **Legitimate authority:** The third principle of the just-war theory poses the question, Who is responsible for resolving this conflict? In the case of the hijacking, the government of country *A* has the responsibility for the welfare of its citizens. A citizens' group from country *A* would not be justified in retaliating against citizens from country *B*. We might also ask whether the group that did the hijacking has the support of country *B's* government. Or is that government also in a sense being held hostage?

The principle of legitimate authority has been called into question by modern revolutions: Can revolutionary forces ever possess legitimate authority? The American Revolution first raised the issue of whether established governments themselves can lose their legitimacy when they act unjustly. Even though revolutionary forces may appear to lack legitimate authority, such struggles can be examined in light of just-war principles.

4. **Proportionality:** The principle of proportionality asks, Does the good likely to result from using violence outweigh the probable damage caused? The just-war theory recognizes that violence and warfare cause great harm and that weighing the cost in human life and suffering is a difficult but crucial task.

For instance, would country *A* be justified in causing the deaths of hundreds of people from country *B* in order to save the five hostages? Would it make a difference if there were fifty or one hundred hostages? Should country *A* allow the deaths of the hostages rather than give in to country *B's* demands? Proportionality attempts to judge the merits of the various options open to those who find themselves faced with a conflict. Obviously the application of proportionality is a difficult issue to assess.

A British hostage being held by rebels in Iraq in 1982

5. Reasonable hope of success: Do the military actions proposed by country *A* hold out a reasonable hope of success? Based on this principle, certain uses of violence might be considered acceptable while others would be rejected. In the example above, it must be asked if a violent attempt to free the hostages will instead cause their deaths.

6. Noncombatant immunity: *Noncombatants* are those persons not directly involved in the manufacture, direction, or use of weapons. In a just war, no military action may be aimed at noncombatants. However, as a result of an action against a military target, noncombatants might be killed. Obviously, modern warfare and weaponry have blurred the traditional distinction between combatants and noncombatants.

In the above case, the principle of noncombatant immunity may apply if, for instance, the hostages are being held at a civilian airport.

7. Last resort: Finally, the just-war theory states that violence must be the last resort; all other means of resolving the conflict must be tried before resorting to violence. As are the applications of the other just-war principles, each case's status as a last resort is also difficult to determine. Often, numerous options for addressing a conflict exist. Sometimes the heat of the moment, a lack of preparation, or simply a lack of knowledge and training in the use of other options make violence appear to be the last resort when, in fact, many other options may not even have been considered.

Originally the just-war theory attempted to name those exceptional cases when violence could be an acceptable means of resolving conflicts. Later in the Middle Ages, violence and warfare came to be seen as often acceptable. Yet voices denouncing violence have emerged throughout the Church's history, and recently the Church has called for a thorough reexamination of warfare.

3. Nonviolent Conflict Resolution: Pacifism Is Not Passivity

When we visualize images of peace, calm and tranquil scenes may come to mind. Of course inner peace and an atmosphere free of conflict are beneficial. Yet, curiously, many of the great voices for peace throughout history have not led tranquil lives: Jesus, Francis of Assisi, Mohandas K. Gandhi, Martin Luther King, Jr., and Dorothy Day were all embroiled in tumultuous conflicts. In the real world, conflicts happen all the time. So

President Harry S. Truman (1945–1953), who felt that atomic bombs were justifiably used in World War II

peacemakers are called to be courageous yet nonviolent fighters.

The concept of *nonviolent fighters* may be confusing because we often identify fighting and conflict with violence. Yet not every conflict leads to violence. Likewise, we usually confuse peace with passivity or even weakness. When we do, however, we lose sight of the forceful, courageous, challenging dimensions of peacemaking—or **pacifism**. The Indian political leader Gandhi—a person revered for his advocacy of nonviolence—once said, "Where there is only a choice between cowardice and violence, I would choose violence."

Pacifism can be described like this:

- an activity, not passivity
- involvement, not noninvolvement
- a passionate concern, not an apathetic detachment
- strong and forceful, not weak and lackadaisical

Most importantly, pacifism involves struggle with conflicts, not avoidance of them. Pacifist conflict resolution, however, is placed on the opposite end of the line from militarist resolution because pacifism rules out any use of physical or psychological violence. Peacemaking advocates nonviolent conflict resolution.

Examining Pacifism: Struggling with Conflicts Nonviolently

Pacifism *Prior* to Conflicts

We can apply the principles of pacifism prior to actual conflicts, as well as during conflicts. These tactics include actively creating a climate of peace and rooting out the causes of conflict.

Creating a Climate of Peace

The interplay between the USSR and the United States in recent history illustrates what a climate of peace is not. The term *cold war* appropriately describes the strained relations that have existed between these countries since World War II. Although not actually at war, the two countries mistrust each other, blame each other for the world's problems, and generally view each other as evil. Each quickly faults the other, insults the other, and threatens the other with deadly weapons. Such an atmosphere is hardly conducive to peace.

In contrast to a cold-war climate, pacifism seeks to create a climate favorable to nonviolent resolutions of conflicts.

1. Creating an atmosphere of peace requires examining our attitudes toward those with whom we might find ourselves in conflict. Paradoxically, a country in conflict with another country often views its opponent's citizens as both *sub*human (that is, not worthy of our respect or concern) and also *super*human (that is, to be feared and fought). Peacemaking requires a more realistic view of other people: we have to recognize that our opponents are just as human as ourselves.

2. A climate of peace also implies examining ourselves. We can have as distorted an image of our own goodness and right-mindedness as we do of other countries' faults and evil intentions. As North American Christians particularly, we should be as alert to the faults of capitalism as to those of Communism.

3. Finally, an atmosphere of peace places a higher priority on peacemaking than on "war-making." This priority involves committing financial, governmental, educational, and other resources to make tools of peace, not weapons of war. For example, offering scholarships to encourage students to visit the USSR promotes both education and peace.

Rooting Out the Causes of Conflict

Actually, we who engage in nonviolent direct action are not the creators of tension. We merely bring to the surface the hidden tension that is already alive. We bring it out in the open where it can be seen and dealt with. Like a boil that can never be cured as long as it is covered up but must be opened with all its pus-flowing ugliness to the natural medicines of air and light, injustice must likewise be exposed, with all of the tension its exposing creates, to the light of human conscience and the air of national opinion before it can be cured. (Martin Luther King, Jr., *Letter from a Birmingham Jail*)

A second principle of pacifism is to root out the causes of conflict. As Dr. King described above in his letter, the sores of conflict often fester when untended. If we are concerned about peacemaking, we seek to uproot the underlying conditions that might explode into violence.

A case in point: The concept of property ownership is so deeply embedded in Western culture that it ranks with life, liberty, and the pursuit of happiness as a fundamental right. In fact, the right of property has often been defended at the cost of human rights if not lives. For example:

> In the northern region of the United States, steel companies have been closing and relocating their plants for the last decade. The reasons are that the need for steel has declined and that steel can be produced more cheaply in other countries where workers' wages are lower and where companies have invested in modern equipment. As a result, unemployment in some steel towns is much higher than the national average.
>
> The steelworkers may feel that the companies owe their communities a better deal because the companies have been making money off the local workers for several generations. By right of ownership, however, the steel companies are free to pursue profitable ventures elsewhere rather than struggling with the communities to develop new or more efficient industries.

If the steelworkers would resort to fighting during a heated exchange with company leadership, such violence would be obvious to all participants and observers. However, high unemployment and plant closings are also types of violence, representing a more subtle violence that underlies the overt violence of the workers' angry response. Pacifism as active peacemaking concerns itself not only with the conflict when it reaches a boiling point, but also with the injustices, frustrations, and pain seething below the surface of potential conflicts.

Pacifism *During* Conflicts: Nonviolent Conflict Resolution

A primary goal of pacifism is to *prevent* violence. This is not the same as avoiding conflicts, which as was said are a natural part of life. In situations of conflict, pacifism demands at least as much energy, creativity, strength, and courage as does the use of violence. **Mohandas K. Gandhi** of India (1869–1948), our modern era's great apostle of nonviolence, compared a nonviolent campaign to warfare. He called nonviolence *satyagraha* (sə-ˈtyä-grə-hə), meaning "truth force." In other words, Gandhi advocated the concept that "right makes might." Both as a leading theorist and as a practitioner of nonviolence, Gandhi serves as our best model for nonviolent conflict resolution.

Seeing Truth on Both Sides

Gandhi believed that both sides in a conflict always possess some truth, even though not always equally so. He regarded *satyagraha* as an attempt to discover the truth of each position in a conflict and then to act according to that truth. He felt that violent ways of resolving a conflict did not lead to true but to false resolutions.

Simply put, domination by one party reveals only which side of the conflict is physically stronger. Domination does not reveal where truth lies. Since truth is not served, the underlying problem remains for future generations to resolve. In addition, the use of violence creates new conflicts between the two groups.

Interestingly, Gandhi held the same reservations about compromise as he did about domination. He saw compromise as each side winning a little, but each side losing a little as well. Likewise, when a judge or court of law decides which side is right, Gandhi believed that the losing side would feel that the truth in their position was overlooked. The losing party might also feel humiliated and thus could cooperate only reluctantly. For Gandhi, neither compromise nor an appeal to law was a true resolution of conflict.

Seeking Truth and Rejecting Falsehood

An opponent is not always bad simply because he opposes. (Mohandas K. Gandhi)

Mohandas K. Gandhi, Indian leader and peace activist

Gandhi chafed at the word *enemy*. He realized that its use obstructs the search for truth. For Gandhi, an opponent in a conflict is not an enemy. The pacifist's task is to see the conflict from the points of view of each of the combatants. One side may have the greater weight of truth, but that does not mean that the other side has no legitimate claims. Gandhi taught that combatants are not enemies; in a conflict only falsehood is the enemy.

Gandhi also believed that a conflict is not resolved until both parties agree to the solution, that is, until former opponents occupy the same side. Such a resolution calls for constant negotiation that seeks to resolve differences. If one opponent fails to negotiate with sufficient honesty, then the other opponent needs to engage in a *nonviolent campaign.* These campaigns may include the activities that we have come to associate with nonviolence: demonstrations, boycotts, strikes, sit-ins, and civil disobedience.

For Gandhi, such activities do not involve coercion—either physical or psychological. Instead of attacking an opponent, Gandhi taught *noncooperation.* That is, Gandhian fighters would not cooperate with falsehood but would act according to their understanding of the truth.

Examples of Nonviolent Conflict Resolution

Gandhi did not deal merely with abstract concepts; he constantly tested his theories in practice. A number of other groups have employed Gandhian nonviolent methods in conflict situations. Let's examine some of these:

■ Under Martin Luther King, Jr., the civil-rights movement in the United States applied Gandhian principles and tactics to the struggle against the discrimination against black people. One tactic employed was the sit-in. In southern states, laws prevented blacks from eating in restaurants or in other public places marked Whites Only. The civil-rights movement wanted those laws repealed. Under Dr. King's leadership, groups of black people simply acted as if the laws did not exist. They sat in sections reserved for whites and suffered the legal penalties, thus exposing the immorality of the laws.

■ The United Farm Workers under the leadership of Cesar Chavez employed the nonviolent tactics—strikes and boycotts—long associated with labor struggles. The farmworkers of California were one of the poorest-paid groups of workers in the United States. The nature of their work afforded them little stability and few opportunities to become organized. Under Cesar Chavez they began a long struggle in which they focused on boycotting California's lettuce, grape, and wine producers.

As news of the struggle spread, many North Americans refused to buy the boycotted products. Throughout the United States, support groups formed to petition local stores not to buy California lettuce, grapes, and wine, and to demonstrate in front of those stores that did not comply. Moved by the "truth force" of the farmworkers' struggle, many church leaders and political figures rallied to their cause. Although the struggle lasted a long time, the farmworkers' union eventually gained recognition—without the bloodshed and violence that had marked many earlier labor struggles.

Civil Disobedience in the Antiwar Movement

Some people in the antiwar movement during the Vietnam war era, and more recently in the movement against nuclear weapons, have employed tactics that may be viewed as testing the limits of nonviolence. While espousing nonviolence, these protesters perform acts of "symbolic violence"—for example, burning draft cards or a U.S. flag. A number of antiwar activists have spent long terms in prison for this type of nonviolent action—called *civil disobedience.*

Civil disobedience normally involves (1) breaking only those laws considered unjust, (2) accepting the legal penalties for breaking the laws, (3) making a clear, public statement of intentions, and (4) ensuring that no violence is involved.

In practice, however, some antiwar activists have broken laws that they did not consider immoral in order to bring to light what they consider to be a graver immorality. Specifically, protesters have broken into draft board offices and poured blood on draft files. In other actions, protesters have destroyed the casings for nuclear weapons, splattered paint on nuclear submarines, and dug symbolic bomb craters on the White House lawn. Such actions violate laws regarding trespassing and the destruction of private property. However, the activists feel justified in breaking even these just laws regarding property in order to make a public statement about what they consider greater injustices regarding people.

The Promise of Pacifism

Does pacifism work? Even though we can point to past successes such as those mentioned above, the question of pacifism's effectiveness in a variety of situations remains unanswered. For instance:

- Would nonviolent tactics have been effective against Adolf Hitler and Nazism during World War II?
- Is there a place for pacifism in global conflicts—such as that between the United States and the USSR?
- To be effective, does pacifism require large numbers of supporters—such as Gandhi drew in India and Martin Luther King, Jr., in the United States?
- Would government leaders ever adopt nonviolent techniques in resolving conflicts?

We do not know the answers to many of these questions about pacifism. A writer once said that Christianity cannot be said to have failed because it has never really been tried. The same might be said of pacifism. Before we reject pacifism for fear that it has its limits, we would do well to explore its possibilities and to treat it as a valid method of conflict resolution. On the other hand, violence already has been given plenty of use in our century, and the resulting deaths and destruction prove it to be usually ineffective.

A final note: For Christians the first question about pacifism is not whether it is effective. Whether pacifism is faithful to the gospel message is the first question that we should look at—and we will in the next section.

Putting Peacemaking into a Christian Perspective

- A Christian is a crusader, one who is ready to take up the sword in the cause of right. When conquering evil is called for, a Christian does not hesitate to fight with whatever means necessary.
- A Christian uses violence only reluctantly. Sometimes violence is acceptable and proper, and a Christian courageously participates in a just war. However, a Christian sees violence as horrifying and limits its use as much as possible.
- A Christian is a pacifist. Violence against others is such an evil and so clearly against the teachings of Jesus that no other evil circumstances can justify its use. A Christian must stand for peace; to resort to violence is a rejection of Christ's message of peace.

A look at the Scriptures and at our Christian tradition reveals that all three of the above opinions on violence and nonviolence can be defended as Christian positions.

In the Jewish Scriptures, God is occasionally portrayed as a warrior God who smites the enemy, and many of the great heroes—for example, Joshua, Samson, and David—employed violence without a hint of disfavor on the part of the biblical writer. Elsewhere the Jewish Scriptures denounce violence strongly. In particular they provide us with beautiful images of a peaceful kingdom and the melting of animosity between enemies:

> Then the wolf shall be a guest of the lamb,
>   and the leopard shall lie down with the kid;
> The calf and the young lion shall browse together,
>   with a little child to guide them.
> The cow and the bear shall be neighbors,
>   together their young shall rest;
>   the lion shall eat hay like the ox.
> The baby shall play by the cobra's den,
>   and the child lay his hand on the adder's lair.
> There shall be no harm or ruin on all my holy mountain;
>   for the earth shall be filled with knowledge of the
>   LORD,
>   as water covers the sea.
>
> (Isaiah 11:6–9)

Jesus: Our Symbol of Nonviolence

Popular culture—and some would say our natural instincts as well—offers us models of resolving conflicts that exalt violence. For example, Hollywood films frequently portray peaceful people who are driven to the breaking point by vicious bullies. When at last the heroes respond with equal violence, we cheer them on. In a similar way, judges and politicians like to speak of "getting tough." When our country faces a crisis with another country, we hear many calls for a show of "strength"— meaning violent retaliation.

In the face of such images of acceptable violence, we Christians encounter Jesus, the person of peace. When we examine his words and actions, we see that Jesus constantly advocated peace and modeled the nonviolent resolution of conflicts. Although his life was surrounded by conflict—with the Romans, with religious and government leaders in his own country, with other Jewish groups, with his fellow townspeople, and with his own followers—Jesus consistently renounced violence. As a result, Christians have always faced the challenge of applying Jesus' message of peace to the conflicts in their lives. His message seems clear: the Christian is to turn and offer the other cheek to violence and to love one's enemies as oneself.

Jesus also lived the message of nonviolence. Although some readers see Jesus' angrily clearing the temple area as an endorsement of violence, most biblical scholars consider this interpretation an exaggeration. Jesus met his persecutors and death on the cross with nonviolence, and he censured the Apostle Peter when in the garden of Gethsemane Peter cut off the soldier's ear. The early Christian writer Tertullian declared, "The Lord, by taking away Peter's sword, disarmed every soldier thereafter."

For Saint Paul, Jesus proclaimed "the gospel of peace," by which Christians are to replace the armor of war with the armor of Jesus' presence. In a passage that sounds remarkably similar to Gandhi's emphasis on truth, justice, and peace, Paul admonishes Christians to "stand fast, with the truth as the belt around your waist, justice as your breastplate, and zeal to propagate the gospel of peace as your footgear" (Ephesians 6:14–15).

In Jesus' constantly repeated message of forgiveness, all traces of the warrior God who destroys enemies vanish. The Sermon on the Mount and especially the Beatitudes prescribe the virtues of peacemaking and the endurance of suffering rather than the inflicting of suffering. The reign of God, a central concept in the teaching of Jesus, emphasizes forgiveness, compassion, wiping out the underlying causes of violence, and an interpretation of the term *neighbor* that includes all people and thus rejects the idea of enemy. In short, for Jesus the reign of God is a reign of peace. Christians are called to be active participants in the creation of God's reign of peace.

The Church Grapples with the Christian Call to Peace

Jesus' renunciation of violence and his call for compassion have created tension for Christians throughout the Church's history. In the early Church, when Christians were an outcast minority, most Christians interpreted Jesus' renunciation of violence in a literal sense. Even into the fourth century, Christians refused military service. For example, Saint Martin of Tours renounced his soldierly profession in these words: "I am a soldier of Christ. It is not lawful for me to fight."

This pacifist attitude of the early Christians was soon to change, however:

> The reign of Constantine [A.D. 306–337] represents a turning point in Christian thinking about the legitimacy of violence and war. By and large writers before him tended to be pacifist in outlook, whereas those following his rise to power argued for the legitimacy of war under certain conditions. (Louis J. Swift, *The Early Fathers on War and Military Service*, p. 27)

After Emperor Constantine's reign, when Christians rapidly gained power within the Roman Empire, their change of status caused many Christians to look on the admonitions of Jesus in a new light. Although acceptance of violence did not settle comfortably upon the Christian conscience, many Christian leaders saw that the responsibility of ruling in a sinful world required the use of force.

As the restrictions of the just-war theory indicate, the acceptance of force and its accompanying violence never was meant to go unchecked. Nevertheless, Christianity has sometimes had a very bloody history, especially during the Crusades. Yet even during the Middle Ages when violence was so much a part of the feudal system of lords and knights, the Church's restrictions on warfare testified to its uneasiness with war and violence. For instance:

- According to a decree called the *Peace of God*, certain groups such as members of the clergy were not to participate in war, and excommunication was promised to all who used violence upon noncombatants.
- The *Truce of God* prohibited fighting on Sundays and

specified holy days, during Lent, in seasons of harvest (15 August to 15 November), and for a part of each week (usually from Wednesday evening to Monday morning). In its final form, the truce allowed only eighty days in the year for war.

- In 1139, the Second Lateran Council forbade the use of "military engines" against people.

Such restrictions reveal that even though warfare became permitted, the tension that the Church felt about violence never completely subsided.

The Modern Era:
Looking at War with an Entirely New Attitude

Within the Church today, war has regained its bad name. Until recently, however, war was often considered not only acceptable but actually appropriate and even at times glorious. For example:

Gordon Zahn, peace activist

- During World War II, U.S. Catholic pacifist Gordon Zahn declared himself to be a *conscientious objector*—that is, one who opposes participation in war for religious reasons. His local pastor told him that it was absolutely impossible for a Catholic to be a conscientious objector.

Since the late 1960s, however, Catholic pacifists have been very influential in the Church and in the United States. Previously in Catholic circles, pacifist thought was considered odd; today those who find violence acceptable are on the defensive side of debates.

In numerous official documents, the Church has grappled with the problems that modern warfare and weaponry pose to the Christian call to peace. Although church statements do not advocate absolute pacifism, they do formally recognize pacifism as a legitimate Christian position. More than any other group of its size, the Church has been a voice calling into question the reliance on military power. In the past twenty-five years, the Church has spoken strongly against violence and for peace. Because of the Church's continuous raising of the issues, we Christians cannot rest easy in our violence-prone world. Called to be peacemakers, we can say along with the bishops of Vatican Council II:

> All these considerations compel us to undertake an evaluation of war with an entirely new attitude. The [people] of our time must realize that they will have to give a somber reckoning for their deeds of war. For the course of the future will depend largely on the decisions they make today. (*The Church in the Modern World*, no. 80)

Responding to the Call to Peacemaking

When the bishops of Vatican Council II ask us to look at war "with an entirely new attitude," what do they mean by *new?* After all, the Gospel they preach is almost two thousand years old.

The Church's teachings on war are new in the sense that for most societies and for many people, peacemaking remains a strange, even foreign, concept. So let's look at peacemaking as a new attitude toward and response to conflict. Based on our discussion so far, we can designate three areas in which a reappraisal of current attitudes may be needed: (1) a new attitude toward others and ourselves, (2) a new attitude toward resolving conflicts, and (3) a new attitude toward our world.

1. A New Attitude Toward Others and Ourselves

How We View Others

In our volatile age, viewing other people, groups, or nations as enemies is both dangerous and counterproductive. In the spirit of Jesus we need to reflect on the times when we have reduced others simply to *the enemy*—with all of the emotional weight that the term carries.

We can apply the principles related to prejudice and racism to our view of others. If we can expand our consciousness to look beyond color, language, and national differences in order to recognize our common humanity, then we are less likely to dismiss or defame others. If we view those with whom we are in conflict as brothers and sisters, then we are more likely to treat their concerns seriously. In short, the fires of war are stoked by the language, emotions, and thought patterns that stem from calling others *the enemy*. The attitude of peacemaking requires that the concept *enemy* be put aside along with the toy guns and toy soldiers of our childhood.

How We View Ourselves

Do our current images of maturity suggest that adults attack problems with their fists or with their minds? Do we consider the use of violence to be strength or brutality? Do we consider the rejection of violence to be cowardice or courage?

Certainly one popular image of maturity portrays fists and violence as forms of strength, not brutality. This is an old image of maturity, going back to the pre-Christian era.

A story about Alexander the Great tells us that he once visited an oracle who presented him with an intricately knotted

SOMETIMES A DIFFERENT PERSPECTIVE GIVES LIFE NEW MEANING...

rope. The oracle prophesied that whoever untied the famous Gordian knot would rule Asia. Alexander settled the problem by slashing through the knot with his sword.

Alexander's solution makes sense if one is only slashing a rope. Current film heroes like Rambo, however, suggest that even problems involving people can be resolved by simply murdering those on the other side of the conflict. The Rambo image of maturity presents a cold-blooded, lethal, muscular, and masculine adult. All others—especially women—are merely victims.

In one of the major documents from the last church council, the bishops teach a very different image of maturity:

> Above all, the education of youth from every social background has to be undertaken so that there can be produced not only men and women of refined talents, but those great-souled persons who are so desperately required by our times. (Vatican Council II, *The Church in the Modern World,* no. 31)

To look at violence with a new attitude implies that we look at ourselves anew. The bishops challenge us to be "great-souled." That is, they ask us to enlarge our sense of compassion. They ask that we cherish harmony over discord and the beauty of working together with others over the brutality of working against them. A new attitude toward war implies a new attitude toward ourselves.

2. A New Attitude Toward Resolving Conflicts

Our View of War

> Even though recent wars have wrought immense material and moral havoc on the world, the devastation of battle still rages in some parts of the world. Indeed, now that every kind of weapon produced by modern science is used in war, the savagery of war threatens to lead the combatants to barbarities far surpassing those of former ages. (Vatican Council II, *The Church in the Modern World,* no. 79)

Common sense declares that "war is hell." Yet for many people this hell holds a morbid yet romantic fascination. A new attitude toward war requires that we see war as the savagery and the suicide that it is. Especially today, when suffering and destruction often are inflicted from great distances and on such large numbers of victims that the human dimension is lost, we have felt forced into viewing war coldly. But we must not allow the fact that incomprehensibly large numbers of people can be killed in modern warfare to numb us to war's evil.

The ancient Roman poet Horace wrote that "it is a sweet and fitting thing to die for one's country." History provides us with a long list of people whom we hold in esteem because they have died for their countries or their faiths or their causes. More often than not, our heroes and heroines are exalted because they have also killed for their country.

Yet a new attitude toward war suggests that we examine our understanding of heroism. Only when peacemakers in our society are exalted, at least to the degree that war-makers are, will we be able to view war with a new, realistic attitude.

Our View of Resolving Conflicts

... Let us profit by the respite we now enjoy, thanks to the divine favor, to take stock of our responsibilities and find ways of resolving controversies in a manner worthy of human beings. Providence urgently demands of us that we free ourselves from the age-old slavery of war. (Vatican Council II, *The Church in the Modern World*, no. 81)

At this juncture in history we are in urgent need of discovering new methods of resolving conflict. Although the threat of war clouds the future, a disproportionate amount of human resources is committed to war-making and preparing for war. Given the limitations of our material resources, our human resources, our time, and our money, we need to make choices. For example, as we will discuss more fully in our next chapter,

- Our government can either purchase tanks and missiles or classrooms and medical supplies.
- Our schools can either train students for war-making or peacemaking.
- Government think tanks can either rely on people trained in violent conflict resolution or in nonviolent conflict resolution.

We may argue, Why can't we have both? Unfortunately, the strain that war-making places on our resources limits what we might put into exploring methods of nonviolent conflict resolution.

The new attitude toward war called for by the bishops of Vatican Council II questions the emphasis that our world places on war and violence. This implies that alternative methods of resolving conflicts need to be examined and taken seriously. For that to happen, we must call upon our government to treat nonviolent forms of conflict resolution as viable alternatives to war and violence. Also, we can challenge other institutions, such as schools, to support the study and practice of nonviolence.

Our Budget Priorities

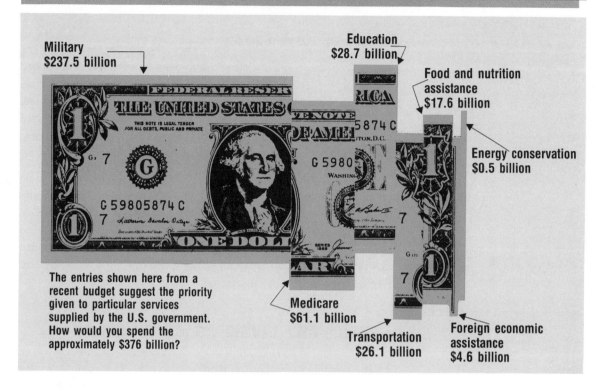

Military
$237.5 billion

Education
$28.7 billion

Food and nutrition
assistance
$17.6 billion

Energy conservation
$0.5 billion

The entries shown here from a recent budget suggest the priority given to particular services supplied by the U.S. government. How would you spend the approximately $376 billion?

Medicare
$61.1 billion

Transportation
$26.1 billion

Foreign economic
assistance
$4.6 billion

3. A New Attitude Toward Our World

Addressing the Underlying Causes of Violence

If peace is to be established, the first condition is to root out the causes of discord among [people] which lead to wars—in the first place, injustice. Not a few of these causes arise out of excessive economic inequalities and out of hesitation to undertake necessary correctives. Some are due to the desire for power and to contempt for people, and at a deeper level, to envy, distrust, pride, and other selfish passions. (Vatican Council II, *The Church in the Modern World*, no. 83)

A world filled with starving children is not a peaceful world. A world where basic freedoms are lacking is not a peaceful world. A world of plenty in which many people are homeless or unemployed is not a peaceful world. A new attitude toward war demands that we examine the underlying causes of war and violence that exist in our world.

Present world conditions lead many people to feel justified in resorting to violence to attain their basic rights, to gain their freedom, or to preserve their security. A new attitude toward war must accompany a new attitude toward existing world conditions.

Making Peace a Reality

> Accordingly, the Council proposes to outline the true and noble nature of peace, to condemn the savagery of war, and earnestly to exhort Christians to cooperate with all in securing a peace based on justice and charity and in promoting the means necessary to attain it, under the help of Christ, author of peace. (Vatican Council II, *The Church in the Modern World,* no. 77)

Jesus desires peace for the world. We who are followers of Jesus seek to move the world closer to the Christian vision of peace. War and violence are a tragic part of our past, intimately tied to human history and culture. The gospel message is that peace is a bright part of our future—if we place our hope in Jesus and live out his message of justice.

Conclusion: Giving Peace a Chance

In the words of the U.S. Catholic bishops, "Catholic teaching begins in every case with a presumption against war and for peaceful settlement of disputes" (*The Challenge of Peace,* summary). Clearly, the Church sees peacemaking as a primary responsibility for itself and for its members in the days ahead. This challenge from Jesus and his Church to be peacemakers leads us to question the violence and the war-making that so permeate our world. By our attempts to create a peaceful world, we live out the Christian vocation named in the Beatitudes:

> Blessed are the peacemakers:
> they shall be recognised as children of God.
>   (Matthew 5:9)

For Review

1. List the two extremes of the continuum of conflict.
2. What is the basic belief behind militarism?
3. What is the historical origin of the just-war theory?
4. List the seven principles of the just-war theory.
5. Explain the principle of proportionality in the just-war theory.
6. Explain why pacifism is an active not passive approach to conflict resolution.
7. Describe the two tactics of pacifism that are used prior to conflicts.
8. Explain Gandhi's concept of *satyagraha.*
9. Describe Gandhi's attitude toward enemies. What did he regard as the enemy in any conflict? Why?
10. What is civil disobedience?
11. What is Jesus' message regarding the use of violence?
12. What was the early Church's position on the use of violence and participation in warfare? How did this position change after the reign of Emperor Constantine?
13. What were the Peace of God and the Truce of God?
14. What are the three major implications of the modern church teaching that we must look at war "with an entirely new attitude"?

For Reflection

1. Write a one-page essay to answer these questions: What are the reasons that young people enter our country's armed services? What functions do young people in the armed services actually serve?

2. In writing, describe examples of how popular culture portrays war. What attitude toward war and violence is presented to us in movies, television, comic books, games, and other expressions of popular culture? What impact do you think these portrayals of warfare have on people, especially on children and young people?

3. Write down your thoughts on the notion that men especially are natural killers. Consider this notion in light of the following conclusion from interviews with over four hundred infantry companies during World War II, conducted by U.S. Army Colonel S. L. A. Marshall:

> He found that on average only 15 percent of trained

> combat riflemen fired their weapons at all in battle.
> The rest did not flee, but they would not kill—even
> when their own position was under attack and their
> lives were in immediate danger. (Gwynne Dyer, *War*,
> p. 118)

4. If you were part of a U.N. committee established to develop principles regulating when the use of violence is acceptable, what principles would you suggest? Outline your recommendations and then compare your principles to those of the just-war theory.

5. Can the principles of the just-war theory be applied to interpersonal conflicts? In writing, describe a conflict situation within a family or group of friends and explain how each of the principles might apply.

   Now recall an argument or conflict that you recently had. How did you resolve it? Looking back, how do you wish you had resolved it?

6. Reflect on these questions: How would you respond to someone who claimed to be a pacifist? How would you feel about that person's position? What would you say to the person? Would you vote for the person for a national political office?

7. Pacifism rules out the use of both physical and psychological violence in resolving conflicts. List some examples of *psychological* violence. Write a one-page essay on psychological violence.

8. Research and report on a local or national conflict that exhibits a lack of a climate of peace. Outline steps that could be taken to help create a climate of peace. How do your steps relate to the attitudes described in the section on climate of peace in this chapter (pages 232–233)?

9. Describe in writing three examples of how enforcing property rights can cause violence against persons.

10. Research and report on a creative demonstration of nonviolent conflict resolution. If you wish, report on the Soviet invasion of Czechoslovakia mentioned on page 226. Provide further details. Explain how the concept of *satyagraha* applied to the event.

11. Write a two-page essay about your feelings and opinions concerning civil disobedience. When would you find it justified? Are there expressions of it that you consider unacceptable? What rules would you propose for those

practicing it? Are there any situations in which you could envision yourself participating in civil disobedience. What would they be?

12. Complete one of the following exercises:
    a. Write an essay describing what you understand to be the Christian perspective on violence and peace. Focus in particular on your interpretation of Jesus' teachings related to the subject.
    b. Read and write a reflection on Matthew, chapter 5, discussing the possibility of living out the idea of "turning the other cheek."

13. Very often people of countries at war attempt to differentiate killing during wartime from killing in peacetime. One way this is accomplished is through depersonalizing the people in the other country. The opposing country's citizens are referred to collectively as *the enemy*—including school children and teachers, older persons and infants, and mothers and fathers who are not soldiers.

    List groups of people whom many North Americans tend to reduce to negative stereotypes. Then answer these questions:
    ■ What are some of the negative stereotypes regarding these people?
    ■ Of these groups of people, which group do you believe could most easily fit into an image of "the enemy" for North Americans?

14. Write an essay entitled "Developing the Attitude of a Peacemaker."

15. Complete one of the following exercises:
    a. Imagine that you are the teacher of a course on non-violent methods of resolving conflicts. Write up a course description. First, provide a rationale explaining why such a course is important. Second, describe the content and some of the techniques that would be taught in the course.
    b. Write a one-page proposal for a national peace academy that will train citizens in conflict resolution by means other than war.

12
Peacemaking in the Nuclear Age

Because of the existence of nuclear weapons in today's world, our response to the Christian call to peacemaking faces new challenges and takes on a new urgency. In recent years the Catholic Church has spoken forcefully and frequently against nuclear weapons. The Church believes that Jesus' message of peace directly opposes the development or deployment of nuclear weapons. For that reason, the Christian call to peacemaking requires us to question the policies and priorities of governments and to seek a new direction for our world.

A War Movie Viewed Backward

Billy looked at the clock on the gas stove. He had an hour to kill before the saucer came. He went into the living room, . . . turned on the television. He came slightly unstuck in time, saw the late movie backwards, then forwards again. It was a movie about American bombers in the Second World War and the gallant men who flew them. Seen backwards by Billy, the story went like this:

American planes, full of holes and wounded men and corpses, took off backwards from an airfield in England. Over France, a few German fighter planes flew at them backwards, sucked bullets and shell fragments from some of the planes and crewmen. They did the same for wrecked American bombers on the ground, and those planes flew up backwards to join the formation.

The formation flew over a German city that was in flames. The bombers opened their bomb bay doors, exerted a miraculous magnetism which shrunk the fires, gathered them into cylindrical steel containers, and lifted the containers into the bellies of the planes. The containers were stored neatly in racks. The Germans below had miraculous devices of their own, which were long steel tubes. They used them to suck more fragments from the crewmen and planes. But there were still a few wounded Americans, . . . and some of the bombers were in bad repair. Over France, though, German fighters came up again, made everything and everybody as good as new.

When the bombers got back to their base, the steel cylinders were taken from the racks and shipped back to the United States of America, where factories were operating night and day, dismantling the cylinders, separating the dangerous contents into minerals. Touchingly, it was mainly women who did this work. The minerals were then shipped to specialists in remote areas. It was their business to put them into the ground, to hide them cleverly, so they would never hurt anybody ever again. (Kurt Vonnegut, Jr., *Slaughterhouse Five*, pp. 73–75)

Examining the Scandal of Nuclear Weapons

Billy Pilgrim, the hero of Kurt Vonnegut's novel *Slaughterhouse Five*, possesses the ability to travel back and forth in time.

When we consider the effect that nuclear weapons have had on our modern world and the threat that they pose for our future, we might wish for Billy Pilgrim's talent. If we could travel backwards in time, we might persuade world leaders of fifty years ago to avoid developing the nuclear weapons that have placed humanity so near annihilation.

Unfortunately we lack time-travel capabilities, and nuclear weapons are an ominous danger to our world. If humankind is to survive, we cannot deny the possibility that nuclear weapons may end human history, but neither should we despair that this will necessarily happen.

Although time travel is not within our reach, Billy Pilgrim's fantasy of reversing the destructive course of the current weapons buildup is not unrealistic. The Christian call to peacemaking challenges us to create a peace-filled world in spite of the advent of nuclear weapons. As we will see, the Church suggests many ways to make peace in our nuclear age.

The Nuclear Peril: A Deadly Duel

When two hostile countries possess large quantities of nuclear weapons, the situation can be compared to a duel between two gunfighters in an old Western movie.

- Each gunfighter faces the other in a state of constant readiness, hand poised just inches from the trigger. Each gunfighter looks for signs of aggression: Is his opponent's hand twitching? Is he reaching for his gun? Each gunfighter refuses to show any signs of weakness and fears letting his opponent get the upper hand.

At this point in the duel, the reasons that these two persons face each other are totally irrelevant. The cruel choices are these: (1) one gunfighter can drop his guard and trust that the other will not open fire; (2) one can open fire and hope that he kills his opponent before getting shot himself; or (3) both gunfighters can stand indefinitely in this precarious state of fear and readiness.

As a witness to this gunfight, you might wish to intercede and suggest that these people simply talk to each other and walk arm-in-arm into the saloon to share a drink. Yet, as long as both people are too afraid to lower their gun hands or to look away, the situation cannot change for the better.

The Current Nuclear Dilemma: Mutually Assured Destruction

A stalemate similar to a gunfight has existed in the world for almost thirty years. The gunfighters, of course, are the United States and the USSR. Both countries have kept massive nuclear arsenals aimed at one another and in constant readiness. This standoff, in which the use of nuclear weapons by one country assures the use of nuclear weapons by the other, is the policy known as **MAD**—the abbreviation for **Mutually Assured Destruction.**

Supporters of this nuclear stalemate believe that the present balance of military power has value as a deterrent. In this view, as long as the use of nuclear weapons by one country assures the destruction of the other, both countries will be deterred from using the weapons. These supporters point out that the fear of retaliation has prevented either nation from employing nuclear weapons for decades. They also suggest that in the future, nuclear weapons will continue to exist. Consequently, they reason, only the threat of retaliation will deter nuclear war.

Acceptance of the deterrent value of nuclear weapons, however, need not rule out negotiations about reductions of nuclear weapons. A balance could be maintained even with huge reductions in the current number of nuclear weapons. The obstacles to such *arms-limitation agreements* revolve around two questions:

- Can an arms-limitation agreement be *mutually verifiable*—that is, can both countries guarantee that the other is complying with the terms of the agreement?
- Can both countries be trusted during times of tension and conflict to remain committed to balance and equality and not to seek an advantage over the other country?

Perhaps more importantly, the current policy of Mutually Assured Destruction need not result in a continuing **arms**

Traditional and modern depictions of the horrors of war:
Top: In Albrecht Dürer's 1498 woodcut *The Four Horsemen of the Apocalypse,* characters representing war, sickness, famine, and death combine to destroy humanity.
Bottom: Pablo Picasso's 1937 painting *Guernica* is a modern portrayal of the havoc and suffering of war.

race—that is, the development and stockpiling of new weapons. In fact, MAD might be the basis on which to scale down each country's nuclear arsenal.

Unfortunately, this aptly named policy, MAD, is based on fear and mistrust. Both the United States and the USSR fear that the balance of military power might swing to the other's favor. Two developments could disturb this balance:

- If a country designed a defensive system invulnerable to enemy attack, then destruction would no longer be assured.
- The deterrent value of MAD would be lost if one country developed a nuclear-weapon system that was capable of destroying *all* of the other country's nuclear weapons, thus leaving the opponent without the possibility of retaliation.

Let's look at these possible developments in more detail. In addition, we will consider one other alternative to MAD—that is, eliminating nuclear weapons.

Alternatives to Mutually Assured Destruction

1. Developing an Effective Defensive System

If a defensive system existed that would effectively prevent the use of nuclear weapons, and if both major powers possessed such a defensive system, then nuclear weapons would be obsolete. This would be the only true safeguard against the use of nuclear weapons.

Such a defensive system has been proposed as a positive alternative to MAD. The proposal holds great appeal. However, valid criticisms have been raised.

- First, a completely effective system would be impossible to develop: no defensive system could be 100 percent effective against tens of thousands of missiles. A less-than-perfect system makes sense only if it is used in conjunction with a first strike, after which a defensive system would only have to deal with the opponent's small number of remaining missiles.
- Second, as long as conflicts continue to occur between countries, the use of defensive systems will only spur on research into new, more deadly offensive systems. As a result, an arms race, which the defensive system proposes to eliminate, might actually accelerate.
- Third, development of such a system requires huge sums of money. Yet the world already allots too much of its resources to military spending.
- Finally, throughout history many similar inventions, which

were originally intended for peaceful or defensive purposes, have been transformed into offensive weapons.

In short, this alternative to "MAD-ness" is fraught with new perils. These pitfalls need to be carefully examined before this path can be considered a realistic one.

2. Developing a First-Strike System

Supporters of a **first-strike system** argue that if an offensive nuclear system existed that could assure the destruction of the other country's entire nuclear arsenal, then the country that possessed that system could negotiate on its own terms because it would not fear retaliation.

A first-strike system faces many of the same problems that are raised by a defensive system. In addition, however, a first-strike system is so dangerous that the concept seldom comes into discussions of alternatives to MAD.

- Imagine the difficulty of assuring the destruction of every nuclear weapon owned by an opponent. Thousands of these weapons are located in land-based silos, in roving submarines, and in long-range bombers. Each of these mobile nuclear carriers would have to be sighted and then destroyed. If only one nuclear submarine escaped, it would be capable of retaliating and destroying at least two hundred cities within one hour.

- The closer one country comes to having a first-strike system, the more likely the other country is to put their own system on a *hair trigger*—that is, a highly sensitized, computerized system that would actually make the decision to attack.

- Moreover, the only way a country could prove it had the capability for a successful first strike would be to attempt it.

- Finally we must acknowledge that if a first strike were carried out, its effects would not be limited to the devastation of the military targets. "The spread of radiation due to the natural winds and atmospheric mixing would kill vast numbers of people and contaminate large areas. The medical facilities of any nation would be inadequate to care for the survivors" (quoted in *The Challenge of Peace*, no. 145). Such nuclear explosions could even result in global climatic changes, which clearly negates the benefit of being free from retaliation.

3. Eliminating Nuclear Weapons

Those people who want nuclear weapons eliminated entirely point out the danger of accidents and remind us of near accidents in the past. Opponents of these weapons also fear that

Dr. Robert Oppenheimer directed the research that led to the atomic bomb, but he later spoke against nuclear armaments.

the mere existence of nuclear weapons makes them accessible to terrorists and other psychologically disturbed persons. Moreover, like our gunfighters, countries armed with nuclear weapons will continue to deal with each other in a spirit of fear and mistrust. No lasting peace can be achieved between armed camps. Finally, nuclear-weapon systems are extremely costly, at a time when many other justice-related concerns need attention.

Victory: A Viable Goal?

Before we can decide upon our response to the current nuclear dilemma, we need to be clear about what we want. Then in regard to what we want, we need to set viable goals. For example, our goal cannot be to win a nuclear war. Realistically speaking, *nuclear war has no winners*. Studies by nuclear physicists, medical doctors, and experts in other fields attest to this fact. Nuclear weapons are terrifically more powerful than traditional non-nuclear weapons—which are called **conventional weapons.** Consider these facts:

- The destructive power of all the conventional bombs dropped during World War II was three megatons (equivalent to three million tons of TNT).
- Incredibly, only one nuclear U.S. Titan II missile contains ten megatons of destructive power.

The Firepower of the World's Nuclear Weapons

The chart shown here helps us to visualize the nuclear threat to our world.

- The single dot in the center square represents all of the firepower of the weapons that were detonated during World War II, totaling three million tons of TNT. During that war, fifty million people were killed.
- Each of the other dots on the chart represents this same amount, that is, three megatons of firepower.
- All the dots on this chart represent the destructive capacity of all the nuclear weapons presently in existence—approximately 18,000 megatons of destructive power, which equals 6,000 World War II's. About half of this amount belongs to the United States and about half to the USSR.

Coupled with their immediate catastrophic destructiveness, nuclear weapons are more dangerous than conventional weapons because they add long-term calamitous effects: Their radiation would poison the earth and the air, our water and our food sources for a long period after a nuclear blast. The human services that we have come to depend upon—governmental, medical, and business—would be eliminated at the very time when they would be needed most. Finally, large-scale nuclear explosions would likely cause a general drop in temperature, called *nuclear winter,* that would threaten the survival of much of the earth's plant, animal, and human life.

In their pastoral letter on nuclear weapons, *The Challenge of Peace,* the U.S. bishops have echoed what many similar studies about the use of nuclear weapons have concluded:

> Recent talk about winning or even surviving a nuclear war must reflect a failure to appreciate a medical reality: Any nuclear war would inevitably cause death, disease and suffering of pandemonic proportions and without the possibility of effective medical intervention. That reality leads to the same conclusion physicians have reached for life-threatening epidemics throughout history. Prevention is essential for control. (Quoted in *The Challenge of Peace,* no. 130)

The Firepower of One Poseidon Submarine

United States

To imagine the destructive power of just one U.S. Poseidon submarine (whose firepower equals nine megatons), suppose that it attacked the United States. The illustration depicts the unleashing of the Poseidon's sixteen missiles, each with up to fourteen independently targeted nuclear bombs. Within one hour, 224 cities could be destroyed.

The firepower of a newer Trident submarine is twenty-four megatons, which equals eight World War II's.

Prevention:
The Goal of Peacemaking in the Nuclear Age

The Catholic Church—and most other Christian groups—has reached this consensus: the use of nuclear weapons must be prevented because it is immoral and can never be justified. The Church has arrived at this conclusion by applying traditional moral principles such as the just-war theory to the unique nature of nuclear weapons. In the conclusion to their pastoral letter, the U.S. bishops stated, "In simple terms, we are saying that good ends (defending one's country, protecting freedom, etc.) cannot justify immoral means (the use of weapons which kill indiscriminately and threaten whole societies)" (*The Challenge of Peace*, no. 332).

The question that the U.S. bishops leave unanswered is how best to prevent the use of nuclear weapons. For that reason, the bishops did not unconditionally condemn a country's possession of nuclear weapons, so long as the goal is deterrence. In the eyes of the bishops, the policy of Mutually Assured Destruction is temporarily acceptable in so far as its aim is the prevention of nuclear war. On the other hand, the bishops condemn the arms race, as well as the building of nuclear weapons that are designed specifically for a first strike. Both activities lead away from peaceful agreements and widen the door to the possibility of nuclear war.

Although the U.S. bishops do not condemn the possession of nuclear weapons, this does not mean that they rest easy with the acceptance of the weapons' value as a deterrent. In the bishops' words, "The political paradox of deterrence has also strained our moral conception. May a nation threaten what it may never do? May it possess what it may never use?" (*The Challenge of Peace*, no. 137). Maintaining a weapon system ready for use at a moment's notice—even when declared as being purely for the purpose of deterrence—certainly strains our common, as well as our moral, sense.

Nuclear Proliferation:
The Spread of Nuclear Weapons

Although the arms race between the United States and the USSR continues on its ominous course, it represents only part of the current nuclear problem faced by our world. No other country has a nuclear arsenal close to the size of these two nations, but Great Britain, France, India, and China have already tested their own nuclear weapons. Estimates suggest that by the year 2000, approximately one hundred countries will possess the raw materials and knowledge necessary to produce nuclear weapons. U.S. officials list South Africa, Iraq, Israel, Pakistan, Libya, and Brazil as among the countries that actually will possess nuclear weapons within the next two decades. Undoubtedly other countries will be able to buy nuclear weapons from countries willing to sell them.

Nuclear proliferation—that is, the spread of nuclear weapons to more and more countries—creates ever-increasing opportunities for the use of the weapons. The image of only two nuclear gunslingers caught in perpetual impasse is fast becoming obsolete. As nuclear proliferation continues, new, more complex problems will arise, and tougher solutions will be required.

Regarding this proliferation, the U.S. bishops note the stinging truth that if the United States and the USSR take no steps to limit their own nuclear capabilities, then the non-nuclear countries will have little incentive for limiting their development of these weapons.

What About the Russians?

The problem of nuclear weapons now extends beyond the USSR-U.S. confrontation. Nevertheless, the popular question What about the Russians? deserves comment. The USSR's nuclear arsenal rivals that of the United States. Although not formally at war and with a surprising number of trade and other agreements, these two nations maintain what the U.S. bishops aptly term "peace of a sort."

The United Nations' Security Council

Ironically, the existence of a capability for mutual destruction results in a paradox—namely, that *the security of the United States is increased when the USSR feels more secure.* The opposite is also true: if the USSR feels less secure, the United States has reason to feel more threatened. For that reason, the United States serves its own interests by seeking to enhance Soviet security.

If this notion seems baffling, recall the scenario of the two gunfighters mentioned earlier. If both gunfighters are capable of killing each other, then the most sensible policy for both people is not to make the other angrier or feel more threatened. A threatened gunfighter is a dangerous gunfighter—unless the other gunfighter is certain that he can kill his opponent without being killed himself. At present, this is not the case in the confrontation between the USSR and the United States. For that reason, both countries might better serve their own interests

by lessening tensions. Unfortunately, both countries more frequently follow a policy of equating greater security with more
weapons. (Imagine our gunfighters strapping on second guns!)
This policy deepens tensions and results in graver risks. In the
words of the U.S. bishops, "In our quest for more and more
security, we fear we are actually becoming less and less secure"
(*The Challenge of Peace,* no. 332).

The Question of Possessing Nuclear Weapons

> We see with increasing clarity the political folly of a sys-
> tem which threatens mutual suicide, the psychological
> damage this does to ordinary people, especially the young,
> the economic distortion of priorities—billions readily spent
> for destructive instruments while pitched battles are
> waged daily in our legislatures over much smaller amounts
> for the homeless, the hungry, and the helpless here and
> abroad. (*The Challenge of Peace,* no. 134)

Although the possession of nuclear weapons and their use are
naturally linked, we can examine the morality of each separate-
ly. The above quotation from the U.S. bishops' pastoral points
out two damaging effects of the very existence of nuclear
weapons: (1) the effect on people's psychological states and (2)
the misdirection of resources.

1. The Psychological Effects

Living under the threat of a nuclear holocaust can leave
psychological scars. Constant awareness of the threat can lead
to depression; however, attempting to ignore the threat requires
psychological numbing.

The usual attitude toward the possibility of a nuclear
holocaust resembles the attitude held by many people toward
the Jewish holocaust during World War II. When news of the
Nazi policy of genocide against the Jews became public, most
people—including most Germans—found the news to be simply unbelievable. Similarly, we find nuclear war to be un-
thinkable: we shudder at the thought of it, and in order to go
on living our lives, we block it from our minds. Consequently,
this see-no-evil attitude damages our mental, emotional, and
moral well-being.

2. The Misdirection of Resources

Every gun that is made, every warship launched, every
rocket fired signifies, in the final sense, a theft from those

who hunger and are not fed, those who are cold and are not clothed.

This world in arms is not spending money alone.

It is spending the sweat of its laborers, the genius of its scientists, the hopes of its children. . . .

This is not a way of life at all, in any true sense. Under the cloud of threatening war, it is humanity hanging from a cross of iron. (President Dwight D. Eisenhower, 16 April 1953)

Many years ago President Eisenhower—himself a former Army general—recognized the huge expense that building and maintaining our modern weapons entails. Money spent on such expensive weapon systems represents tax money that is not spent on education, health care, housing, and other social programs. This allocation of resources is what the U.S. bishops mean when they say that money spent on nuclear weapons is a "distortion of priorities."

Some people feel that spending large amounts of money on armaments is good for the economy. They suggest that the economic depression of the 1930s ended only with the munitions

A Seattle production line building B-17 bombers during World War II

buildup that was triggered by World War II. They further argue that missile programs create jobs and therefore help feed people by providing them with employment.

Actually, recent studies indicate that military spending creates fewer jobs than almost any other form of government expenditure. A study of the MX-missile program documented the following figures:

- One billion dollars spent on MX-missile construction would result in 53,000 jobs.
- By contrast, one billion dollars spent on mass transit would create 79,000 jobs.
- The same amount spent on day care would lead to 120,000 jobs—well over twice as many jobs as missile construction would generate.

In addition, most of the jobs created by military spending are for highly skilled labor. Consequently, the defense industry fails to employ those people most in need of work—the unskilled and the poorly educated people in the ranks of the unemployed.

In short, the U.S. bishops not only condemn the use of nuclear weapons and the nuclear arms race, they also raise questions about the possession of nuclear weapons.

Putting the Nuclear Scandal into a Christian Perspective

Misreading the Scriptures

In 1982, A. G. Mojtabai, a New York author, took up residence in Amarillo, Texas. Mojtabai wanted to find out how the religious vision of the citizens of Amarillo related to their view of nuclear war. The nuclear issue confronts Amarilloans daily because the city is the home of Pantex, the final assembly plant for all the nuclear weapons built in the United States.

In fact, Mojtabai found a widespread belief that nuclear war might be the showdown between good and evil that the Bible calls Armageddon (Revelation 16:14–16). Accompanying this view was another belief that when this last battle takes place, devout Christians will be "raptured"—that is, lifted off the earth and saved from the final holocaust. Mojtabai's natural reaction was one of concern: if many North Americans share the view that negotiation is unnecessary and war is inevitable, then nuclear war becomes all the more possible.

Although the Bible is a book for all ages, to read it as a book of prophecies about our current world crises is to misread it. The Bible does speak about war and peace, justice and injustice, which are universal and timeless issues. As such, the

Bible contains many truths applicable to modern warfare, modern weaponry, and international relations.

The Bible also makes clear statements about evil and points out the harm resulting from certain attitudes and actions. Yet it does not portray evil and destruction as inevitable or triumphant. On the contrary, the Bible offers hope that God is with us even in the midst of difficult times. So, although the Scriptures can shed light on our current nuclear crisis, they are misused when they fuel the flames of despair and hatred.

Jesus' Teaching on Love: A Value for a Nuclear Age

When we consider the virtues advocated by Jesus, we come quickly to the word *love*. He summed up all the commandments in "love the Lord your God" and "love your neighbor as yourself" (Matthew 22:37,39). Not content with a limited understanding of "love your neighbor," Jesus universalized and intensified its meaning. For Jesus, our enemy is equally our neighbor (Matthew 5:44), and our *attitudes* toward others are as important as our actions toward them (Matthew 5:21–22).

Jesus advocates love of enemies even in the face of their hate: "You have heard the commandment, 'An eye for an eye, a tooth for a tooth.' But what I say to you is: offer no resistance to injury. When a person strikes you on the right cheek, turn and offer him the other" (Matthew 5:38–39). Moreover, Jesus describes love of enemies as a positive activity. As one biblical scholar puts it, our enemies are to be "blessed," "prayed for," "fed," "given drink," "lent to," and "healed."

This teaching on love of enemies is not on the outskirts of Jesus' message; rather, this love is at its heart. As modeled in the life of Jesus, we are challenged to reflect the intense and universal love that God has for all people. Therefore, this teaching forms a Christian basis upon which to address nuclear war and nuclear weapons.

A nuclear policy based on hostility and mistrust does not reflect the spirit of Jesus' teaching on love. A nuclear policy that seeks superiority over another goes counter to Jesus' teaching. Finally, the use of nuclear weapons against others clearly would violate Jesus' teaching to love your neighbor—including enemies—as yourself.

The Challenge of Peace: The U.S. Bishops Confront Nuclear Weapons

Love of enemies and nonretaliation (as in "turn the other cheek") are clearly the teachings of Jesus. However, as stated in the last chapter, the just-war theory emerged as an attempt by the Church to restrict and regulate violence in a world that did not measure up to the Christian ideal. Church documents since the advent of the nuclear age have applied both the teachings of the Scriptures and the traditional just-war theory to the use and possession of nuclear weapons.

The most complete, recent church statement on nuclear weapons is the 1983 U.S. bishops' pastoral letter, *The Challenge of Peace: God's Promise and Our Response,* which has been quoted frequently in this chapter. In the letter, the bishops grapple with the many issues surrounding war and peace in the nuclear age. As the letter's title indicates, the bishops realize that peace is the great challenge facing humanity today. Because the weapons that threaten us are so powerful, our efforts to create and maintain peace must be equally great.

In their pastoral letter, the bishops employ the Scriptures, the just-war principles, and the findings of modern social sciences to arrive at general principles related to nuclear weapons. They also make specific recommendations about nuclear policies. Some of their principles and policy suggestions have already been referred to earlier in this chapter. The real power to implement or reject the recommendations lies in the hands of government leaders. However, the letter ends with suggestions for individual Christians who seek to respond to the challenge of peace in the nuclear age.

Responding to the Nuclear Scandal

On a Personal Level

Our response to the challenge of peace as stated by the U.S. bishops can be divided into three categories: the personal, the interpersonal, and the structural. In *The Challenge of Peace*, the bishops recommend the following practices on the personal level:

1. **Forming conscience:** "We must learn together how to make correct and responsible moral judgments" (no. 281). The bishops encourage us to open our eyes to the problems and to become informed and educated about the issues of war and peace. Only in that way can we make conscientious decisions in response to those issues.

2. **Linking peace with reverence for life:** "Violence has many faces: oppression of the poor, deprivation of basic human rights, economic exploitation, sexual exploitation and pornography, neglect or abuse of the aged and the helpless, and innumerable other acts of inhumanity" (no. 285). Here the bishops point out that we abhor the destructiveness of nuclear war because we revere life. They remind us that our no to nuclear war sounds hollow unless we also speak out against violence as it manifests itself throughout our society.

3. **Praying:** "Through [prayer], we seek the wisdom to begin the search for peace and the courage to sustain us as instruments of Christ's peace in the world" (no. 293). Prayer leads us to truth and love because it involves spending time with God, who is the source of truth and love. Through prayer, we realize our communion with all people. In this realization we achieve a hint of God's reign of peace. The bishops particularly recommend the Mass as a powerful prayer for peace.

4. **Doing penance:** "As a tangible sign of our need and desire to do penance we, for the cause of peace, commit ourselves to fast and abstinence on each Friday of the year. We call upon our people voluntarily to do penance on Friday by eating less food and by abstaining from meat" (no. 298). The bishops link doing penance, such as fasting, with conversion to Christ. Their suggestion to do penance reminds us that we need to repent, to change our lives, so that we can become more like Christ. By becoming more Christlike, we will become more fully persons of peace, as Jesus was.

On an Interpersonal Level

We must develop a sense of solidarity, cemented by relationships with mature and exemplary Christians who represent Christ and his way of life. (*The Challenge of Peace,* no. 277)

■ In 1956 Bob Aldridge began work as an engineer at Lockheed Missiles and Space Company. He worked there until 1973. During his time at Lockheed, Bob was actively involved in the production of nuclear weapons.

In Bob's mind, this was a work of peace: he was helping to keep the United States safe from aggression. However, toward the end of his time at Lockheed, Bob encountered other Christians who were seeking to apply Jesus' message of peace to the nuclear age. Bob began to realize that from what he could see, his company was more interested in gaining lucrative contracts than in preserving peace. He also realized that he was now building offensive and not defensive weapons. Challenged by these new awarenesses, Bob left his job in 1973. He knew that he would never again be offered work in the defense industry and that this type of work was the only kind for which he was professionally suited. Even so, with the support of his family and other friends, Bob knew he had made the right and necessary choice. (You can read how Bob and other Christians relate their faith to concern about nuclear weapons in the book *Peacemakers,* edited by Jim Wallis.)

■ Terry McHugh's life demonstrated that Catholic schools can work. Early in high school at West Catholic in Philadelphia, Terry became involved in service projects through the school's branch of Community Service Corps. She loved the contacts with a variety of people, the community atmosphere, and the spirit of caring that she found through her involvement. After high school, Terry's commitment to serving the poor people of Philadelphia intensified. She also came to recognize more and more that poverty and prejudice are intimately linked with the issues of war and peace.

For Terry, becoming involved with local people working for peace represented a natural outgrowth of her years of church and community service. Her involvement with peace groups led to surveillance by the FBI and the threat of imprisonment. Terry's unfailing spirit and the support of her many friends carried her through these times of harassment. She remained active in matters of service and justice until an accident ended her life at the age of twenty-six. (You can read more about Terry's life in the book *Her Life for His Friends,* by Cecelia Johnson.)

In the above cases, Bob and Terry both came from their own starting points to take steps toward becoming active peacemakers. Similarly, we each must address the issue of nuclear weapons starting with our own particular perspectives. For example, workers in defense industries have a different perspective from social workers or doctors. As a student, you will naturally want to learn all that you can about this vital issue. As a young person, you can speak about nuclear weapons and the future with a unique voice. As a member of a family, you can raise concerns about how policies related to nuclear weapons might affect your family members.

Both Bob and Terry found the courage to be active peacemakers from the support and spirit of solidarity that they experienced within their Christian communities. We also need to recognize the communities to which we belong and from which we receive encouragement. Working alone may seem heroic, but it is not the way of the Christian. We must foster community while pursuing ways, as part of that community, to help preserve our world.

On a Structural Level

> The virtue of patriotism means that as citizens we respect and honor our country, but our very love and loyalty make us examine carefully and regularly its role in world affairs, asking that it live up to its full potential as an agent of peace with justice for all people. (*The Challenge of Peace,* no. 327)

The U.S. bishops encourage us to be political. In other words, they want us to ensure that the challenge of peace always remains a primary concern in our own country's policies and practices. In a quotation from the Second Vatican Council's document *The Church in the Modern World,* the bishops describe the virtue of patriotism:

> Citizens must cultivate a generous and loyal spirit of patriotism, but without being narrow-minded. This means that they will always direct their attention to the good of the whole human family, united by the different ties which bind together races, people, and nations. (Quoted in *The Challenge of Peace,* no. 327)

For the U.S. bishops, the concept of *patriotism* is clearly different from *nationalism*. **Patriotism** means a genuine love of one's country that nevertheless admits its shortcomings and seeks to right its faults. **Nationalism** means a spirit of one-upmanship and lording it over other countries whenever possible. Patriotism is a positive virtue; nationalism is a selfish, narrow-minded vice.

Patriotism does not exclude identifying oneself as a world citizen. As a virtue, it recognizes that citizens of every country can make positive contributions to solving common problems. On the other hand, the vice of nationalism places the good of one's own country above the needs of every other country.

While extolling the virtue of patriotism, the U.S. bishops call for a perspective that is *cosmopolitan* (meaning "having the characteristics of a citizen of the world"). Specifically, they want a global body to oversee the regulations concerning war and nuclear weapons. They believe that at the present time such a body can be formed and that modern technology can make it effective. A patriotic spirit would not prohibit such a development; a nationalistic spirit, however, would hesitate to relinquish power from one's own domain.

Conclusion: Where Are We Going?

On the president's chair in Independence Hall in Philadelphia is a carving of half a sun at a horizon. After the signing of the Declaration of Independence there, Benjamin Franklin reportedly remarked that "only time will tell whether the sun is setting or rising." Because of the destructive power of nuclear weapons, humankind again finds itself at a crisis point with our future in question. The actions we take now will determine whether our sun is rising or setting.

For Review

1. Describe the policy known as Mutually Assured Destruction.
2. Define the following terms: *mutually verifiable arms-limitation agreement* and *arms race.*
3. What problems accompany the development of a nuclear defensive system?
4. What are the dangers behind the concept of a first-strike system?
5. What arguments are offered by those who wish to eliminate nuclear weapons entirely?
6. How are nuclear weapons different from conventional weapons?
7. What does the term *nuclear winter* refer to?
8. What is the goal of peacemaking in regard to nuclear weapons?
9. What is nuclear proliferation?
10. List two problems raised by the U.S. bishops regarding the possession of nuclear weapons.
11. In what way are the Scriptures sometimes misinterpreted in regard to our modern nuclear crisis?
12. Describe Jesus' attitude toward enemies.
13. How does the U.S. bishops' pastoral letter *The Challenge of Peace* suggest that we respond to nuclear weapons on a personal, an interpersonal, and a structural level? Outline the bishops' recommendations.

For Reflection

1. Complete one of the following exercises:
   a. Imagine that you can travel backward in time to an era before the development of nuclear weapons. Write a proposal to the world leaders of that time containing your understanding of the current nuclear-weapons crisis. Then write a paragraph describing what you think would be their response to your description.
   b. Imagine that you can travel forward in time to an era when humanity has advanced to the degree that warfare is obsolete. In writing, explain to the world leaders of that time your understanding of the current nuclear-weapons crisis. Then write a paragraph describing their response to your description.

2. The present U.S. nuclear policy is nicknamed *MAD*, for Mutually Assured Destruction. Create your own nickname for a safer, saner nuclear policy.

3. This chapter describes a number of positions on the development of new nuclear weapons. In writing, explain your position on this complex issue.

4. Certain films offer graphic portrayals of the probable results of a nuclear war. Do you believe that such films should be *mandatory, voluntary,* or *prohibited* viewing for the following groups? In writing, briefly explain your reason for each decision.
   a. U.N. representatives
   b. public officials
   c. eligible voters
   d. high school students
   e. elementary school students

5. Research and write a report on the probable effects of a nuclear war.

6. Imagine that you are discussing the dangers of nuclear weapons with a friend. She asks, "But what about the Russians?" Explain in writing your response to her.

7. Imagine that Jesus addresses the United Nations on nuclear weapons. What do you think he would say? Imagine that after his address you interview representatives from four different countries. Identify each country, and record how you think the representative from each country would respond.

8. The Church asks us to be informed about nuclear weapons. Find a newspaper or magazine article addressing an issue related to nuclear weapons. Write a review of the article, focusing on the following questions:
   ■ What message(s) regarding nuclear weapons does the article convey?
   ■ Do you agree or disagree with the article?
   ■ What questions would you like to ask the author of the article?

9. Albert Einstein, the famous scientist whose research helped to develop nuclear weapons, once remarked, "nuclear weapons have changed everything, save our modes of thinking, and thus we drift toward unparalleled catastrophe." In writing, describe what you believe is the necessary

change in thinking that the existence of nuclear weapons requires.

10. The U.S. bishops link peace concerns with other life issues (see page 266). Write an essay explaining how one of these other life issues has an effect on our society's attitudes and policies regarding nuclear weapons.

11. Complete one of the following exercises:
    a. Read *The War Prayer,* by Mark Twain. Write an updated version of it that includes references to our current nuclear-weapons crisis.
    b. Create a political cartoon or poster about the arms race.

12. Identify three religious practices that people could perform on a regular basis that would help them become peacemakers in our nuclear age. Then explain in writing how these practices would help them become peacemakers.

13. Read about someone who has attempted to be an active peacemaker today. Write a report on that person. Include in your report a statement about what that person has to say to us about peace in the nuclear age.

14. Based on your reading about patriotism in this chapter, complete the following sentence in four different ways: "A true patriot is someone who . . ."

15. Develop a questionnaire and interview a group of people to determine their feelings and opinions regarding nuclear weapons. Report on your findings.

16. Write an essay entitled "Even in Our Nuclear Age, Peace Is Possible."

Conclusion

Cultivating Justice and Peace

This course began with a parable about a topsy-turvy world in which a despised Samaritan acted neighborly toward a stranger in distress. Although the story of the good Samaritan sounded radical and perhaps shocking to Jesus' audience, the parable actually describes a world that reflects God's original design. In this world of justice and peace, God reigns and people help others in need regardless of apparent differences. This world—in which people treat others with the same care and respect that they profess toward God—is the pearl of great worth and the heavenly banquet proclaimed by Jesus.

We are called to view the people and problems that we meet in light of Jesus' vision. As Christians, we recognize our responsibility to continue the work of Jesus, to be cocreators of a just world. Because we have Jesus' word that God is with us, we can pursue this goal with great hopes.

Throughout the course, we have been reminded that concerns about justice and peace must be addressed on a personal, an interpersonal, and a structural level. Three virtues may serve as reminders of these three dimensions of our response. These key virtues are compassion, community, and creativity.

Compassion: "Be Compassionate, As Your Father Is Compassionate"

> Compassion asks us to go where it hurts, to enter into places of pain, to share in brokenness, fear, confusion, and anguish. Compassion challenges us to cry out with those in misery, to mourn with those who are lonely, to weep with those in tears. Compassion requires us to be weak with the weak, vulnerable with the vulnerable, and powerless with the powerless. Compassion means full immersion in the condition of being human. (Donald P. McNeill, Douglas A. Morrison, and Henri J. M. Nouwen, *Compassion*, p. 4)

Compassion marks a first step toward answering our Christian call to justice and peace. Compassion means that we are touched by others and are moved to help them. Perhaps we hear the story of someone who is struggling in life, or we view a film about someone who is suffering. We find the story or the film touching; it is a moving experience for us. On an elementary level, this is what compassion means.

Our capacity to feel with others moves us to become involved in their lives and to seek changes that will ease their pain, including the pain of injustice. When moved by compassion, we hesitate to contribute to others' suffering through the destructiveness of violence and war. In this sense, compassion relates to peacemaking in that it is akin to the "disarmament of the human heart" described by the U.S. bishops in their pastoral letter (*The Challenge of Peace*, no. 284).

Compassion sparks a concern for those who are in our family, school, and community. It also leads us to want to learn more about the ways that people who are beyond our immediate circle are in need. Finally, compassion draws us toward greater involvement in working to overcome the suffering around us.

Community: "Love One Another"

> In a society like ours, the only effective way to be able to cut down on possessions, to view the possessions we do have in a different way, to give ourselves a basic level of security while creating desirable alternatives for ourselves and our children, is to work at it within a sustaining and supporting community. Building community on a personal or neighborhood or parish level is also a way of concretizing the concept of interdependence—how we need each other. (Kathleen and James McGinnis, *Parenting for Peace and Justice*, p. 11)

Community is both a goal and a means to the goal. As a goal, it represents a place where people support and encourage one another, learn from one another, and celebrate together. As a means to a goal, community provides a setting for performing the works of justice and peace.

As a virtue, community needs to be cultivated and worked at. In our modern world, community can be elusive. For instance, we can be active and involved throughout high school. Then, upon graduation we may discover that the community that we thought was so close-knit is quickly unraveling. Only renewed effort on our part can sustain this community or lead to a community in another setting.

Together with *working* at community, *celebrating* in community is equally important. We are reminded of this link between celebration and community in the life of Jesus. Although an undaunted advocate of justice, Jesus was noted for celebrating with his friends. The Gospels make frequent mention of Jesus' enjoying meals with others, and he himself refers to

Top: Missionaries in Haiti helping to build a hospital
Bottom: In the Philippines, refugees being trained in the use of tools and in the English language required to explain their use

the reign of God as a banquet. In the Christian community, working for justice and peace and joyfully celebrating go hand in hand.

Developing the virtue of community means that our response to the call to justice and peace is a group effort and not an isolated one. Our response is meant to be work but not a chore; it is a joyful and life-affirming celebration. In short, community means sharing our compassion with others and rejoicing in what we can be together.

Creativity in a Time of Crisis

A period of crisis can be a period of imminent breakdown. But it can also be a period of imminent breakthrough. Rather than reading the signs of our times as signs of human history winding down, we can read these times as a pregnant period in which the human spirit is challenged to new heights of creative effort. Beneath all the surface evidence of upheaval and confusion, there is evidence that these times could be the advent of a positive thrust forward in human history. (Gerald and Patricia Mische, *Toward a Human World Order,* pp. 5–6)

The Misches, who have studied our current world order, tell a parable titled "The Coat That Got Too Small." In the story they describe a group of people bundled up in coats that are much too small for them: "Buttons and zippers were being strained to the limit and seams threatened to tear at the sides. Their bodies bulged against the overstretched fabric as if the contents had been stuffed in with tremendous effort" (*Toward a Human World Order,* p. 1). Of course, in this confined condition the people found any movement, even breathing, to be a difficult chore. Moreover, a great deal of irritation and clumsiness accompanied every social interaction.

Asked why they wore such restricting clothing, one member of the group responded that they had worn these coats since youth. They had grown accustomed to the coats. Although the coats constricted growth and caused many problems, they made the people feel secure. To this explanation a visitor remarked: "Maybe you should get a new [coat] that fits you better. It looks like this one has served you in the past, but now it is more like a straitjacket than a coat" (p. 2).

Applied to today's world, this story suggests that the social structure of our human community reflects an order more appropriate to the past than to the present. The "coat" that previously fit us comfortably now confines us like a straitjacket.

For that reason, we find ourselves at a crisis point, in danger of bursting at the seams.

Throughout our course, we have considered critical issues of justice and peace. You may have been struck by the realization that these issues are interconnected and hold both personal and global implications. To address these concerns adequately, we need to do more than operate solely in our local communities. To complete our response to the call to justice and peace, we need to recognize how social structures—the coats that we wear—affect ourselves and others. In doing so, we will recognize that this time of crisis can be a time of break*through* rather than of break*down*.

To foster a breakthrough toward a more just and peaceful world, we need to address current problems and potential solutions with a spirit of creativity. When we approach choices about the current structure and future world order creatively, we are acting as cocreators of God's Kingdom—as Jesus commissioned us to be. In short, creativity is an essential ingredient in our response to the Christian call to justice and peace.

Bibliography

Abbey, Edward. *Desert Solitaire: A Season in the Wilderness.* New York: Ballantine Books, 1968.

Abzug, Bella. *Gender Gap Nineteen Eighty-four: How Women Will Decide the Next Election.* Boston: Houghton Mifflin Co., 1984.

Adams, Richard. *Watership Down.* New York: Macmillan, 1972.

Aquinas, Saint Thomas. *See* Thomas Aquinas, Saint

Augustine of Hippo. Quoted in *The Faith That Does Justice,* edited by John C. Haughey, p. 118.

B., Javier Torres. "The Hunger of Others." In *Solidarity with the People of Nicaragua and Peru,* by James McGinnis, p. 70. Saint Louis: Institute for Peace and Justice, 1982.

Benestad, J. Brian, and Francis J. Butler, eds. *Quest for Justice: A Compendium of Statements of the United States Catholic Bishops on the Political and Social Order, 1966-1980,* Washington, DC: United States Catholic Conference, 1981.

The Bishops of Appalachia. *This Land Is Home to Me.* In *Renewing the Earth,* edited by David J. O'Brien and Thomas A. Shannon, pp. 474-515.

The Bishops of Midwestern United States. *Strangers and Guests: Toward Community in the Heartland.* Sioux Falls, SD: Heartland Project, 1980.

The Bishops of Northeast Brazil. *The Marginalization of a People.* Quoted in *Heralds of a New Reformation,* by Richard Shaull, p. 102.

The Bishops of the United States. *See* National Conference of Catholic Bishops

Brown v. *Board of Education.* Quoted in *Twenty Years After Brown: A Report of the United States Commission on Civil Rights.* Washington, DC: U.S. Printing Office, 1977.

Butler, Robert N. *Why Survive? Being Old in America.* New York: Harper & Row, 1975.

Byers, David M., ed. *Justice in the Marketplace: Collected Statements of the Vatican and the U.S. Catholic Bishops on Economic Policy, 1891-1984.* Washington, DC: United States Catholic Conference, 1985.

Carrigan, Ana. *Salvador Witness: The Life and Calling of Jean Donovan.* New York: Simon & Schuster, 1984.

Catholic Relief Services. *Narrowing the Gap: An Introduction to Third World Poverty and Development Issues.* New York: Catholic Relief Services, n.d.

Chrysostom, John. Quoted in *The Faith That Does Justice,* edited by John C. Haughey, pp. 118 and 141.

Clement of Alexandria. Quoted in *The Faith That Does Justice,* edited by John C. Haughey, p. 136.

Development Education Centre. "Development and Underdevelopment: Two Sides of the Same Coin." In *Development Education Viewpoint #1.* Toronto: Development Education Centre, 1975.

Dyer, Gwynne. *War.* New York: Crown Publishers, 1985.

Eisenhower, Dwight D. Speech on 16 April 1953. Quoted in leaflet. Washington, DC: A Citizen's Organization for a Sane World.

Finnerty, Adam Daniel. *No More Plastic Jesus.* New York: E. P. Dutton, 1978.

Gabel, Medard. *Ho-Ping: Food for Everyone.* In *World Hunger: Learning to Meet the Challenge,* pp. 15-16. New York: Impact on Hunger, n.d.

Gandhi, Mohandas K. Quoted in *Fighting with Gandhi,* by Mark Juergensmeyer, p. *vii.* San Francisco: Harper & Row, 1984.

Gish, Arthur G. *Beyond the Rat Race.* Scottdale, PA: Herald Press, 1973.

Gutiérrez, Gustavo. *We Drink from Our Own Wells.* Translated by Matthew J. O'Connell. Maryknoll, NY: Orbis Books, 1984.

Hart, John. *The Spirit of the Earth.* New York: Paulist Press, 1984.

Haughey, John C., ed. *The Faith That Does Justice: Examining the Christian Sources for Social Change.* New York: Paulist Press, 1977.

Heilbroner, Robert. *The Great Ascent.* New York: Harper & Row, 1963.

Impact on Hunger. *World Hunger: Learning to Meet the Challenge.* New York: Impact on Hunger, n.d.

Inter-Religious Task Force for Social Analysis. *Must We Choose Sides? Christian Commitment for the 80's.* Oakland, CA: Inter-Religious Task Force for Social Analysis, 1979.

Johnson, Cecelia D. *Her Life for His Friends: A Biography of Terry McHugh, 1950–1977.* Chicago: Fides/Claretian, 1980.

John XXIII. *Peace on Earth (Pacem in Terris).* In *Justice in the Marketplace,* edited by David M. Byers, pp. 150–170.

Kemper, Vicki. "Poor and Getting Poorer." *Sojourners* 15 (March 1986): 15–18.

King, Martin Luther, Jr. *Letter from a Birmingham Jail.* In *The Life and Words of Martin Luther King.* New York: Scholastic Book Services, 1968.

Kipling, Rudyard. Poem. In *Learning About Peoples and Cultures,* edited by Seymour Fersh, p. 24. Evanston, IL: McDougal, Littell & Co., 1974.

Kownacki, Mary Lou, ed. *A Race to Nowhere: An Arms Race Primer for Catholics.* Chicago: Pax Christi, 1980.

Lappe, Frances Moore, and Joseph Collins. *World Hunger: Ten Myths.* San Francisco: Institute for Food and Development Policy, 1977.

McCullers, Carson. Quoted in *The Passionate Life,* by Sam Keen, p. 231. San Francisco: Harper & Row, 1983.

McGinnis, James B. *Bread and Justice: Toward a New International Economic Order.* New York: Paulist Press, 1979.

McGinnis, Kathleen, and James McGinnis. *Parenting for Peace and Justice.* Maryknoll, NY: Orbis Books, 1982.

McKenzie, John L. *Dictionary of the Bible.* New York: Macmillan, 1965.

McNeill, Donald P., Douglas A. Morrison, and Henri J. M. Nouwen. *Compassion: A Reflection on the Christian Life.* Garden City, NY: Doubleday, 1985.

Malavez, L., "La Vision Chretienne de l'Historie." *Nouvelle Revue Theologique* (1949): 260–261. In *Christianity and Science,* by Jean Abele, translated by R. F. Trevett, p. 138. New York: Hawthorn Books, 1961.

Marx, Karl. Quoted in *The Faith That Does Justice,* edited by John C. Haughey, p. 48.

Miller, Alan S. "The Environmental and Other Bioethical Challenges for Christian Creation Consciousness." In *Cry of the Environment: Rebuilding the Christian Creation Tradition,* edited by Philip N. Joranson and Ken Butigan, p. 386. Santa Fe: Bear & Co., 1984.

Mische, Gerald, and Patricia Mische. *Toward a Human World Order: Beyond the National Security Straitjacket.* New York: Paulist Press, 1977.

Mojtabai, A. G. *Blessed Assurance: At Home with the Bomb in Amarillo, Texas.* Boston: Houghton Mifflin Co., 1986.

National Conference of Catholic Bishops. *Brothers and Sisters to Us: United States Bishops' Pastoral on Racism in Our Day.* Washington, DC: United States Catholic Conference, 1979.

———. *The Challenge of Peace: God's Promise and Our Response.* Washington, DC: United States Catholic Conference, 1983.

———. *Economic Justice for All: Catholic Social Teaching and the U.S. Economy.* Washington, DC: United States Catholic Conference, 1986.

———. *Society and the Aged: Toward Reconciliation.* In *Quest for Justice,* edited by J. Brian Benestad and Francis J. Butler, pp. 333–340.

———. *Statement on the World Food Crisis: A Pastoral Plan of Action.* In *Quest for Justice,* edited by J. Brian Benestad and Francis J. Butler, pp. 102–105.

The New American Bible. Washington, DC: Confraternity of Christian Doctrine, 1970.

Newland, Mary Reed. *The Saint Book.* New York: Seabury Press, 1979.

O'Brien, David J., and Thomas A. Shannon, eds. *Renewing the Earth: Catholic Documents on Peace, Justice, and Liberation.* Garden City, NY: Image Books, 1977.

Paul VI. *On Promoting the Development of Peoples.* In *Justice in the Marketplace,* edited by David M. Byers, pp. 203–223.

Romero, Oscar. Speech of 27 November 1977. In *The Church Is All of You: Thoughts of Archbishop Oscar Romero,* translated by James R. Brockman, p. 6. Minneapolis: Winston Press, 1984.

Seattle, Chief. Speech. In *Gamaliel,* pp. 72–73. Washington, DC: Community for Creative Nonviolence, 1976.

Senior, Donald. "Jesus' Most Scandalous Teaching." In *Biblical and Theological Reflections on "The Challenge of Peace,"* edited by John T. Pawlikowski and Donald Senior. Wilmington, MD: Michael Glazier, 1984.

Shaull, Richard. *Heralds of a New Reformation: The Poor of South and North America.* Maryknoll, NY: Orbis Books, 1984.

Shea, John. *An Experience Named Spirit.* Chicago: Thomas More Press, 1983.

Silverstein, Shel. *The Giving Tree.* New York: Harper & Row, 1964.

Simon, Arthur. *Bread for the World.* Rev. ed. New York: Paulist Press, 1984.

Steinem, Gloria. Quoted in "Liberation's Next Wave, According to Gloria Steinem," by Betsy Carter. *Esquire* 101, no. 6 (June 1984): 203.

Swift, Louis J. *The Early Fathers on War and Military Service.* Wilmington, MD: Michael Glazier, 1983.

The Synod of Bishops. *Justice in the World.* In *Justice in the Marketplace,* edited by David M. Byers, pp. 249–263.

Teresa of Calcutta. Quoted in "Mother Teresa, the Myth and the Person," by Eileen Egan. *America* 148 (22 March 1980): 239–243.

Teresa of Calcutta. Quoted in *Something Beautiful for God: Mother Teresa of Calcutta,* by Malcolm Muggeridge, p. 68. New York: Harper & Row, 1971.

Thomas Aquinas, Saint. Quoted in *Aquinas,* by F. C. Copleston, p. 230. Harmondsworth, Middlesex: Penguin Books, 1955.

Toton, Suzanne C. *World Hunger: The Responsibility of Christian Education.* Maryknoll, NY: Orbis Books, 1982.

Tutu, Desmond. "Into a Glorious Future: Nobel Laureate Speaks to the Press." *Sojourners* 14 (February 1985): 22–25.

Twain, Mark. *The War Prayer.* New York: Harper & Row, 1984. [Originally published in 1923 as part of Twain's *Europe and Elsewhere.*]

U.S. Midwestern Bishops. *See* The Bishops of Midwestern United States

V., Orlando Perez. "Prayer." In *Solidarity with the People of Nicaragua and Peru,* by James McGinnis, p. 71. Saint Louis: Institute for Peace and Justice, 1982.

Vatican Council II. *Pastoral Constitution on the Church in the Modern World.* In *Vatican Council II: The Conciliar and Post Conciliar Documents,* edited by Austin Flannery, pp. 903–1014. Northport, NY: Costello Publishing Co., 1975.

Vonnegut, Kurt, Jr. *Slaughterhouse Five.* New York: Dell Publishing Co., 1969.

Wallis, Jim, ed. *Peacemakers: Christian Voices from the New Abolitionist Movement.* New York: Harper & Row, 1983.

Wiesel, Elie. *The Gates of the Forest.* Translated by Frances Frenaye. New York: Avon Books, Bard Books, 1966.

Index

Acknowledgments (*continued*)

The scriptural quotation on page 246 is from the Jerusalem Bible, published and copyrighted © 1985 by Darton, Longman & Todd, Ltd., London, and by Doubleday & Company, Inc., New York.

All other scriptural quotations used in this book are from the New American Bible. Copyrighted © 1970 by the Confraternity of Christian Doctrine, Inc., Washington, D.C. Reprinted by permission of the copyright owner. All rights reserved.

The woodcuts on pages 36, 173, 215, and 238 are by Fritz Eichenberg, from *The Green Revolution*, by Peter Maurin (Fresno, CA: Academy Guild Press, 1949).

The Ziggy cartoons on pages 76, 156, and 242 are by Tom Wilson. Copyright © 1977, Universal Press Syndicate. Reprinted with permission. All rights reserved.

The excerpt on pages 96–98 is from *The Great Ascent*, by Robert L. Heilbroner, pages 33–37. Copyrighted © 1963 by Robert L. Heilbroner. Reprinted by permission of Harper & Row, Publishers, Inc.

The excerpt on pages 102–103 is from *Heralds of a New Reformation: The Poor of South and North America*, by Richard Shaull, pages 119–121. Copyrighted © 1984 by Orbis Books. Reprinted by permission.

The illustration on page 135 is used by permission of Catholic Relief Services.

The excerpt on page 187 is from *Why Survive? Being Old in America*, by Robert N. Butler, M.D., pages 6–7. Copyrighted © 1975 by Robert N. Butler, M.D. Reprinted by permission of Harper & Row, Publishers, Inc.

The excerpt on page 216 is from *The Spirit of the Earth*, by John Hart, page 109. Copyrighted © 1984 by Paulist Press. Reprinted by permission.

The excerpt on page 252 is from *Slaughterhouse Five*, by Kurt Vonnegut, Jr., pages 73–75. Copyrighted © 1969 by Kurt Vonnegut, Jr. Reprinted by permission of Delacorte Press/Seymour Lawrence.

Photo Credits

Cover: UPI/Bettmann Newsphotos (top center and top right), Reuters/Bettmann Newsphotos (top left), The Image Bank (bottom)

Half-title page: Art Resource, Inc.

Title pages: Taurus Photos (far left and right), Frost Publishing Group (left), The Image Works (far right)

Art Resource, Inc.: pages 35, 37, 49, 55 (left), 83, 109, 134, 158 (bottom), 172 (bottom), 174, 208 (bottom), 210, 254 (top and bottom)

Bettmann Archive: pages 32–33 (top), 33 (bottom), 54, 55 (right), 56, 57, 58, 59, 61, 62 (top), 64, 74, 94, 113, 130 (right), 137, 149 (top), 154 (right), 169 (top), 170 (top and right), 191 (left), 202 (left), 208 (top), 214 (bottom), 231, 235, 250–251 (top), 255, 264

Bettmann Newsphotos: pages 41, 42, 73 (bottom), 76, 77, 79, 91, 101, 168 (bottom), 169 (bottom), 176 (bottom), 214 (top), 229 (bottom), 233, 256

EKM-Nepenthe: pages 7 (bottom), 10 (bottom), 11 (top), 14–15 (top), 15 (bottom), 21 (top), 23, 24 (bottom), 28 (bottom), 80, 81, 84, 85, 92–93 (top), 93 (bottom), 130 (left), 145 (bottom), 147, 153, 154 (left), 155 (right), 158 (top), 159, 165 (bottom), 170 (bottom), 175 (bottom), 176 (top), 184 (bottom), 185, 188 (top and bottom), 189, 194, 201, 202 (right), 209, 218 (top), 236, 240, 262, 276

Frost Publishing Group: pages 6–7 (top), 8, 10 (top), 12, 17, 18 (left, middle, and right), 20, 21 (bottom), 24 (top), 27 (left), 28 (top), 38 (bottom), 39, 63 (left), 107 (right), 128, 132, 155 (left), 192, 195, 196 (bottom), 203, 204, 207, 216 (middle), 218 (bottom), 219 (bottom), 225 (bottom), 251 (bottom), 260

The Image Works: pages 9, 11 (bottom), 22, 26, 27 (right), 44 (left), 63 (right), 78, 88, 97 (top), 98, 123 (bottom), 124, 151 (left and top right), 152, 164–165 (top), 167 (right), 177 (top), 183 (bottom), 186, 193, 204, 211, 216 (bottom), 227, 229 (top), 230, 231, 275 (bottom)

Jean-Claude Lejeune: pages 140, 148 (top), 149 (bottom)

Northwind Archive: pages 154 (middle), 168 (top), 175 (top)

Norman Provost, FSC: page 206

Religious News Service: pages 29, 43, 47, 53 (bottom), 68, 72–73 (top), 86, 100 (bottom), 110, 129, 131, 217 (top), 241

Rising Hope: page 191 (right)

James L. Shaffer: pages 13, 44 (right), 52–53 (top), 62 (bottom), 108, 133, 136, 144–145 (top), 157, 182–183 (top), 197, 223, 244, 253, 266, 279

Taurus Photos: pages 25, 38 (top), 97 (bottom), 99, 100 (top), 104, 106, 107 (left), 115, 121, 122–123 (top), 127 (top and bottom), 148 (bottom), 151 (bottom), 167 (left), 172 (top), 177 (bottom), 178, 184 (top), 187, 190, 196 (top), 216 (top), 219 (top), 224–225 (top), 228, 234, 268, 272, 274–275 (top), 277 (top and bottom)